Joseph Cowen and Popular Radicalism on Tyneside,
1829-1900

For Richard

Joseph Cowen
and
Popular Radicalism
on Tyneside, 1829-1900

Joan Allen

MERLIN PRESS

First published 2007 by The Merlin Press Ltd.
96 Monnow Street
Monmouth
NP25 3EQ
Wales

www.merlinpress.co.uk

ISBN. 9780850365849 paperback
ISBN. 9780850365832 hardback

British Library Cataloguing in Publication Data
is available from the British Library

Printed in the EU by L.P.P.S. Ltd. NN8 3PJ

Contents

Illustrations

(between pages 54 and 55)

1.   Map of Northumberland, 1921

2.   Joseph Cowen, c. 1860

3.   Joseph Cowen, c. 1881

4.   'Joe', *Vanity Fair*, 27 April 1878

5.   '*The Incorruptible Brick*'

6.   "*The Reason Why' Parliament was dissolved*'

7.   '*When is he going to stop?*'

8.   '*Going to Parliament*'

9.   The Unveiling of the Cowen Memorial, Newcastle upon Tyne, 7 July 1906

Sources: 1: P. Anderson Graham, *Highways & Byways in Northumberland*, London, 1921; 2-4: Laing Art Gallery, Newcastle; 5-8: R. W. Martin, *North Country Elections from 1826*, Robinson Library, Newcastle University; 9: Local Studies, Newcastle City Library.

Acknowledgments

During the long gestation in which this book took shape and was written I have become deeply indebted to many institutions, funding bodies and colleagues as well as to close friends and family for their support and encouragement. First and foremost I would like to record my thanks to Newcastle University and the Arts and Humanities Research Council for providing study leave and financing the final stages of the work. An AHRF award supported additional research and conference grants from the British Academy in 2004 and 2005 enabled me to test my findings among an international audience.

It all began with a conversation with my then undergraduate tutor, Bill Lancaster, who waxed enthusiastic about Joseph Cowen's political activities and suggested that a study of his life and career would be a good topic for a doctoral thesis. The British Academy generously supported my postgraduate work and, with the appointment of Robert Colls as co-supervisor, I set out to make sense of the vast archive of papers which Cowen left behind. I was indeed fortunate in having a superb team of labour historians to provide such wise counsel and expert guidance. Both Bill and Rob gave generously of their time and knowledge, and made helpful comments that significantly improved the thesis which finally emerged. I have called upon their assistance many times in the intervening years and I have always appreciated their continued interest in my work. During my postgraduate studies, Northumbria University gave the work an intellectual home and, subsequently, provided this fledgling historian with employment and convivial company in the Department of Historical and Critical Studies. During this period, too, Northumbria University gave me a small research grant which facilitated essential visits to archives in Hull, Glasgow, London and Amsterdam.

I appreciate all the help I have received from the librarians and archivists of numerous libraries and archives. In the North East, I was assisted by staff at Northumbria University Library, the Robinson Library, Newcastle University (especially Melanie Woods and her staff in Special Collections), the Laing Art Gallery, Northumberland Record Office, Gateshead Library and other libraries throughout North Tyneside who all responded helpfully to my countless requests for materials. Richard Potts and his staff at the Tyne and Wear Archives provided advice and assistance, as well as making the Search Room a comfortable and friendly place in which to work. Staff in the Local Studies Department of Newcastle City Library, at great inconvenience to themselves, indulged my preference for handling manuscript volumes of newspapers. Elsewhere, the late Peter Carnell facilitated my search through the Mundella/Wilson/Leader Papers at Sheffield University as well as helping me to find accommodation in the city. I have drawn heavily upon the patience and good humour of staff at the British Library (St Pancras and Colindale), Bishopsgate Institute, the Bodleian Library in Oxford and the Cooperative Archive, Holyoake House, Manchester. In this regard I would like to register my particular thanks to Gillian Lonergan whose extensive knowledge of the Co-operative Movement never ceases to amaze. She has responded cheerfully and efficiently to my many requests for information. I made two visits to the International Institute of Social History, Amsterdam, and on both occasions staff made great efforts to ensure that I was able to fully access their collections. I am grateful to them all.

This book and its author have benefited from other acts of generosity. Thanks are due to Mrs F. Harris who allowed me to read the manuscript of the late Keith Harris. Since my appointment to Newcastle University in 1999 I have enjoyed many interesting conversations about Cowen's European connections with my colleague David Saunders. I am very grateful to David for locating a microfilm copy of the long lost papers of W E Adams at the International Institute of Social History in Amsterdam, and for facilitating attempts to trace the originals which are held in the Moscow State Archives.

Friends in the Society for the Study of Labour History welcomed me into their ranks; collectively and individually they helped me to develop my interest in the field. I am grateful to Chris Wrigley and Maggie Walsh for generously supporting my many efforts to find work and to secure funding. That I managed to do both is a minor miracle and it could not have been achieved without their assistance. I have enjoyed the company of all those who have attended the annual Chartist conferences and benefited from their helpful feedback on my conference papers. I am glad to have this opportunity to state how much I value the friendship of Owen Ashton at Staffordshire University's Centre for the Study of Chartism. We first met in May 1991 at the launch of his biography of W.E. Adams and quickly found that we had much in common. And so it has proved. I have benefited from his extraordinary generosity countless times during the last sixteen years. We have collaborated on a number of projects and I have never ceased to be impressed by his modesty and unfailing good humour. I have come to count on him in more ways than I can say here. On this occasion, he read the entire manuscript and offered invaluable suggestions for its improvement. I hope that I have done justice to his advice while any infelicities in the text are entirely my own responsibility.

I would like to thank the following friends and colleagues for supporting my endeavours: Jo Alberti, Tony Barrow, Richard Bott, Dave Byrne, Ray Challinor, Malcolm Chase, Sandra Chilton, Hilary and Ian East, Neil Evans, Martin Farr, Susan-Mary Grant, Hazel and Gordon Horsley, Gilbert Hugman, Tim Kirk, Don MacRaild, Norman McCord, Roger Newbrook, Archie Potts, Luc Racaut, Stephen Regan, Dave Ridley, Ted Royle, Patrick Salmon, Rosie White, and the staff in the School of Historical Studies, Newcastle University. I am delighted that this book is to be published by Merlin Press and grateful to Tony Zurbrugg and Adrian Howe for their assistance and encouragement. By one of those curious tricks of fate my cousin, David Anderson MP, is now the elected member for the Blaydon constituency. I hope he will enjoy reading about the skirmishes, parliamentary and revolutionary, of his famous predecessor, the 'Blaydon Brick'.

As every writer knows only too well, it is the personal sacrifices made by close family members that make it possible for anything worthwhile to be achieved. In different ways and at different times my family have given me the support I needed to see the project through to completion: my children, Jonathan and Louise, may have been bemused by my liking for dusty books and newspapers but have always encouraged my efforts; my sister Margaret's hot line to St Rita worked its own special magic; I have been cheered on by the entire Allen clan, not least the historian among them to whom I have turned constantly for advice. Richard Allen enthusiastically read his way through several drafts, corrected the many oddities in my footnotes and propped up my faltering confidence at every turn. As in everything else, this has been a shared enterprise and this book is dedicated to him.

Abbreviations and Conventions

AP	Adams Papers
BL	British Library, London
CDP	Charles Dilke Papers
CP	Cowen Papers
DMA	Durham Miners' Association
FLA	Freehold Land Association
GLRO	Greater London Record Office
HJWP	H. J. Wilson Papers
AIISH	Amsterdam, International Institute of Social History
INLL	Irish National Land League
IRB	Irish Republican Brotherhood
JCM	Jane Cowen Manuscript
LC	Leader Correspondence
MP	Mundella Papers
NALU	National Agricultural Labourers' Union
NCLLS	Newcastle City Library, Local Studies
NFAC	Newcastle Foreign Affairs Committee
NLF	National Liberal Federation
NMA	Northumberland Miners' Association
NPU	Northern Political Union
NRU	Northern Reform Union
NUMI	Northern Union of Mechanics' Institutes
PDS	Polish Democratic Society
RLSC	Robinson Library, Special Collections
RSWP	Robert Spence Watson Papers
SUSC	Sheffield University, Special Collections
TWAS	Tyne and Wear Archive Service

Introduction

The public appetite for biography has always been strong and yet it may be said to have gone into overdrive in recent years as lesser-known celebrities and royal servants vied with the usual crop of actors, writers and politicians to scale the bestseller lists. Political biographies which are viewed in some quarters as part of this populist aesthetic have attracted harsh criticism, not least from Patrick O'Brien who considers that such gratuitous outpourings represent 'a triumph of form over substance'.[1] Leaving aside the vexed issue of guilt by association, the problem with O'Brien's analysis is that he assumes too narrow a definition of what history is or should be, and he is wedded to the idea that the lives of politicians cannot significantly extend our knowledge of political history.[2] The snares and traps he associates with the genre are certainly real enough, as anyone who has ever written a biography will testify. The need to demonstrate that a given individual possessed unique or virtuous qualities has steered many a biographer into a hagiographic *modus operandi*, while the fears of presenting an incomplete biography have all too often produced an unwieldy and unreadable manuscript. Biographers must accept that even where there are rich collections of personal papers and other documents there will always be aspects of a life which remain hidden or only partially revealed. Nonetheless, the challenges of writing a scholarly political biography should not be regarded as greater or more intractable than those with which other historians must contend. A persuasive argument can still be made that such biographies offer insights into the past that cannot be found in any other form.

At first glance, the subject of this political biography, Joseph Cowen MP, may appear to be an unlikely candidate for demonstrating the intrinsic merits of the genre. After all, he was only in office for the twelve years between 1874 and 1886, and his parliamentary career as a Liberal member for Newcastle can hardly be described as illustrious. In that time his name was not linked with the passage of an important reform act or other piece of landmark legislation; he was not a member of Gladstone's cabinet, nor was he one of the new working-class members of parliament. This being the case, can he have any claim upon the attention of historians? Certainly, in his own lifetime, his life and career was considered worth capturing for the public record. E.R. Jones' biography was given a warm reception by Cowen's many admirers, even though it glossed over the political conflict that had left him isolated at Westminster.[3] Like Jones, William Duncan who produced his study a few years after Cowen's death was still too much in awe of his subject to produce a critical analysis and it was to be almost a century later before Cowen's life was appraised by a modern historian.[4] The intention here is to demonstrate that Cowen's extraordinary career does indeed warrant further historical scrutiny, and that a study of his life can help to address questions that still remain about how Radicals and Liberals negotiated and shared power.[5]

Cowen was a wealthy man who falls neatly into that category of activists which Owen Ashton and Paul Pickering have defined as 'Friends of the People'.[6] His father left a considerable estate of lands, business interests and money which the younger Cowen substantially augmented, even though he plundered these resources to finance his many causes and campaigns.[7] He left a formidable collection of nineteenth-century letters and documents spanning the period 1833 to 1937 and which his daughter Jane Cowen collated after his death.[8] It was Jane who ruthlessly censored all of the personal correspondence, no doubt in accordance with her father's wishes. Cowen himself deliberately destroyed most of the material which referred to his clandestine republican activities, particularly those papers which related to his involvement in Felice Orsini's plot to assassinate Napoleon III in 1858. Understandably, he judged the correspondence to be much too sensitive. Nevertheless, despite the lamentable loss of some documents, the *Cowen Papers* are an unusually rich resource which offer rare insights into the realm of nineteenth-century popular politics. The lack of material on Cowen's family life or social activities is more than compensated for by the richness of other material, on radical activities and international affairs as well as on the workings of the Radical/Liberal alliance. The Minute Book of the Northern Reform Union (1858-62), for example, charts the day-to-day progress of the campaign, while the accompanying correspondence reveals Cowen's efforts to regenerate the call for reform in every major town and city. The activities of the Reform League are also well documented and give both a national and a local perspective on the events surrounding the Second Reform Act. The collection includes extensive material relating to working-class organisational and associational life. Cowen's involvement in temperance activities, mechanics' institutes and, in particular, his role in the spread of Co-operation in the North East are all detailed in numerous letters, memoranda and circulars.

The significance of the *Cowen Papers* lies mainly in the composite picture they provide of Cowen's extensive network of radical and revolutionary contacts. Thus letters from John Bright and Joseph Chamberlain, George Jacob Holyoake and George Julian Harney are held alongside those from Giuseppe Mazzini and Giuseppe Garibaldi, Henry Hyndman and Peter Kropotkin. This correspondence gives the collection a relevance and value which extends beyond the usual parameters of political memorabilia. Membership lists of both foreign and domestic radical movements are invaluable because so many proved to be short-term initiatives, and the available published information tends to be sparse and piecemeal. Finally, Cowen's career as an MP can be readily charted from extensive transcripts of his parliamentary speeches, together with related correspondence from his political colleagues.

The *Cowen Papers* are augmented by the extensive files of Cowen's early journals and the *Newcastle Chronicle* archives.[9] His editorial control was particularly in evidence in the pages of the *Daily Chronicle* which also carried his regular 'London Letter' column. Press sources afford unusually detailed accounts of radical activities and associational life, not least because the *Chronicle* offices acted as the operational headquarters for many of Cowen's political campaigns. His flamboyant career quite naturally provided good copy for countless national and provincial newspapers. Here the resources of the British Library (Colindale) offer a less privileged barometer of his wider impact and political status. In this regard the files of the *Pall Mall Gazette* during John Morley's and W.T. Stead's periods of editorship are particularly useful as they convey both metropolitan and provincial perspectives.

Other manuscript collections, too, are relevant to the reconstruction of Cowen's career, notably the *Mundella Papers,* the *Leader Correspondence* and the *Henry J. Wilson Collection.*[10] The *Mundella Papers* mainly comprise correspondence with prominent members of the Liberal Party and local Liberal Association executives, but they also contain some crucial material on Mundella's role as arbitrator in the 1871 Engineer's strike on Tyneside. The *Leader Correspondence* greatly illuminated the role of the Liberal press in Sheffield and the extent to which Mundella, unlike Cowen, was dependent upon Robert Leader's good offices in providing sympathetic and favourable publicity. As might be expected, all three collections are complementary and can be usefully interrogated together. Given Cowen's range of activity the collections that might be consulted are elastic but of these Holyoake's Library at Bishopsgate Institute, the Charles Dilke Papers (British Library), the Liberation Society records[11] and the long lost papers of Cowen's editor and friend W. E. Adams – recently re-discovered – provided insights that were not readily found elsewhere.[12]

Nineteenth-century British radicalism has received a good deal of scholarly attention,[13] but the absence of any national organisation or official leadership gave the movement a remarkable fluidity which has posed particular problems for historians. The challenge is how to analyse a movement whose manifestations varied according to local circumstances, community leadership and the political exigencies of the day. At the end of the 1850s the Liberal Party which emerged was a loose alliance of divergent opinions. Generally speaking, the party was dominated by the Whigs, a wealthy, right-wing group of landowners who monopolised most of the key political positions, and a much smaller group of Radicals who mostly represented the nonconformist, manufacturing interests of the new industrial constituencies. Throughout the nineteenth century the Liberals appealed to a broad cross section of the British public and elicited massive popular support, not least by exploiting the popular press in its 'golden age' of innovation and expansion. Despite the existence of a large corpus of work on nineteenth-century Liberal politics, significant gaps in our knowledge remain, not just in terms of the workings of the Radical/Liberal alliance at Westminster but also in the realm of provincial and regional politics.

While the remarkable resilience of the Liberal majority on Tyneside has been well documented,[14] the role of two generations of the Cowen family in that political success has scarcely registered in the relevant historiography. In the case of Sir Joseph Cowen (1800-1873) the oversight is understandable: his career, though laudable enough in its own way, was not exceptional and his subsequent knighthood rewarded his work as Chairman of the River Tyne Commission rather any major contribution to national political life. However, in wresting control from the Whig clique in 1865,[15] and providing Tyneside with a Radical member of parliament, the elder Cowen established a power base which his son, Joseph Cowen Jnr, was later able to exploit.

The neglect of the younger Joseph Cowen by generations of Liberal historians is an altogether more serious omission. Cowen's wide-ranging political activities and parliamentary career placed him in the forefront of almost every noteworthy progressive movement, both at home and abroad, and on that basis alone his relegation to the faddist fringe is as inappropriate as it is misleading.[16] The negotiated political compromise, by which Cowen agreed to represent the Liberals, ensured that Tyneside did not fall prey to the tide of reactionary feeling sweeping the country in 1873 and, more importantly, enabled the party leadership to regard north-east England as a secure bastion of Gladstonian Liberalism. The fact that Cowen was at odds with the Liberal Party for almost his entire parliamentary career, and actively opposed key areas of policy, is not reflected in the official statistics. Wholly unreliable as a description of the prevailing political realities, the Liberal epithet nevertheless prevailed, helped on by summary electoral returns and published histories of Victorian politics. Ultimately, Cowen's marginalisation has been so thorough that the ingrained traditional radicalism he inherited and sustained, and with which Tyneside was unquestionably associated at the time, has been effectively subsumed; subordinated to the rank of other contributory 'isms' (viz. Chartism, secularism, republicanism, etc.) which fed into rather than challenged the triumph of popular Liberalism.

Inevitably, much of the published work has focused upon national issues, parliamentary reforms and Cabinet ministers and, while the importance of such analyses is indisputable, they have not gone far enough towards advancing our understanding of popular Liberalism. The evidence suggests that local issues loomed large in the consciousness of the electorate, especially in the period prior to the 1868 Reform Act. Even in the closing decades of the century, as the greatly enlarged voting public grew accustomed to a more sophisticated style of political campaigning, such as that associated with Gladstone's Midlothian campaign, and the ad hoc flurry of activity at election times was replaced by a more permanent bureaucracy, local economic and social factors continued to exert considerable influence upon political postures and allegiances.[17] Clearly, the intricacies of parliamentary activity need to be balanced by an equally rigorous scrutiny of the workings of local politics, and the relationship between the two carefully evaluated.

Widespread acceptance that nineteenth-century Liberalism had a specific geography serves to underscore the point.[18] Where certain regions and localities are shown to have exhibited unusually consistent political allegiances, an explanation may legitimately be sought at the grass roots. Despite the continuing emphasis upon the importance of Gladstone's charismatic leadership,[19] neither personal popularity nor the appeal of his political message can be held to wholly account for such consistency. More often than not, it was the local politician or activist who assumed responsibility for fleshing out the parameters of Liberal policy in an accessible form, and undertook the delicate task of mediating the effects of individual measures. Provincial politicians had to be capable of tapping into the sensitivities of their immediate communities. Acceptance of the Liberals' retrenchment policy, for example, was often determined by the manner in which it was decoded and explained to any given local community. During the crucial 1874 elections, Biagini states that candidates 'took upon themselves the business of filling the gaps in the premier's manifesto and interpreting it so that it would look more attractive'.[20] On Tyneside, the Liberals' fiscal policy was carefully cast by Cowen in terms of providing 'the free breakfast table' by increasing levies on the frivolous consumerism of the wealthy – a concept which voters and non-voters alike might be expected to wholeheartedly endorse. And, of course, the economic advantages to be gained by the establishment of 'an absolutely free port' were relentlessly pressed home.[21] In this instance and in many others, provincial politicians had a crucial role to play in harnessing and maintaining the popular vote.

Joseph Cowen, was not just famous, he was infamous. He became renowned for his outspoken radicalism, his uncompromising defence of Irish nationalism and Home Rule, and his entrenched opposition to the Gladstonian Liberal policy of the 1880s. In ordinary circumstances, Gladstone and Cowen might have been good friends. After all, it was Gladstone who had secured a knighthood for Cowen's father. Parliamentary nepotism should have prevailed in favour of the son and conferred upon him the usual inherited honours and political success. Cowen was, however, no ordinary career-minded politician. He was greedy for power, but lacked the diplomatic skills that would have eased his path amongst the notables of Westminster; he sought to extend his influence but would not compromise to secure his political position. This was both a badge of honour and his Achilles heel.

On his home territory he fared rather better. As David Eastwood has observed, it was shared activities which 'translated urban individualism into social solidarities'.[22] In this respect, Cowen's acclaimed oratorical powers were a singular asset and one for which he became nationally renowned. In print and in his many speeches, Cowen persuaded large numbers of working people on Tyneside and throughout north-east England to take up the cause of electoral reform. They joined mechanics' institutes that welcomed ordinary workers and encouraged members to debate the religious and political questions of the day. As members of the Northern Reform Union and the Reform League they fought for 'the Charter and Something More': they pledged themselves to temperance, co-operation and religious tolerance; to the pursuit of knowledge and wider access to education; to trade unionism and labour representation.

Under Cowen's leadership, politics diversified and embraced international causes such as the American Civil War, Italian unification, and Polish and Hungarian liberation. These campaigns were personalised through his close friendship with Garibaldi, Mazzini, Kossuth and other prominent republicans. By his oratory, Cowen encouraged the entire Tyneside community – not just the supposedly radical wing – to engage directly in political struggles. Their commitment to the radical agenda had to extend beyond signing petitions and applauding sympathetic speeches, and, to that end, penny subscriptions proved to be an excellent strategy for ensuring maximum popular participation. Apart from giving financial support they were invited to house, feed and employ political refugees, even to enlist in a volunteer force and fight alongside Garibaldi.

Cowen's republican activities brought him into close association with other British radicals, notably W. J. Linton, P. A. Taylor and George Dawson, a Birmingham Unitarian and prominent radical who was also editor of the *Birmingham Daily Press*.[23] Linton and Taylor were the prime movers of the People's International League (1847-50), which became the parent association of a raft of internationalist organisations in the 1850s. Although Leicester did not benefit from Taylor's influential radical connections until later, a nascent republican group was established in 1851 by John Sketchley, the long suffering secretary of the South Leicestershire Chartists.[24] Moreover, John Biggs, who was MP for Leicester between 1855 and 1862, was considered sufficiently sympathetic to the cause of European freedom to warrant Cowen approaching him in 1859 for a subscription to the Mazzini Fund. Potential subscribers had to be trusted friends for, in effect, they were being asked to finance revolutionary activity. In return, they were promised absolute confidentiality.[25] Taylor's subsequent election in 1862 ensured the longevity of Leicester republicanism. Joseph Chamberlain, on the other hand, is noticeably absent from the subscription and membership lists of nationalist movements. His republican activities seem to be a development of the early 1870s and, unlike Cowen or Taylor, there are no detectable links with prominent European nationalists. According to Richard Jay, Chamberlain's fervour in 1871 was partly, if not wholly, a 'useful political bandwagon'.[26] In contrast, Cowen's revolutionary republicanism was legendary, not just in Britain but in towns and cities in Europe too. His Russophobia, particularly at the time of the Eastern Crisis, placed him at odds with many senior Liberals, while his aggressive independence so infuriated the Newcastle Liberal Association that they sought to replace him with a more accommodating representative. He was not an Irishman and yet he became an executive member of the Irish Land League; he was not an Italian and yet an Italian delegation were present at the unveiling of the Cowen memorial statue in 1906.

Cowen's press empire adds another important dimension to this study. In 1859, when he acquired his first newspaper, the public appetite for print had grown exponentially. It would be difficult to exaggerate the advantages this conveyed or the importance of the radical press in proselytising the reform agenda.[27] W. T. Stead, who edited the *Northern Echo* and the *Pall Mall Gazette*, believed his position required him to interpret as well as convey public opinion.[28] Press historians have long argued for the 'centrality of the press' in facilitating a better understanding of modern British society and politics; the press, it is claimed, can reveal a good deal about the 'power relations within society'.[29] Equally, political historians such as David Eastwood have maintained that Victorian print culture 'helped to shape and define the public domain of urban England'.[30] In north-east England where Cowen's popularity was strong, his newspapers achieved an extensive circulation but they also commanded a national and international readership. The global distribution of his newspapers undoubtedly enhanced his profile in the United States and Europe.

The political orientation of the local press played a major role in the formation of public opinion, particularly after the stamp duty was repealed, and this often determined the precise nature of the Radical/Liberal alliance. A brief survey of some key radical constituencies illustrates how this worked. For instance, the *Sheffield Independent* and the *Birmingham Daily Post* were both owned by

Liberal activists.[31] Robert Leader, founder of the Sheffield Liberal Association and a close friend of A. J. Mundella, ensured that Gladstonian Liberalism was given the highest possible profile in the pages of the *Independent*.[32] Sheffield's most prominent radical, H. J. Wilson, was no match for this assemblage of power and influence and, until his election as the member for Holmfirth in 1885, he was cleverly outmanoeuvred at every turn. Mundella was shrewd enough to recognise that connections with the radicals would have to be strengthened if the Liberal party was to retain its hold upon the constituency. Hostile press coverage had soured relations with the Sheffield radicals in the early 1870s, and as Wilson's wife had come under particularly heavy fire for her involvement in the campaign to repeal the Contagious Diseases Act, Mundella was at pains to point out the necessity for greater restraint.[33] Writing to Leader after the 1874 election, he stressed 'the desirability of having Wilson and co. as friends instead of enemies'.[34] In the event, Mundella placated Wilson with a 'frank apology' from Leader and brought him into the fold as secretary of the Sheffield Liberal Association.[35] In the aftermath of the Liberals' disastrous showing at the polls, there was always a risk that the opposition would take advantage of any internecine wrangling and this must have contributed to Wilson's apparent willingness to make peace. Ultimately Mundella handled the situation remarkably well and the tensions that remained rarely surfaced.

Joseph Chamberlain was just as fortunate. Under the proprietorship of J. T. Bunce, the *Birmingham Daily Post* proved to be a powerful ally, backing Chamberlain's entrée into Liberal politics and supporting him even when he made his dramatic exit to champion the Unionist cause.[36] In addition, Bunce was also directly involved in the establishment of the National Liberal Federation (NLF) in 1875. The NLF which introduced a tightly organised party structure militated against the independent stance which Radical members had always cherished and was seen to act as a break upon the flow of progressive ideas. The *Daily Post* became a staunch advocate of the caucus and even Chamberlain himself was obliged to adopt a more moderate pose and a less contentious programme of reform.[37]

Although Leicester radicals had a constant struggle for access to the press, the *South Midlands Free Press* gave them a platform after 1859. This offered an important counterbalance to the orthodoxy of the leading daily, the *Leicester Mercury*, which was owned by the vice president of the Leicester Liberal Association.[38] Thus the harmonious Liberal alliance that operated in Leicester from Taylor's election in 1862 onwards appears to have been mirrored by the local press.[39] Taylor, Mundella and Chamberlain were all to a lesser or greater degree dependent upon the good offices of newspaper proprietors to promote their agenda and generate popular support at election time. In all three burgeoning cities the press favoured the continuing hegemony of the Liberals in the political compromise that was reached and in doing so helped to suppress dissenting radical voices that might otherwise have been a more oppositional force within the parliamentary party.

In contrast, the advantages which accrued to the Tyneside radicals from Cowen's ownership of the *Chronicle* newspapers are all too apparent. As a proprietor who was also a politician, Cowen not only interpreted and conveyed political opinion, he created it, proselytising the full spectrum of radical interests. Trade unions, cooperatives, friendly societies and mechanics' institutes were all presented as essential components of this radical fraternity. Publicity in the *Chronicle* press ensured that campaigns and demonstrations were meticulously coordinated and had maximum impact. In 1873 local miners had particular reason to be grateful to the Cowen press, not only for championing much-needed mining reforms but also for backing the election of the miners' leader, Thomas Burt.[40] The unprecedented journalistic support given to local trade unionists, especially during the 1871 Nine Hours Campaign, delivered incalculable dividends in terms of political cohesion. This can be compared with the Lib-Labism of the Leicester trade unionists who are said to have renounced their radical politics in favour of sectional interests.[41] In the same way, the success of arbitration and conciliation mechanisms so keenly promoted by the powerful nonconformist lobby and Mundella helped to draw Sheffield trade unionists into partnership with mainstream Liberals, away from the militant activity so notable in 1866.[42] Jonathan Spain's study of the 1875 labour law reforms has noted that the well organised trade unionists in the North East were far less dependent upon statutory legal protection.[43] Although the issue was an important factor in the Liberal defeats of 1874 its impact in the North East was minimal. Cowen's success at the polls cannot be attributed to the Liberal manifesto to repeal the Criminal Law Amendment Act; it owed rather more to the services he had already rendered.[44] On Tyneside, Cowen's electoral success turned most of all upon the support of the influential Irish vote.

The cohesion of radical politics cannot be fully understood without due reference to Tyneside's large Irish population. Potentially, the Irish could have been an extremely divisive force. Cowen's espousal of the Irish cause, his close friendship with the Nationalist MPs, and his outspoken defence of Home Rule protected local radicalism from schism and reaped dividends at the polls. In other 'Irish' strongholds, notably Lancashire, prevalent sectarianism had fuelled a strong Tory reaction in 1874.[45] The relative quiescence of Anglo-Irish relations on Tyneside can be attributed to the way that the politically active Irish engaged with the agrarianism that lay at the heart of local radicalism. As a result of Cowen's positive intervention, radical interests became so interwoven with those of the Irish as to be scarcely distinguishable.

In Sheffield, the Radical/Liberal alliance was relatively untroubled apart from the tensions which prevailed over the Irish question. Unlike Cowen, Mundella had a poor relationship with the Irish nationalists and he could not count on their votes at election time.[46] As Alan O' Day has noted, the potential impact of an unpredictable Irish vote was an important consideration for politicians of both parties.[47] Mundella's high profile support for Gladstone's coercion policy in the early 1880s did not endear him to his Irish constituents, especially as many of them had already been alienated by his opposition to denominational education.[48] Wilson continually argued that Irish reforms should be prioritised and repressive measures regarded only as a last resort but Mundella remained unconvinced. He insisted that

> No government can apply any remedy to the Land laws or any other laws until they have first convinced the Irish people that Parliament and not Parnell and Co. are the real Government of the Country … I knew that my connection with the Government would sooner or later prove a trial to you and some others of my friends. I believe I am a member of a government more just and humane than any which has ever preceded it.[49]

As Irish antagonism to the Liberals mounted in the early months of 1881, Mundella urged Robert Leader to 'manfully oppose them. They deserve no quarter.'[50] Wilson had little real political muscle and his efforts to accommodate the needs of the Sheffield Irish were rendered ineffectual by the entrenched opposition of his Liberal partners.

Anglo-Irish relations in Birmingham were equally problematic. Sectarian violence spilled over onto the streets of both Birmingham and Sheffield, fuelled by the vitriol of William Murphy and the scaremongering that followed in the wake of the Fenian outrages of the 1860s.[51] Birmingham subsequently became an important organisational centre of the early Home Rule movement and Chamberlain assisted Butt in his bid to contest the Sheffield seat in 1874.[52] By 1880, however, when the Irish question threatened to squeeze out his plans for domestic land reform, his support was gradually withdrawn. Chamberlain's attitude to the Home Rule question was complicated by his own political ambitions and the policy adopted by Bright, who was the senior member for Birmingham at that time.[53] His knowledge of the Irish problem was almost entirely second hand, relations with the Irish nationalists were barely civil, and he had no direct knowledge of conditions in Ireland. Roland Quinault argues persuasively that Chamberlain was constrained by the Unionist stance adopted by the local press and all but one of his Liberal colleagues, and that he was therefore in no position to support Home Rule in 1886.[54] On balance, most would accept that Chamberlain's radicalism was a weaker mutation which, notwithstanding his enthusiasm for land reform, responded more to the political exigencies of the moment than the ideological principles of the past.

Graham Goodlad suggests that the majority of Liberal politicians were ignorant of what Irish Home Rule entailed[55] but this was not the case on Tyneside. The *Newcastle Daily Chronicle*, which served as a *bona fide* Irish newspaper, had given Irish issues unprecedented coverage and the Home Rule question had been extensively debated. Cowen's links with the Irish nationalists, and his direct participation as an executive of the Irish Land League, placed Irish affairs at the centre of radical politics. Irish reform rested firmly within the agrarian and internationalist tradition which had moulded and shaped Tyneside radicalism for generations and this ensured the continuing solidarity of local radical politics.

This study of Cowen's remarkable life and career has found much that would support those analyses which have argued in favour of radical continuities in the Victorian period.[56] But it does not subscribe to those views which insist upon viewing Liberal culture as an 'untroubled unity'.[57] The evidence shows that, as directed by Joseph Cowen, radicalism in the North East retained its traditional roots and continued to be the politics of opposition. For a time it seemed that Cowen's legacy was not to last beyond his lifetime. The Liberal Party's hold on the affections and loyalties of the Tyneside people[58] were a shadow of what they had been in Cowen's heyday and, for a time, radicalism became increasingly identified with the agenda of the Irish nationalists.[59] Yet, when the ILP finally broke through on Tyneside in 1906, it was Cowen's archetypal radicalism that offered the best model for their bid to progress towards a wider democracy.[60]

Chapter 1
Rights and Privileges:
Tyneside's Radical Tradition, 1775-1832

The ultra-radicalism which distinguished Joseph Cowen from so many of his contemporaries was undoubtedly a reflection of his remarkable intellectual agility. He was a skilful political tactician and a charismatic leader whose campaign for progressive reform has long been regarded as a singular factor in Newcastle's reputation as one of the foremost radical cities in the nineteenth century. Yet even though Cowen is widely held to have moulded Tyneside politics in his own image, he was the legatee of a much older political tradition. Radicalism in north-east England, as elsewhere, was not a nineteenth-century phenomenon for its roots stretch backwards into the eighteenth century and beyond.[1] To make any sense of Cowen's republican ideas and modernizing agenda due account must taken of those formative influences, familial as well as political, which helped to shape his distinctive political philosophy. It has been argued that 'for most people, politics was the politics of the town in which they lived their lives'[2] and, notwithstanding the distorting effects of such a sweeping generalisation, the role of community and locality in shaping the political culture must be recognised.[3] Essentially, the 'community politics' which E. F. Biagini has linked to the emergence of charismatic leaders such as Cowen must be viewed as a symbiotic process.[4] At home he gained a political apprenticeship from his parents whose political activism constituted a powerful exemplar of democracy in action; from Tyneside and his immediate community, the village of Winlaton, Cowen assimilated that potent amalgam of chauvinism and radicalism for which both were so renowned.[5]

The precocious industrialisation of the North East which, from the sixteenth century onwards, was largely built upon the 'perfection of coalery' anchored Tyneside's later reputation as 'the Black Indies'.[6] As the regional capital, the lion's share of this hothouse of trade and production flowed into Newcastle coffers and established the 'Eye of the North' as one of the foremost English urban centres in the eighteenth century.[7] But as countless historians have recognised, the process of industrial change brought great hardship for the many as well as profits for the few.[8] The relentless pace of change created tensions in the workforce which all too frequently spilled over into conflict and violent confrontation. In the North East 'collective bargaining by riot' was not just the stock-in-trade of the keelmen in the seventeenth century, though their organised defence of wages and traditional working practices has been described as 'a primitive form of trade union'.[9] Other sections of the workforce, especially colliers, were just as combative in protecting their customary rights and privileges.[10] A rare surviving account of the 1734 dispute at Newbottle Colliery in County Durham reveals just how acrimonious such clashes often were. In this instance, it cost the life of the pitman John Gray.[11] In the mid-eighteenth century a panoply of friendly societies were already providing a raft of protective benefits and increasingly they offered an organisational structure through which trade disputes could be aired and protested.[12] Recent historiography has questioned the extent to which London radicalism was indebted to the provinces and there is certainly some evidence for this.[13] Thus, in 1768 coal-heavers in London are said to have taken their lead from a coal dispute in the North East and strengthened their demand for better pay.[14]

Some would have it that this incipient trade unionism was apolitical and not linked to the rise of radical politics in the region,[15] but the pressing concerns that prompted workers to resort so readily to strike action throughout this period should not be viewed in a vacuum. A sophisticated print culture, especially in Newcastle which supported four weekly newspapers at the time of the Wilkes' controversy, facilitated the spread of radical ideas, not least by circulating copies of the Middlesex petition in June 1769.[16] The enormous popular celebrations which were held throughout the region after Wilkes' release from prison in 1770 suggest that this propaganda campaign had an impact far beyond the narrow concerns of an intellectual coterie.[17] With more than 1,700 people in Northumberland and Durham employed in some aspect of the book trade between 1626 and 1860, printing was a vital element in the city's commercial success and the national reputation of the engravers Thomas Bewick and Ralph Beilby helped to underpin Newcastle's claim to be a centre of publishing expertise.[18] The circulation of new ideas, whether by newspaper or tract, helped to foster the growth of religious dissent as well as political radicalism and in the eighteenth century most of the major Nonconformist denominations had taken root in the region: Baptists, Methodists, Quakers, Presbyterians and Unitarians had all established their own independent congregations.[19] It is scarcely surprising that some of those who espoused a nonconformist position in matters of faith should be in the vanguard of radical politics. It was a Glassite community in Newcastle that cultivated and informed the revolutionary ideas of Thomas Spence.[20]

Thomas Paine is generally considered to be the key figure in the development of late-eighteenth century radical ideas and, until recently, recognition of
the role of Thomas Spence has been correspondingly thinner. Those who did
acknowledge Spence's contribution tended to concentrate upon the influence
of the Spencean Philanthropists and their subsequent adaptation of Spence's
ideas. The view put forward by G. D. H. Cole and Raymond Postgate, for instance, is typically dismissive: 'his importance lies not so much in himself as
in the organisation he left behind, the "Spencean Philanthropists" whose innocence was to enable the government's agents to use them for an exceedingly vile
purpose'.[21] Studies by Malcolm Chase and David Worrall have since helped to
redress the balance and this is to be welcomed on a number of counts.[22] In the
first place, Chase's research has effectively established the centrality of Spence's agrarian critique by demonstrating the considerable overlap with the ideas
of Paine, and then highlighting Spence's altogether more rigorous approach.[23]
This in turn has prepared the ground for a substantial reappraisal of Feargus
O'Connor and his Land Plan, long regarded as an aberration which seriously
damaged the Chartist movement.[24] Of more immediate significance here, is the
way that Chase focused upon Spence's activities on Tyneside in the 1770s and
this supports the view that Spence was the product of an existing radical tradition, drawing from as well as contributing to the 'strong political consciousness' of late eighteenth-century Tyneside.[25]

The influence of Revd James Murray (1732-1821), leader of the High Bridge
Glassite Congregation reputed for its 'advanced opinions', is said to have been a
salutary influence.[26] The radicalism of later organisations such as the Political
Protestants in the 1820s can be traced back to that same dissenting community.
Murray was an eloquent and influential radical who campaigned for electoral
reform and was heavily involved in raising the profile of the Wilkes' affair.
He exploited Tyneside's rich publishing resources and his polemic tracts obtained a wide circulation. Murray and Spence were also fellow members of the
Newcastle Philosophical Society which, together with various political clubs
such as the Robin Hood Society and the Constitution Club, provided a forum
for lively political debate.[27] In 1775, when Spence delivered his famous lecture
proposing agrarian reform, it was Murray who advocated its publication in
pamphlet form and later vigorously challenged the Society for expelling him.[28]
Spence's writings also reflected his engagement with key local events such as
the dispute over enclosure of the Town Moor in 1771, and the 1774 elections.
The judgement embodied in the Town Moor Act (1774) was regarded as an
irrefutable vindication of the ancient rights of the people and celebrated with
numerous demonstrations and ceremonies.[29] The elections that year were notable not simply for Murray's vigorous satire of the rampant corruption, but

for the adoption of a radical electoral pledge which anticipated the Charter on three counts: shorter parliaments, fairer representation and an extension of the franchise. It is notable too that Jean-Paul Marat's *The Chains of Slavery* polemic had been circulated widely among patriotic societies in Newcastle at that time, and that he regarded them as the 'most pure in the realm'.[30] Mary Ashraf notes that while a similar pledge was drawn up by the London Burgess Party, the Newcastle pledge was much more precisely formulated – the implication being that even at this early stage, the Newcastle radical party was no mere provincial satellite. Granted, its vision may have had a community-centred inflection, but that need not necessarily detract from what were still unusually progressive policies.[31]

The 'Rights of Man' which became a popular motto for radical banners is commonly attributed to Paine but Spence also used the same phrase as the title of his Newcastle lecture.[32] Spence's idea that 'the land is the people's farm' was not an attack on property per se but an expression of his belief that land owner-ship was a perversion of natural justice; the source of all poverty and tyranny which threatened the peace and liberty of society.[33] Paine's 'Agrarian Justice', on the other hand, fell short of condemning land ownership. Instead he advo-cated the imposition of a system of ground rents which would constitute a Na-tional Fund for meeting the special needs of those reaching the age of maturity (21 years) or retirement.[34] Spencean agrarian theory embraced the inherent social and political injustices of the system whereas Paine's perspective appears to be locked into the economic issues. The other key difference was that Spence wrote for a popular audience, publishing cheap tracts and broadsheets which would be more accessible to the poorer classes.

Spence's departure for London after Murray's death in 1782 did not mark the end of radical activity on Tyneside and the years leading up to the French Revo-lution were notable for the proliferation of debating societies and clubs. With the backing of Solomon Hodgson at the *Newcastle Chronicle* political reform remained a live issue and branches of the Revolution Society and the Society of the Friends of the People, among others, continued to proliferate.[35] These radi-cal organisations may have scarcely impacted upon the poorer classes in the way that Spence hoped but nevertheless their activities and publications helped to create a political milieu in which parliamentary reform was strongly sup-ported. They also provided subsequent radical movements with an articulate and confident leadership which could take the reform question forward after the end of the century. Most of all, it is the influence of Spence's ideas that is most clearly detectable in the writings, speeches and policies of later genera-tions of north-east radicals. Cowen and other Tyneside activists consistently campaigned for the abolition of the laws of primogeniture and entail which had produced 'an unnatural centralisation', arguing that the working classes were the producers of all wealth, that their labour was a form of property and that the ills of society were not caused by overpopulation but by an unjust distribution of wealth.[36] This line of argument closely resembles Spence's own conclusion to *The Rights of Individuals* (1797):

> Slaves and Unfortunate men have cultivated the earth, adorned it with buildings and filled it with all kinds of riches. And the wealth which enabled you to set these people to work was got by Hook or by Crook from Society ... All riches come from Society, I mean the Labouring Part of it.[37]

If Cowen's politics were vitally informed by these subversive intellectual undercurrents they were also a product of his upbringing in the village of Winlaton. At the beginning of the nineteenth century, Winlaton was an isolated though well-populated village on the outskirts of Tyneside. The Crowley ironworks which were established in Swalwell and Winlaton in 1691, and the largest of their kind in Europe in the eighteenth century, dominated the local landscape and the lives of the inhabitants.[38] With a reputation both at home and abroad for producing high quality manufactured goods, the Crowley Works were extremely prosperous until the end of the Napoleonic Wars wrought severe economic dislocation. By then, it seems, Crowley's were no longer being efficiently managed and their over-dependence upon military contracts proved disastrous. Unable to compete effectively, the ironworks were finally closed, creating serious hardship and, more crucially, a strong political reaction. In the aftermath, 'Crowley's Crew', as the workers were known, abandoned their Tory loyalties and embraced a strident and uncompromising radicalism.[39]

This ideological somersault emanated from more than just economic privation: the entire social fabric of the village was affected by the firm's collapse. The paternalist experiments introduced by Sir Ambrose Crowley had transformed the village of Winlaton into a model community, with a panoply of innovative social and welfare provisions.[40] Education and medical facilities, and a progressive benefit system, provided villagers with an exceptional degree of social and economic security. Even though Crowley assumed overall responsibility for his workers' everyday needs, this was not just patronage; the costs of most services were met by joint contributions and both employer and employed gained from the good relations that were forged.[41] The highly-skilled workforce, which included women nail makers, were paid good wages and all disputes were settled by an appointed Arbitrators Court.[42] Crowley's welfare system had helped to instil a spirit of independence and a strongly rooted artisanal pride. The closure of the ironworks created a climate of intense class antagonism as workers were forced to accept the less-favourable working conditions imposed upon them by their new employers.[43] In the event, the political deference[44] engendered by the Crowley ethos of mutuality was rapidly replaced by an aggressive radicalism, firmly rooted in a profound sense of injustice and fuelled by a nostalgic desire to recapture a seemingly halcyon past.

At the turn of the century the Cowen family were scarcely distinguishable from any other skilled working-class family in Winlaton, but in the space of three or four decades they had acquired sufficient wealth and status to lend them substantial local influence. Joseph Cowen's grandfather, John Cowen, had worked as a blacksmith for Crowley's before setting up his own workshop. Later he diversified his business interests by moving into brewing and retailing, creating a string of businesses that gave employment and wealth to his growing family.[45] John's son, Joseph Cowen Snr, who later became Liberal member for Newcastle and received a knighthood for his work on the Tyne River Commission, had begun life as an apprentice chain-maker before joining the family business.[46] The propitious marriage in 1819 of his sister Mary to Anthony Forster, a local brick manufacturer, provided the opportunity for Cowen Snr to become a businessman in his own right.[47] Underhand dealings were rumoured but there seems little doubt that his entrepreneurial skills and hard work were responsible for the brickyard's continuing success.[48] Capitalizing on the growing demand for clay products and the availability of fine quality, iron-free clay at Blaydon Burn, he painstakingly developed and patented a unique firebrick which won several awards at the Great Exhibition. As the business grew profitable and expanded into national and international markets he began to invest his spare capital in other lucrative ventures. Beginning with the purchase of a colliery at Blaydon Burn, he gradually acquired coal staithes, a small railway line and a number of substantial tracts of neighbouring land.[49]

Winlaton radicals were in the forefront of local demonstrations protesting against the Peterloo Massacre of 1819,[50] while the concealed arms that were carried by some of the protesters were reputedly manufactured in the village by some of Crowley's former ironworkers who had set up their own independent blacksmith workshops.[51] In 1832, the Winlaton contingent demonstrated their continuing commitment to reform when they marched to the protest meeting at Spital Fields in Newcastle bearing immense oak saplings.[52] And, when the reform campaign was rekindled at the end of 1837, their presence at Chartist meetings was invariably singled out for special recognition. Dr John Taylor's address at the 1838 Christmas Day meeting thus began with a tribute to the men of Northumberland and Durham, and especially 'you men of Winlaton who in 1819 so nobly did your duty'.[53] The Winlaton Band was regularly pressed into service to supply the martial music considered so important a feature of local

Chartist gatherings while the women of Winlaton, too, received their share of praise for turning out in such large numbers.[54]

In 1854, Cowen's journal, the *Northern Tribune,* gave this account of Winlaton's role in north-east Chartism:

> In 1839 it was the headquarters of Chartism in the North East. During the incipient rebellion of that year, pikes and other warlike instruments were made in large numbers by the Winlaton smiths, many of whom were employed exclusively in their manufacture for some time. Almost all the leaders of the movement visited the village and were feted in grand style... The Sacred Month was better observed in Winlaton than most places and few villages in the district contributed so formidable a contingent to the 'Battle of the Forth'.[55]

Even if his heroic account is discounted as over-exuberant pride in his native village, contemporary newspaper reports verify that Winlaton Chartism was of the 'physical force' variety. At a meeting in June 1839, when 'the whole village was on the *qui vivre*', banners bore the uncompromising warning that the marchers were there to demand their liberty, by force if necessary: 'Hereditary Bondsmen, know ye not Who would be free themselves must strike the blow.'[56] And, the decision of the Winlaton Political Union to circulate a special address to their 'Brother Radicals of the United Kingdom' is an indication of the strength of their resolve. 'Fellow Slaves' were offered every assistance and reminded that the resort to arms had enabled the United States to win their independence.[57] That the village could act as host to leading Chartists, such as George Julian Harney and Dr John Taylor, speaks volumes for Winlaton's reputation as a 'bastion of revolutionary politics'.[58] It was in this stronghold of political radicalism that Joseph Cowen Jnr spent his formative years, and undoubtedly culled many of his more revolutionary notions.

By the time that Cowen Jnr was born in 1829 the family had already begun to acquire the capital, property and disposable income that would enable them to move in smart middle-class circles. His father had, by then, purchased a large house near the brickworks at Blaydon Burn, a small hamlet on the outskirts of Winlaton which consisted of little more than a cluster of workingmen's cottages. According to Cowen's daughter, Jane, the men employed in the brickyard 'lived as neighbours to their employer and his children'.[59] The relative isolation of the Blaydon Burn community seems to have bred an easy familiarity and it is said that Joseph 'often escaped from his mother to help push the tubs of clay. Many a time the servant lass caught him and took him home, washed him and changed him.'[60] Local legend would have it that Cowen was born in one of those same workingmen's cottages,[61] but whether there is any truth in this or not, Cowen's childhood certainly gave him that intimate understanding of working-class life and experiences which was to inform so much of his later politics. He was, of course, much too young to have participated in early Chartism but he must have garnered something of the strength of local feeling from the children he mixed with so freely. In particular, the local impact of the prolonged and bitter mining strike in 1844 must have had a lasting impact. The Great Strike, as it was called afterwards, led to violent clashes as 'blackleg labour' was recruited and local miners' families were summarily evicted. As Robert Colls notes, what began as a dispute over pay and conditions 'ended as a straight fight for trade unionism in the coalfield'.[62]

These key formative experiences were reinforced by the political education he received first-hand from his own parents and through their friendship with prominent local radicals who were frequent visitors to the family home at the time when he was, perhaps, at his most impressionable. Some of these radical connections had been forged in 1819 when his father had led his 'class' of Winlaton blacksmiths at the Peterloo demonstrations on the Town Moor.[63] His mother, Mary Newton, was the leader of a branch of Female Reformers who had a reading group and also walked in the procession that day.[64] In addition, Cowen Snr's membership of the Northern Political Union (NPU), which is said to have played a pivotal role in securing the successful passage of the 1832 Reform Act, brought him into contact with activists such as Thomas Doubleday, Charles Larkin and Charles Attwood.[65] Much later, in the 1850s, Joseph Cowen Jnr was able to capitalize upon his easy familiarity with this older generation of radicals, drawing them into his Foreign Affairs Committee and the Northern Reform Union.[66] Doubleday, especially, became a regular correspondent and Cowen used him as a sounding board for some of his reform ideas and strategies.

After 1832 the political affiliations of the Cowen family becomes rather ambiguous. Sir Joseph Cowen reputedly 'engaged in a little social climbing', taking his family to society balls and soirees, and identifying himself with the Anti-Corn Law League and Poor Law Reform.[67] It is unclear whether this political trimming was motivated by a desire to make advantageous business connections, or by serious political ambitions which would have required him to cultivate those who had local influence. It is tempting to surmise that his wife's avoidance of these social functions indicated a continuing allegiance to the radicalism of her youth, but such speculation is unhelpful.[68] On the one hand, the appointment of Sir Joseph Cowen to the Gateshead Board of Guardians suggests that he had no serious misgivings about implementing the 1834 Poor Law Amendment Act but, on the other, surviving records show that the Board did press for substantial reforms during his time as Chairman. The petition that the Board presented to parliament in 1845 bore the explicitly radical statement that the working population had 'in exchange for their labour the inalienable right to existence from the land which gave them birth'.[69] The *Gateshead Observer* bragged of the Board's largesse in not discriminating between the resident and casual poor, and asserted that 'in no part of the kingdom can the Poor Law be more faithfully administered than in this and the neighbouring Union'.[70] This was no idle boast and it is noteworthy that the Poor Law Board considered it necessary to recommend some modification of the Gateshead Board's dietary provision, on the grounds that it was 'decidedly higher in nutrient than the average'.[71]

Cowen paid this tribute to his father's political radicalism after his death in 1873:

He preserved to the end the ardent political opinions of his youth and he died as earnest and advanced a Radical as he was when, fifty years ago, he marched at the head of his brother blacksmiths to the famous political gathering on the Town Moor. It sometimes happens that a change in a man's circumstances alters his political principles. That was not the case with the gentleman to whom I now refer ... I know of no man more conscientious in the beliefs he entertained, and more consistent in upholding them.[72]

No mention was made of his father's flirtation with Whig orthodoxy, for Cowen was at great pains to present himself to the electorate as the 'natural' successor and rightful heir to the Radical candidacy. Political pragmatism apart, his father's reputation as an even-handed and generous employer, and his record of service to the Tyneside community, could justifiably be viewed as the practical application of radical principles. Sir Joseph was one of the few local employers to continue the Crowley system of caring for their workers. Both disabled and elderly employees were provided with a weekly pension which was further supplemented by the provision of accommodation and fuel. He also commissioned the building of a row of cottages to house local widows, and when employment was scarce he organised work schemes such as the planting of Brockwell Wood at Blaydon Burn.[73] It was this kind of paternalism that was so much in evidence when Sir Joseph addressed a meeting of the Newcastle Farmers' Union in 1850 and urged upon them 'the importance of erecting cottages for those labourers in remote districts of Northumberland who are now compelled to live in mud hovels'.[74] Beyond these immediate community concerns he also served as a Town Councillor for Newcastle and on countless charitable committees. When

Gladstone formally recognised his public service, including his Chairmanship of the River Tyne in 1871, with a life peerage it was said to be 'well deserved'.[75]

Cowen learned to emulate his father's work ethic and dogged determination, and to share his conviction that superior wealth and status carried with it a burden of responsibility that could not be shirked. 'Power', Cowen said, 'to the very last particle of it, is duty.'[76] Like his father, he became a hard-headed entrepreneur who never allowed sentiment to interfere with the smooth running and expansion of his business interests. Although he always denounced the acquisition of wealth for its own sake, he made no apology for his resolute pursuit of profits, arguing that 'there may come a time when we must advocate a cause which does not meet with popular approval, then a balance at the bank is very useful'.[77] The possession of wealth, as Cowen discovered, had provided his father with an enviable degree of independence, and the opportunity to take a leading role in the political fabric of Tyneside life. Notwithstanding the sincerity of his desire to serve the local community, Cowen evinced a palpable appetite for power. Fortunately, he did not have to indulge in any sycophancy or compromise his political principles in order to realise his ambitions; when the time came, he was able to follow in his father's footsteps with every conceivable advantage – money, status and political experience all helped to smooth his path.

As already shown, the value system that informed Cowen's politics in later life was demonstrably a composite of the local radical tradition and the family's own code of ethics. But, equally, the direction of his political and philosophical ideas was also shaped by the progressive education he received. His first taste of school, as a boarder at Burnopfield, Co. Durham, appears to have been uneventful. What is interesting is that he was later taught by Henry Allison, the former schoolmaster at Crowley's.[78] Before long, he had progressed to Mr Week's Academy at Ryton. Weeks was no country tutor but a man of means, serving as a Poor Law Guardian and taking an active role in local politics.[79] More importantly, he was an innovative teacher who encouraged his students to read widely and to engage in group discussion. And it was Richard Weeks who, amongst other things, introduced Cowen to the literature of Walter Scott.[80]

Most of all, Cowen grew intellectually and politically during his years as an undergraduate arts student at Edinburgh University. When Cowen took up his place there in November 1845, Edinburgh was the focus of religious controversy and a hothouse of literary and philosophical debate. He boarded with his personal tutor, Dr John Ritchie, who was a United Presbyterian Minister and a leading member of the Free Kirk movement.[81] Ritchie was well known in Newcastle as an advocate of Teetotalism and beyond as the 'Goliath of the voluntaryists'.[82] These temperance and nonconformist credentials may explain why he was selected as Cowen's mentor. Even though his stay in Edinburgh proved to be relatively short-lived, this extrovert character exerted a powerful influence over Cowen. Ritchie was a renowned radical activist, taking a prominent part in Scottish Chartism and often holding meetings in his chapel, as well as eloquently championing the cause of anti-slavery and temperance.[83] Through Ritchie, Cowen was brought into close contact with other Free Kirk leaders, such as Dr Candlish and Robert Chalmers.[84] Moreover, the abolition of slavery campaign was then just beginning to gather momentum and many of the leading protagonists visited Edinburgh, circulating tracts and delivering lectures. The speeches he heard by George Thompson, Thomas B. Wright and Frederick Douglass are said to have exerted 'a profound influence',[85] and he became firmly committed to the 'total and immediate abolition of slavery, not just in the United States, but throughout the world'.[86] This was no idle commitment. Alongside W. E. Adams,[87] Cowen subsequently gave full press backing to the campaign of 1861-2, earning generous praise from the abolitionist William Lloyd Garrison for his efforts: 'Many thanks to you for the handsome manner in which you introduced me to the people of Newcastle, through the columns of the *Chronicle*.'[88]

Although Cowen displayed little interest in his academic studies, he threw himself enthusiastically into the city's radical causes and became Chairman of the University's Eclectic Debating Society. It was in this capacity that Cowen brought forward a motion of censure, protesting against the Home Secretary's controversial interference with the private mail of Giuseppe Mazzini, the renowned Italian nationalist.[89] Mazzini's letter had contained sensitive information regarding the seditious activities of the Bandiera brothers, and a storm of protest broke out when the brothers were executed by the Austrian government.[90] Cowen wrote to Mazzini expressing his horror at the shootings. The 'cordial and encouraging' reply he received marked the beginning of a prolific correspondence and a serious commitment to the cause of Italian unification.[91] Mazzini introduced Cowen to a network of European revolutionaries and their friendship, as he later recalled, 'influenced my political course'.[92]

By 1846, Cowen's professed 'ultra-radicalism' was beginning to cause his parents considerable anxiety. Dr Ritchie, he admitted in his diary, had enabled him to see 'many things in a different and better light'.[93] His profession of radical beliefs was broad, encompassing the abolition of hereditary titles, sinecures, laws of entail, state churches, food taxes and slavery; he declared himself committed to fight for the Six Points of the Charter, religious freedom and social reform. Clearly, some of his diary entries would have been considered highly seditious, especially the pronouncement that 'When governments fail to secure to the people life, liberty and the pursuit of happiness, it is their Right and their

Duty to alter or abolish them'.[94] Despite the unequivocal opposition of both family and friends, and his own fear that his political opinions would force him to leave home, he remained 'determined to stick fast to my present views'.[95] Urgent attempts were made to persuade him to concentrate more on his studies and moderate his political views. His aunt, Mrs Allison, was despatched to Edinburgh to ensure that he complied but, in the event, the ploy proved to be a complete failure when she also became caught up in Edinburgh's religious warfare.[96]

Why Cowen should have left Edinburgh in 1847 without completing his studies is not altogether clear.[97] There are suggestions that he suffered from ill-health, but the more likely explanation is that his parents were eager to channel his energies into more orthodox pursuits. According to his daughter, Jane, his employment in the family business as a clerk had been planned long before his year at University and there seems to have been no possibility that he might choose his own career.[98] Working up to twelve hours a day, and frequently deputizing as manager in his father's absence, does not appear to have had the desired effect; it neither curtailed his political studies nor sapped his enthusiasm for radical causes. He took out a subscription to Julian Harney's *Democratic Review* and the *Red Republican*, and joined the People's International League,[99] whose members included such radical luminaries as Thomas Cooper, W. J. Linton and Henry Vincent.[100] As a result, his network of radical contacts began to expand, helped on by his friendship with Mazzini and, of course, Harney.[101]

Although Cowen had drawn up a precocious testimony of belief by this stage, his politics were still in a state of flux. At the same time as he denounced the aristocracy in forthright and uncompromising terms, he yet expressed a naive faith in the integrity of the middle classes. Citing Robert Burns, William Blake, Oliver Goldsmith and Richard Cobden as examples, he claimed that 'the strength and honour of a nation depends on her middle class'.[102] However, within the space of a few brief years, he was forced to re-evaluate his opinions. Beginning in his own local community, Cowen embarked upon three reform projects at the end of 1847 and it was this experience, more than any other, which led him to renounce the middle-class gradualism espoused by his father and into a commitment to fundamental working-class reforms.

The least successful of these early ventures was the formation of a branch of the Anti-State Church Association 'for the liberation of religion from all state interference'.[103] A founding conference had been held in London at the end of April 1844 following a series of articles in the *Nonconformist*. As Dr Ritchie was one of the delegates it seems likely that Cowen's interest in the organisation originated from his Edinburgh days.[104] Initially, he had planned to hold a series of public meetings in the Nonconformist chapels of Winlaton and Blaydon, and to engage a representative of the parent association as guest lecturer.[105] In 1848 he paid 7s 6d for some Association literature[106] and invited several local radical activists to address the branch, including Charles Larkin, but unfortunately they all declined. Despite his efforts, Cowen was not able to generate enough local interest or raise the necessary subscriptions to make the project viable, and he was forced to abandon it.[107] It is typical of Cowen to assume that everyone would share his views or, if they did not, that he could persuade them to reconsider. Ritchie's influence was doubtless significant and he seems to have scarcely registered the furore that his 'ungodly' activities would unleash in such a small village. To his credit, Cowen did not lose faith in the wider campaign and he continued to represent Newcastle on the Association's Council by coordinating subscriptions.[108] In 1853 the Association merged with the Liberation Society, together with a number of Nonconformist congregations, and under these new auspices it became an effective lobby for disestablishment.[109] For Cowen, the experience taught him an important lesson in political expediency. Future campaigns, as he now appreciated, would have to be more carefully planned.

When he launched the Winlaton Sanitary Association, he deliberately set out to cultivate the support of the most respected members of the community, thus defusing any potential opposition and ensuring that there would be no financial difficulties. Insanitary conditions were endemic at that time, and even though medical opinion was beginning to attribute recurrent outbreaks of cholera to environmental pollution, improvements still depended upon local initiatives.[110] His father was appointed Chairman and, this time, Charles Larkin agreed to lend his support. In his opening speech Cowen Jnr appealed to the gathered residents to work cooperatively in the interests of the whole community. The Crowley ethics of mutuality were clearly to the fore and his understanding of the problem had almost certainly been informed by his regular subscription to the *People's Journal*.[111] Deploring 'the abundance of putrid heaps of dung and stagnant pools', he accused the wealthy of shirking their responsibilities. For their part, working men were urged to be self-reliant; to realise that, 'If you are to be elevated, you must do so yourselves'.[112] Subscriptions were fixed at the modest sum of 1s per annum to encourage the widest possible participation. The success of the project is difficult to assess for beyond an account of the inaugural meetings there are no other surviving documents. Improvements could not have been very significant for in April 1850, when the *Newcastle Guardian* ran a series of articles on the condition of the working classes, Winlaton was still described as an 'insanitary and dirty' village.[113]

Ignorance, as Cowen was beginning to discover, was the greatest obstacle to progress and his decision to establish a Literary and Scientific Society in Winlaton emanated from a firm belief that 'political bettering of the people must rest on the heels of moral and intellectual elevation. Education must be its precursor'.[114] At that time, mechanics' institutes tended to cater for the skilled working classes, subscriptions were prohibitive and lectures too high flown and intellectual.[115] Although Cowen's initial proposals suggested that the aims of the Winlaton Institute were not substantially different from those of other institutes, his opening address proved otherwise. Cowen's criterion that such institutions should be 'open to all' was not just empty rhetoric: women as well as men were to be admitted as members.[116] Subscriptions and other levies were adjusted downwards and the original rules were revised to ensure that at least half of the committee were drawn from the working classes.[117] Within six months a mechanics' institute had been established at Blaydon and Cowen embarked on a 'missionary' tour of all of the outlying villages.[118] Success, and the prestige that flowed from it, fuelled his ambitions. While his own community were always the first to benefit from his initiatives (the first co-operative store was established in Blaydon in 1859), he began to look for a much bigger challenge: 'Our special field of labour will be the North of England, with Tyneside for our centre; our object the Education of the People.'[119]

As the 1840s drew to a close, local radicalism faced an uncertain future. Mass support was dwindling fast and without a viable leadership it had begun to lose all sense of purpose and direction. Cowen was well placed to assume a leading role. He was sufficiently distanced from Tyneside Chartism to make a dispassionate assessment of its weaknesses and shortcomings. Sound local knowledge enabled him to capitalise on its existing ideological strengths, and his early experiences in business and politics, equipped him to devise feasible tactics to ward off the encroachments of reformism. Initially, temperance organisations provided a useful platform from which to launch his public image as a skilful mediator of middle and working class interests, while his quiet campaign to extend educational opportunities to isolated communities helped to produce the groundswell of support upon which his political career would ultimately rest.

Chapter 2
Printing and Preaching:
Chartists, republicans and reformers

In the 1970s historians were mostly inclined to stress the disconnectedness of radical campaigns and, for Tyneside, to regard the activities of protesters and reformers as merely a response to short term grievances by 'small, dedicated minorities.'[1] Subsequently, however, the work of Kate Tiller and Bill Lancaster, and an important edited volume by Eugenio Biagini and Alastair Reid, established clear lines of continuity between early forms of radicalism and its later manifestations.[2] The case for continuity has proved very persuasive and, if anything, the Tyneside example strengthens this analysis. Close scrutiny of local membership lists reveals that a core group of radicals articulated shared aims and concerns from 1819 to 1868, and that a small number of individuals were still active beyond that date.[3] This evidence offers a persuasive counter argument to those readings which have emphasised the inherent weakness of British radicalism: its failure to sustain the Chartist movement; its redundancy at the hands of an astute, manipulative government and its subsequent absorption into Liberalism.[4] The basic premise is that Tyneside radicalism was a powerful force, retaining its grip on local politics largely because of the sophistication of its print culture and the way that successive generations of radicals maximised its propagandist potential. The politics of print which served eighteenth-century radicals such as Murray and Spence was mobilised in the nineteenth century to even better effect, engaging the attention of the literate working classes and 'hear read' by countless more in Tyneside's public houses and reading rooms.[5] In the first half of the nineteenth century, nothing demonstrates the advantages this conveyed more than the remarkable impact which the *Northern Liberator* had upon north-east Chartism. The dynamic collaboration between Tyneside Chartists and the *Liberator*'s editorial team demonstrated that press coverage was the essential ingredient of any radical campaign.[6] Equally, it will be shown that the fight for social reform and the 'Six Points' was not abandoned after 1848, even though, as Margot Finn contends, Chartist energies thereafter flowed into European republicanism.[7]

Republicanism in the North East was a persistent and strongly rooted strand of radical faith which appears to have accentuated rather than replaced the call for domestic reform.[8] Electoral reform had been consistently demanded from the time of the Peterloo Massacre onwards: in the declarations of the Political Protestants and the radical platform of the Northern Political Union (NPU).[9] Far from being consigned to the ashes, the rallying cry of radical forces in the 1850s and 1860s was 'The Charter and something more'[10] – a flagship slogan that continued to energise the reform campaign and was assiduously promoted by Joseph Cowen in his many journalistic ventures: the *English Republic* (1854-55), the *Republican Record* (1854-55), the *Northern Tribune* (1854-55) and the *Northern Reform Record*. If the Radical/Liberal alliance is to be regarded as something of an ideological compromise, some of that accommodation lay with the newly formed Liberal Party in the sure knowledge that the adoption of a radical programme was a prerequisite of political success.[11] The Northern Reform Union (NRU)[12] which Joseph Cowen formed in 1858 successfully roused the North East and then went on to revive radical allegiances in cities such as Birmingham and Manchester where, to all intents and purposes, reform was a dead issue.[13]

Essentially, what is being stressed here is that after 1848 Tyneside radicalism gathered new strength and a certain respectability. The vexed issue of 'physical force' Chartism has all too frequently served to cloud matters, the tendency being to view its advocacy as the apogee of radicalism, and the subsequent return to constitutional norms as clear evidence of diminishing fervour.[14] The radicalism of the 1850s and 1860s expressed its dissent differently and, in a sense, more confidently. Some of this confidence can doubtless be ascribed the rise of the Co-operative Movement and the proliferation of working-class organisations such as mechanics' institutes which, on Tyneside, were instrumental in sharpening popular perceptions that 'knowledge is power'.[15] But, arguably, the crucial factor was local leadership. A generation of leaders had been lost, either by the punitive actions of the authorities or driven into self-imposed exile overseas;[16] countless others had given up the struggle and moved onto less confrontational causes such as education or temperance. Joseph Cowen, who had been neither tested nor exhausted by the Chartist struggles, was able to inject a new energy into local radicalism which transformed it almost beyond recognition. European internationalism was nurtured by him through his long standing friendship with Harney and W. J. Linton, and his vast network of republican and revolutionary contacts. Ultimately, the 'something more' for which Tyneside radicals clamoured owed much to Cowen's boundless energy and his faith in the power of the 'paper pulpit'.[17]

It has been argued that radicalism was 'first and foremost a vocabulary of political exclusion'.[18] Given that this political exclusivity rested upon property qualification it is not surprising that the contentious issue of land ownership should be of overriding concern to successive generations of radicals, or that they should repeatedly call for land reform. Widespread popular support for Feargus O' Connor's Land Plan, Karl Marx's Land and Labour League, and Joseph Chamberlain's English Land Restoration League, to mention but a few, demonstrate the tenacity of the response.[19] The importance of English agrarianism as a vital strand in Tyneside radical ideology can scarcely be overstated. The influence of Spence's writings resonated half a century later in the speeches and activities of local reformers such as Robert Lowery[20] who re-launched the NPU in 1838 by reminding the crowd of their inalienable rights:

> Did not Lord John Russell know that the right of the people to a maintenance from the soil was older and better than the right of his father to his lands?... The improvements in society ... had all been produced by the people.[21]

In this context it is worth registering the symbolic significance of the Town Moor as the preferred meeting place for radical demonstrations. The success of the 1774 campaign to oppose enclosure of the Moor has already been noted. Radicals who gathered there in their thousands did not do so simply because it was conveniently situated and large enough to contain vast crowds; there are grounds for arguing that they also derived immense satisfaction from demanding their rights in that particular place. The nuances and subtleties of such symbolism are important, especially when it is remembered that nineteenth-century literacy levels were considerably lower than they are today. Symbolic modes of communication were an essential element of any popular campaign.[22] For instance, the carrying of large oak saplings by the Winlaton radicals in 1832 was obviously intended as a militant display of defiance and strength and, as such, was extremely effective.[23] But equally, the choice of oak was not arbitrary and such agrarian imagery would also have been instantly recognised by the crowd. The Winlaton contingent deliberately tapped into an emotional register, conjuring up nostalgic images of Old England, of a timeless landscape where natural rights were sacrosanct. At an NPU dinner shortly after the passage of the 1832 Reform Act, Charles Larkin reaffirmed the view that power should be invested in 'not only the owner of the soil, but the cultivator'.[24] In similar vein, the 80,000 Chartists who gathered on the Town Moor on Coronation Day in 1838 were called upon to assert their 'rights of human nature...to worship at the *altar of freedom*'. Robert Lowery reminded the crowd that the crown was held in trust for the people – that it was the property of the people, and could be resumed when the people were wronged....It was a principle that did not depend upon the decree of Lords or Commons, it emanated direct from the throne of the Almighty.[25]

Even though the majority would have been unable to hear the speeches, they could still participate by marching behind a banner bearing their own eloquent message. It is no accident, either, that the banners carried that day included one bearing a few lines of Goldsmith's poem, The Direful Effects of Luxury: 'Our fenceless fields, the sons of wealth divide/ and even the bare-worn common is denied'. Goldsmith, like Robert Burns, was popular with north-east radicals, his poetry frequently quoted in the radical press, especially the Northern Liberator. In 1839, the Northern Liberator, described the crowds who assembled on the Town Moor as 'a goodly clustre of bees round the hive of liberty' – a handsome tribute to Spence's bookshop in Holborn which readers would doubtless have appreciated.[26] Time and again, prominent radicals employed agrarian metaphors in their speeches to reinforce their demand for a return to natural justice and a 'renewal' of the constitution. When Julian Harney addressed the 'brave men of the North' on Christmas Day 1838 he began by reminding them that 'They were met with their feet on God's own earth, with God's own sky for their canopy…would they take the oath – the oath to live free or die?'[27] His few words were something akin to a benediction; the campaign thus legitimized could be regarded as a moral crusade and, like the crusades of old, physical force was accepted as an unavoidable expedient.

Some historians, notably T. J. Nossiter, have played down the revolutionary character of Newcastle Chartism, arguing that despite the vast quantities of pikes sold at regular Saturday markets, they posed little real threat to law and order. Nossiter dismisses the letters of old Chartists published in 1884 by Cowen's Newcastle Weekly Chronicle as 'romantic journalism', arguing that such accounts emphasised its moderate character.[28] Thomas Devyr's Odd Book of the Nineteenth Century, which maintained that the Northern Liberator's offices were used to make shells and that the leaders were involved in the procurement of arms, has also been ridiculed as the ravings of a man eager to claim his place in the annals of the movement.[29] But if there was no real threat of public disorder, why did the authorities consider it necessary to swear in hundreds of special constables? Close scrutiny of the Northern Liberator, which was in press between October 1837 and December 1840, suggests that the recourse to arms was no idle threat.[30] In January 1839 those who gathered in Winlaton following the arrest of Revd J. R. Stephens vowed to support the cause 'to the death if necessary'.[31] This can, perhaps, be dismissed as emotional rhetoric. However, the decision to cite Blackstone's *Commentaries on the Law of England*, which confirmed the right to bear arms in an editorial preface, instead of the customary lines from Byron, suggests otherwise. Thereafter, readers were given advice on how to manufacture cartridges and on strategies for street fighting, and reminded that 'hand grenades can be cast by any workman of the thousands of the NPU employed in iron foundries'.[32] A letter to the *Northern Star* in December 1838 from the 'Men of Winlaton' asked 'Where are those physical force men?' and promised to support O'Connor 'against all cowards, whether Birmingham or Edinburgh'.[33] Banners and hymns blatantly proclaimed this new martial agenda until Frost's trial in January 1840 forced local Chartists to adopt a more restrained strategy.[34]

The land schemes which proliferated during and after the Chartist years proved enormously attractive to Tyneside radicals and, although ostensibly they were calculated to secure voting rights at county elections, many shareholders believed that they were reclaiming the land for the people. Unusually then, and despite its obvious agrarian appeal, the Anti-Corn Law League proved to be the source of sharp division and hostility.[35] While local radicals roundly condemned the Corn Laws as a 'revival of the serfage of the Middle Ages',[36] they had little faith in the loyalties of the middle classes, fearing that 'as soon as they get the Corn Laws repealed they would turn their backs upon the people again'.[37] An 1840 handbill which called upon the middle classes to support Chartism threatened to burn their houses if they refused: 'vengeance, swift and terrible, will then overtake you...and one black ruin overwhelm England'.[38] Evidence such as this suggests that class antagonism lay at the very heart of local radicalism.[39] Many feared that the repeal campaign was a middle-class ploy to divert Chartist energies away from suffrage reform.[40] As it turned out, support from Newcastle was noticeably lacking.[41] At a meeting to debate the issue, Lowery argued that raising the price of bread

> springs from a Political Power for their own interest. This Land and the Aristocracy have got knit together so much that they study their own interest only, but the very persons who supported the Corn laws have found it out that they have been deceived by this middle class...has not the Working Men of England a right to go to the root of the disease and carry universal suffrage?

Working men, he argued, would ultimately suffer if the Corn Laws were repealed before the Charter:

they [the Masters] have brought them down to the very lowest, to the starving point…they tell me the very weavers go clothed in Rags. There is thousands of acres of land that might be employed to advantage if we had a good government.[42]

The uneasy alliance between the Whigs and the radicals, which ended in bitter recriminations after the 1832 Reform Act, was unlikely to be sustained other than on a short term basis.[43] The main protagonists on both sides continued to be politically active, and in a tight-knit community such as Tyneside perceived betrayals were not easily forgotten, much less forgiven.[44] Membership of the League was, in any case, beyond the means of the average worker.[45] Voting subscriptions were fixed at £50 p.a. – a sum easily affordable by Sir Joseph Cowen for instance – but not necessarily by his tenants or his workforce. Nonetheless, radicals did borrow from the League's successful strategy of contesting local elections, and later repeal provided a much needed incentive to those seeking other reforms.[46]

As to the Chartist Land Plan, for many years both Feargus O'Connor and his Plan had a singularly bad press.[47] On Tyneside the Plan can be regarded more as a unifying force than a 'reactionary' strategy,[48] and north-east Chartists, including miners, invested £1,270 – an amount significantly higher than the national average.[49] Notably, it was not just Chartists and radicals who could unite under an agrarian banner, but also trade unionists. The involvement of north-east miners in Chartism was exceptional given that, nationally, miners reputedly had 'minimal links' with the movement.[50] The 'St. Lawrence Colliery' and 'King Pitmen' banners flew alongside the Shoemakers 'Bundle of Sticks, Cap of Liberty' at the Town Moor Chartist meeting in May 1839.[51] And the upsurge in support is amply demonstrated by the way that Wallsend colliers 'laid in their colliery and came every man to the demonstration, though an agitating meeting never had been held in the neighbourhood'.[52] Securing the affiliation of local miners was considered to be crucial and reports of NPU weekly meetings are dominated by 'missions' to mining communities.[53] In 1842 large numbers of miners were questioned about their 'considerable part in Chartist disturbances' during an inquiry into Children's employment in mines.[54]

It is clear that Roy Church's criteria of 'experiential degradation' and community solidarity are both met: the first, by the declining conditions and prices, and the dangerous conditions in which miners worked, and then the harsh evictions carried out whenever industrial protest threatened the coal owners' profits; the second, by miners' involvement in the full range of radical organisations. Given the sheer scale of mining accidents in this period, it seems somewhat specious to argue for the 'irrelevance to miners of the factory reform movement' as an explanation for their supposedly limited involvement.[55] Any improvement in factory conditions was bound to have implications for miners whose claim for redress was, if anything, even more cogent. In this instance, active participation in the Chartist Land Company need not necessarily be interpreted as evidence of the miners' underlying conservatism, but rather as a demonstrable commitment to local radicalism and its agrarian roots. As Patrick Joyce has observed, land ownership was more than just 'the politics of nostalgia'.[56] The influence of trade union leaders such as Martin Jude and Tommy Hepburn would have been significant too. The Miners' Association solicitor, W. P. Roberts, was a close friend of O'Connor and an enthusiastic supporter of the Land Plan. In his election address in 1847, Roberts declared his unequivocal opposition to the laws of primogeniture and to a property-based voting system. His expert defence of colliers and Chartists would have earned both their loyalty and respect.[57] And, if any further endorsement of the Plan was needed, Thomas Slingsby Duncombe's backing would have given it impressive credentials.[58] North-east colliers received their radical education from the pages of the *Miners Advocate* and through the harsh realities of eviction, particularly during the bitter 1844 strike.[59] In the circumstances, O'Connor's Land Plan would have offered a much-needed lifeline.

Despite the collapse of the Land Plan, other schemes flourished. In 1849 the Newcastle Freehold Land Association [FLA] attracted over 700 subscribers within two weeks of its inaugural meeting. Subscriptions were fixed at 3s per fortnight 'to enable working men who were "frugal and industrious" to work out their own freedom'.[60] Once again an opportunity occurred for collaboration between different radical groups. Local Chartists organised and addressed meetings while temperance associations provided suitable venues for the collection of regular payments.[61] Sir Joshua Walmsley MP, speaking at a Parliamentary and Financial Reform Association meeting in Newcastle, called upon working men to support the FLA:

> He called upon the mechanics who could afford it – and he was sorry so many could not afford it – to do what they could to get hold of the franchise by buying retail plots at wholesale prices and thus obtain a 40/- franchise for something like £20.[62]

Nationally, the response to the scheme was mixed. Both Harney and Linton remained 'vociferously opposed' to the FLA, though their antipathy doubtless had much to do with its links with the Parliamentary and Financial Reform Association.[63] Harney, who was deeply committed to Spencean ideas, poured scorn on the FLA arguing that

The object of Cobden with his freehold land scheme, and Walmsley with his 'little charter' is, clearly, to so far extend the suffrage as to swamp the house with representatives of the 'Manchester School'. In short, the policy of both is to make use of the proletarians to establish bourgeois suprema-cy...The proletarians need another sort of reform...[With that view] the land must be made national property.[64]

Such entrenched opposition was significant because Harney had long-stand-ing ties with the Tyneside radicals and both men became close friends and sup-porters of Joseph Cowen.[65] The question of land ownership persistently domi-nated the pages of Harney's *Democratic Review*. An unidentified contributor, 'Terrigeneous', contributed many articles addressed to 'Brother Owners of the Soil', insisting that the land was a God-given inheritance to all and quoting ex-tensively from the Book of Genesis to substantiate his claims.[66] Clearly, Harney regarded land reform as a priority and not a peripheral issue; alongside his call for 'the Charter and Something More', Harney advocated 'The Charter, The Land and the organisation of labour'.[67] The few lines of Southey's verse printed on the first page of the *Red Republican* eloquently convey the essence of Harney's belief in equality, international brotherhood and natural justice:

If it be guilt –
To preach what you are pleased to call strange notions;
That all mankind as brethren must be equal;
That privileged orders of society
Are evil and oppressive; that the right
Of property is a juggle to deceive
The Poor whom you oppress; – I plead me guilty.[68]

It is said that the land question became a point of contact with the Liberals, facilitating both a radicalisation of the Liberal Party and a liberalisation of the radical movement.[69] Given the centrality of agrarianism in radical ideology, one thing is certain: without a demonstrable commitment to land reform, the Liberal Party would not have secured radical support. It can also be argued that agrar-ianism fed directly into republicanism which obtained unusually high popular support on Tyneside after 1848. In their fight for their own political and social freedom, Tyneside radicals automatically identified with the struggles of other oppressed peoples. Time and again, glasses were raised at meetings to toast the 'glorious French Revolution' and to commemorate the Polish Revolution of 1830.[70] A radical assembly in 1838 concluded their proceedings with three resounding cheers for the *Northern Liberator*, universal suffrage and the National Guards of France; the 'Cap of Liberty' which adorned countless banners was a striking symbol of this same solidarity;[71] and in 1854, when the Italian cause was not considered remotely 'fashionable', a penny subscription from the Tyneside community rather than the doles of an elite paid for a presentation to Giuseppe Garibaldi in memory of his visit to Tyneside.[72]

The contention here is that the internationalist ideas that informed Tyneside radicalism helped to sustain its remarkable resilience and longevity. In the main, other centres of radicalism appear to have been more parochial and, inevitably, this begs the question why local radicalism should be so fundamentally different. Clearly, the answer cannot be located in any lack of community sentiment for, if anything, the opposite was the case. In what has been viewed by some as the golden age of independent politics,[73] endemic local loyalties invariably outweighed national considerations and, therefore, the influence of leading activists must be considered the key factor. For instance, Augustus Beaumont, the founding editor of the *Northern Liberator*, had fought with the National Guards in Paris in 1830.[74] As the elected member for Kingston, Jamaica, he was an ardent abolitionist, and as the proprietor of the 'best selling journal on Tyneside' he repeatedly called for 'an end to Irish oppression and colonial tyranny'.[75] Beaumont's influence was not diminished by his premature death. In the minds of the faithful, he had become a martyr, one who had

> sacrificed his health, and ultimately his life, to his principles....By what means can we prove ourselves worthy of his labours? By diligently following the course which he has pointed out to us – by redoubling our exertions in the practice of those principles which he inculcated...the cause of the millions of suffering humanity.[76]

Gentlemen leaders[77] like Beaumont, Harney and Cowen helped to disseminate the belief that liberty had to be fought for by all men, acting together. And if, for a time, international solidarity dominated the agenda, perhaps it was because the stalwarts of physical force Chartism needed a level of participation unavailable to them at home.

If the fight for reform was one side of the coin, the fight against tyranny was the other. In 1840, many local radicals regarded Russia as the tyrant *par excellence* After all, in a milieu where expressions of fraternal solidarity were a commonplace, Tyneside was the perfect breeding ground for David Urquhart's 'Russophobia' to take root.[78] Charles Attwood, the NPU leader was an early convert to Urquhart's foreign policy.[79] His radicalism was markedly different from the moderate Tory reformism of his brother Thomas, the MP for Birmingham.

Although there had been close collaboration between the Birmingham Political Union and the NPU, Charles seems not to have shared his brother's obsession with currency reforms.[80] Under his guidance the local movement embraced both international and national reforms. Thus, in 1830, local radicals and Whigs met at the Turks Head public house in Newcastle to affirm 'the sympathy of Englishmen with the cause of liberty in France'.[81] Since Tyneside had a large Irish population, their concerns were also targeted by the NPU who sent an 'Address to the People of Ireland', inviting them to join the campaign: 'Will Irishmen continue slaves…or will they join heart and hand with their brothers of England, of Scotland, – aye and of France – and swear by the spirit of their fathers that slavery shall exist no longer?'[82]

The enthusiasm of leading activists such as Thomas Doubleday, Robert Lowery, John Mason and Charles Attwood persuaded many sceptics that Urquhart's analysis was sound. Some historians claim that local support arose from a form of economic protectionism; that traders, merchants and bankers feared the loss of established trading links.[83] J. H. Gleason, for example, notes Urquhart had most success in Newcastle and Glasgow, and suggests that both were responding to economic pressures.[84] There seems to be some dispute, however, about the extent to which Glasgow Chartists succumbed to Urquhart's monomania. While some aspects of the campaign gained support it has been claimed that 'the purity of Glasgow Chartism was preserved'.[85] The language used in the disclaimer suggests a certain determination to protect the reputation of Glasgow but, notably, R. G. Gammage also held that 'Newcastle almost alone paid any particular attention to the subject.'[86] In any event, the economic argument offers, at best, only a partial explanation. Those Chartists willing to risk unemployment, jail or even transportation were unlikely to be deflected from their purpose by economic concerns alone. A more plausible explanation is that some relished the opportunity to support a campaign which was so blatantly anti-Palmerstonian and which also encompassed the clear principle of defending oppressed people. When anti-Russian feelings resurfaced in the early 1850s an impassioned speech by Cowen on the eve of the Crimean War reasserted the moral imperative for defending Turkey: 'What was the right course for one man was right for the nation…we should defend Turkey against the unprovoked attack by Russia even if it would damage trade and commerce.'[87] Notwithstanding these arguments, the importance of Urquhart's campaign on Tyneside lies in the way it informed the international dimension of local radicalism. In the early 1850s the Polish and Hungarian Refugee Committee was able to tap into this Russophobia and elicit popular support for the Polish exiles.[88]

The preoccupation with foreign affairs may be said to have served a dual purpose. In the first place, anti-Russian sentiment aroused latent but passionate patriotic emotions which helped to bring together the radical middle and the working classes at a time when alliances over domestic issues had proved largely unsuccessful. More crucially, this détente had special ramifications in the sphere of domestic politics, especially at mid-century when Liberalism was in a state of flux. The Liberals came to respect the radicals' remarkable grasp of foreign affairs, and the possibility of their working cooperatively became not just feasible but desirable.[89] The Paris Peace Congress of 1849 provided an ideal forum for both groups to explore their mutual interests and begin to move towards a rudimentary working partnership.[90] A large local delegation attended the Congress, including George Charlton, J. A. Cockburn, Robert Lowery and Sir Joseph Cowen.[91] However, the conference recommendation for a policy of non-intervention in the domestic affairs of Italy and Hungary provoked controversy, infuriating ultra-radicals such as Linton who was frankly dismayed that prominent Chartists should associate themselves with it.[92] Henry Vincent, for instance, was a founder member of the People's International League which purported to promote the cause of freedom and self-government, and had close links with the Italian movement.[93] Linton's antipathy to the policy was caustically expressed in his illustrated alphabet:

> M is the Middle Class Movement, sir! It's quite a new invention.
> You see it's impossible to leap without due circumspection
> It's borrow'd from that diplomatic dodge-non-intervention
> Which means to let the devil work, and help him with intention.[94]

For Harney, the Paris Congress was little more than 'a solemn farce':

> under the appearance of peace, the rich oppressor and the poor oppressed are at daggers drawn...how futile the proceedings of this Congress appear. How many of the veritable sons of labour graced that assemblage by their presence? Look over the list. You will find manufacturers, lawyers, parsons, bankers, adventurers and speculators of all grades and names who, like the voluptuous aristocracy of Vienna, desire peace that they may enjoy themselves in safety.[95]

Despite the attempts to broker more conciliatory class relations, there were contradictory forces at work. Harney anticipated renewed class conflict, not harmony,[96] and pressed ahead with initiatives to unite the working classes of all countries.[97] Notwithstanding O'Connor's determined opposition, the pages of the *Northern Star* were regularly given over to the discussion of European nationalism in a bid to improve working-class knowledge of foreign affairs.[98]

As already noted, Harney had long been an influential figure on Tyneside It is, then, hardly surprising that his style of aggressive radicalism should carry substantial weight, especially in view of his deepening friendship with Joseph Cowen. Both were close friends of Mazzini and their involvement in various national and local societies which promoted Italian, Polish and Hungarian liberation gave them frequent opportunities to exchange ideas. Access to a national network, largely effected through Cowen's contacts with the radical elite, was crucial to the continuing progress of Tyneside radicalism. That being said, it is important to note that Cowen was not Harney's protégé, as some have suggested.[99] Nor was Harney able to dictate the policy of the Tyneside radicals through his friendship with Cowen, even though Schoyen creates the misleading impression that he was the controlling force behind the Newcastle Foreign Affairs Committee (NFAC).[100] Cowen was far too shrewd to be manipulated by anyone else, and his tight financial control of the Committee ensured that he remained, as he always intended, both policy maker and power broker. Harney and local radicals such as Josiah Thomas, William Hunter, James Watson and John Kane provided the vital strand of continuity so essential to link the early and late radical movements. Appendix I, which traces the activities of some twenty-six prominent Chartists, demonstrates the extent to which radicalism retained its grip in the locality, and the way that foreign affairs engaged radical energies at mid-century. When the complete membership of the NFAC is scrutinized (Appendix II) almost 50 per cent can be identified as former Chartists. Given that a reasonable proportion of them would have been lost to the cause through old age, death or emigration, the picture which emerges is one of quite remarkable resilience and one which suggests that the language of radicalism was far from bankrupt on Tyneside. The claim advanced here is that there was a radical network of talented core activists who moved between the various disparate groups acting as communicators, propagandists and coordinators. A more detailed study of this network will be offered in the next chapter. For the present, it can be noted that core members were prominent in trade unions and friendly societies; executive members of temperance organisations and mechanics' institutes; and, after 1859, when Cowen introduced co-operative retailing into the region,[101] a large percentage were also committed co-operators.

In 1848, north-east Chartists, like their compatriots elsewhere were in notably quiescent mood. They lacked an effective leadership and meetings were reportedly 'thinly attended'.[102] The *Gateshead Observer,* eager to promote the formation of the Newcastle and Gateshead Reform Association, took the opportunity to assert that local Chartists had little local influence and no real power:

the Chartists…are an unimportant body in Newcastle. Great in noise but few in number – violent in print but weak in purpose and power – their insignificance might excuse us from all notice of their proceedings; but gladly recognising in their councils, with all their error and follies, a visible amendment we are disposed to reason with them…and convince them, if we can, of the injustice of their reckless assertions.[103]

It was into this more conciliatory political climate that Cowen first began to make an impact. Initially, as his early writings and activities reveal, he was convinced that a class alliance was the best way forward. It was to the middle class, he claimed, that 'the nation has to look both for the hand of support and the eye of intelligence, these are a nation's strength'.[104] His stirring speech at a large public meeting of the Parliamentary and Financial Reform Association powerfully conveys this optimism. Calling upon the 'Middle and Productive classes' to support the Association, he expressed regret that the motion had not been presented by a working man:

He was not one himself, though he would endeavour to be their exponent that evening. He must avow himself a Chartist. He knew that the Chartists had committed excesses but that did not affect the justice of their claim. He was for universal suffrage and he accepted the proposed measure as he would accept 7/6d in the £, when he could get nothing else…He called upon every sincere reformer to stand forward and work with the certainty that they would ultimately triumph. In all their efforts they must evince a sympathy with the people. He had found good and noble minds amongst the people. Some people thought because the people had dirty hands they had dirty minds. That was not only an error but a lie. (*Hear, hear, and applause*)…He did not put much faith in political revolutions. They might have a good pick axe but it would be of no benefit if they did not use it. The good institutions which were now in operation were not worked with half the energy they ought to be…A virtuous and intelligent population never would be slaves. Reformers should have clean hands…and the Chartists might thank their own inconsistencies for having struggled for so many years in vain.[105]

In those early years, Cowen doggedly courted the support of the middle classes, but he had only limited success. By the early 1850s his views were beginning to shift, as this letter defending the use of physical force demonstrates:

There are some people so dead to all sense of honour, of righteousness and of truth that the only way of reaching their consciences is through their hides or their stomachs. They can only be thrashed or starved into subjection.[106]

The reasons for such a dramatic *volte-face* may be said to be two-fold. Firstly, the profound class antagonisms which permeated Tyneside radicalism persuaded Cowen that he needed to take control of the local movement. Moreover, his friendship with a great many exiled revolutionaries led him to identify with their causes and to conclude that 'peace cannot be attained before justice, and justice cannot be wrung from the European despots save by arms'.[107]

The international dimension of Tyneside radicalism may not have been engendered by Cowen but his enthusiasm for foreign affairs certainly ensured that it retained a high profile on the radical agenda in the ensuing decades. Cowen was no mere passive observer, but an active participant; a revolutionary in the cause of Italian and Polish Liberation who readily supplied money, seditious literature, asylum and even arms. His close friendship with Mazzini brought him into contact with other like-minded activists, particularly those who were members of the People's International League.[108] Linton, who was Secretary of the League, hoped it would be 'a successful association of the best minds in the country' and actively solicited Cowen's support.[109] The League stressed international responsibilities, the folly and immorality of an isolationist foreign policy and the importance of educating the public:

Though many, the nations of Europe are one and all members one of another. In the well-being of each all are interested, for all share consciously or unconsciously in the mixed good and evil which affects each…Englishmen should be cognisant of the processes through which the progressive destinies of Europe are being worked out, so that whenever European affairs may call for interference, they may be in no doubt as to the course to be pursued.[110]

The League's programme aimed to benefit oppressed nations and 'infuse new strength, morality and prosperity into England's social life'.[111] Mazzini's *Address* which outlined the League's proposals obtained an enormous international circulation and much has been made of its availability in the period immediately preceding the 1848 revolutions.[112]

Cowen collaborated with Linton on a number of projects, and he became the chief sponsor of Linton's ambitious publication, the *English Republic*.[113] This important journalistic venture also brought Cowen into contact for the first time with W.E. Adams,[114] who was to become a life long friend and fellow activist. Cowen was fully alive to the potential power of the press and to that end he canvassed sympathetic provincial newspaper proprietors, impressing upon them the importance of publicizing radical issues. He financially supported radical publications such as the *Democratic Review* and the *Red Republican* in a bid to ensure their continued circulation, and also published two periodicals, the *Northern Tribune* and the *Republican Record*, before finally purchasing the *Newcastle Chronicle* in 1859. Even before that date, the *Chronicle* was effectively promoting Cowen's political views for he had already negotiated partial control over its contents in return for financial assistance.[115]

In 1851 more than 250 Polish-Hungarian refugees arrived in Liverpool seeking asylum following the war against Austria and Russia, and British radicals combined forces to assist them and block attempts to resettle them in America.[116] Addressing a large meeting in the Nelson Street Lecture Hall, Cowen introduced the Newcastle contingent of twelve led by Konstanty Lekawski as steady, sober, industrious, intelligent and virtuous men, and reminded his audience that they were 'merely doing for their country what our own Cromwell and his colleagues did for England'. Naturally, the emphasis upon sobriety was essential if Cowen was to recruit the assistance of the influential Methodist and temperance memberships.[117] When all twelve refugees were settled, the final debts were left to Cowen to disburse and although he was disappointed at so much 'lip patriotism' he still maintained that his own good conscience was 'a higher and better reward than the plaudits of a noisy public'.[118] Stanislaw Worcell, Lajos Kossuth and Alexander Herzen were already members of Cowen's circle of friends and after 1851 this group included Konstanty Lekawski. Subsequently, Cowen became closely involved in the clandestine activities of the Polish Democratic Society [PDS].[119] Surviving correspondence shows that he was personally involved in assisting Ludwik Bulewski, another leader of the PDS, to travel incognito to Danzig via Belgium as well as smuggling seditious literature and arms by sea. Bulewski persuaded Cowen to sell some artwork to raise the money for his trip and to provide letters of introduction to 'continental firms'.[120]

The extent of Cowen's illicit activities, including his part in the Orsini bomb plot,[121] will probably never be known but his commitment to the republican cause was absolute. As he stated in his welcoming speech for Kossuth in 1851: 'Worse things may befall a country than a war for liberty...despotism is worse'.[122] The beginning of 1852 found Cowen and Linton engaged in the launch of the Friends of European Freedom subscription fund, and copies of a circular address were distributed to every liberal newspaper in Britain and Ireland.[123] Subscriptions were fixed at 1s per head, with all funds raised to be used by Mazzini and Kossuth 'in whatever manner it may seem good'.[124]

Unfortunately, despite Cowen's best efforts, the campaign was a failure; at the end of twelve months only £57 7s 6d had been raised for the cause.[125] Like the editor of the *Monas Herald*, who complained in March 1852 that Kossuth had spent $50,000 on arms, many questioned how the money would be spent.[126]

In 1854 Cowen launched a new republican journal, the *Northern Tribune* which was published alongside the *English Republic* at Brantwood in the Lake District by Linton and W. E. Adams.[127] As with the *English Republic*, Linton supplied the engravings for the *Tribune* and a number of eminent radicals, including Kossuth and Mazzini contributed articles. The *Northern Tribune* was widely condemned for its extreme republicanism but Cowen refused to modify either tone or contents to increase its profitability. He insisted that they would 'write neither for pay nor pastime and to forego one principle of our democratic creed would be to play traitor to our conscience'.[128] The urgency of the journal's chosen motto, 'Light! More Light!', was mirrored by the upbeat tone of its contents. The first issue is reputed to have sold 4,000 copies and it quickly moved to a weekly circulation cycle the following December.[129] With Cowen as editor, the *Tribune*'s cast of writers also included George J. Holyoake, Samuel Kydd, Thomas Cooper, Gerald Massey and Linton. Readers were provided with a mixed diet of political and literary material, and, most notably, local affairs. Ironically enough, Cowen's campaign to repeal the newspaper Stamp Duty was a contributory factor in the *Tribune*'s failure. The competitive climate which followed repeal squeezed out less populist journals and, in March 1855, Cowen sold the *Tribune* to Holyoake, who incorporated it into his own anti-clerical publication, the *Reasoner*.[130]

In any event, Cowen had more pressing concerns. The groundswell of interest in foreign affairs became more focused in 1854 when events in the Crimea became a source of local as well as national concern, precipitating the regeneration of the NFAC.[131] Although Urquhart was undoubtedly responsible for the establishment of Foreign Affairs Committees in a number of cities and towns, he did not visit Tyneside until October and, by then, the reorganisation of the NFAC was well in hand.[132] Charles Attwood reappeared in radical circles, writing to Cowen in December about the urgent need for action:

> We must work. Newcastle is now the very anchor of the nation's safety. If it be saved at all, it will be through her determined and continued energy. If it be lost, it will be through her not being got sufficiently excited to her own grand office of protecting it.[133]

Attwood's fears that the radicals would be unresponsive proved entirely unfounded. The NFAC had already swung into action, holding a large demonstration on 29 November, the anniversary of the Polish Revolution. Attwood was elected President and Cowen took on the role of Secretary.[134] Although many former Chartists and radicals responded to Urquhart's anti-Russian appeal the vast majority did not subscribe to his political views. Urquhart was popularly believed to be the arch-conspirator who had betrayed the Welsh at the time of the Newport rising in 1839.[135] He was an outspoken Tory who, by his own admission, had 'no time for popular uprisings' and, in any event, his outspoken criticism of Kossuth and Mazzini would hardly have endeared him to Cowen. The blatant republicanism that informed the NFAC agenda was completely at odds with the Urquhartite foreign diplomacy that almost invariably dictated the aims and activities of Committees elsewhere.[136] In March 1855, conflict between a handful of Urquhart's supporters and the rest of the Committee resulted in the establishment of a rival group, led by George Crawshay.[137] Anxious to distance himself from Urquhart's views, Cowen issued a public disclaimer in the *Northern Tribune*: 'we cannot count ourselves as enrolled in the ranks of the faithful, although on many points we accord with Mr. Urquhart's opinions, appreciate his patriotism and admire his talents'.[138] Perhaps the key to their strange relationship lies in another stirring speech Cowen gave in December 1853. Whenever the honour and independence of the nation was threatened, he said, he would 'bury all party war cries, all party badges and rally to one common watchword': patriotism, Cowen believed, was the guiding precept, 'the string that bound them together'.[139]

The Committee included some strong personalities, notably Charles Attwood, George Crawshay, Robert Peddie and John Fife, but Cowen exerted tight financial control and this ensured that he could impose his own authority upon them.[140] The Republican Brotherhood emerged from the ranks as a separate, more extreme grouping around Cowen and his allies with its own publication, the *Republican Record*, and moved quickly to distance itself from the NFAC which Cowen claimed was best suited 'to undertake the mission of the *present*, [while] ours is rather the mission of the *future*'. Their aim was not just to circulate information about foreign affairs but to set in motion 'a thorough reconstruction of society'.[141] Universal suffrage remained an absolute priority but the Brotherhood looked far beyond parliamentary reform:

> The members of the Republican Brotherhood will seek, by instructional means, to indoctrinate their fellow countrymen with republican principles, leaving to the national will of the future to determine the means of reforming or changing the institutions of the country.[142]

The influence of both Harney and Linton is clearly detectable in the Brotherhood's slogan: 'the government of the people, by, and for, the people'.[143]

Cowen drew foreign nationals and eminent radicals like a magnet: Felice Orsini, Kossuth, Worcell, Lewkawski, Harney and Holyoake all enjoyed his hospitality at Stella Hall and gave generously of their time in return, speaking at mechanics' institutes, making speeches at soirées and dinners, and writing provocative and illuminating articles for his many radical publications. As for the people of Newcastle, they became more and more drawn into foreign issues, understanding and sympathizing with the exiles to such an extent that the customary divide between foreign and domestic politics became ever more blurred.

Of all the foreign nationals to visit Newcastle, Giuseppe Garibaldi was the one who most captured the imagination and the heart of the Tyneside people.[144] In April 1854, he spent some three weeks on Tyneside enjoying Cowen's hospitality and, in return, he visited and gave a talk to the Winlaton Mechanics' Institute. Although Garibaldi was anxious to avoid publicity, Cowen's Friends of European Freedom raised a penny subscription and presented Garibaldi with a handsome gold and steel sword, and an engraved telescope.[145] Cowen did not meet Garibaldi again until 1864 but they remained in close contact, especially during the Sicilian War when both money and arms were sent by Cowen to assist the campaign. After the Battle of Milaggio, Garibaldi wrote to Cowen to convey his heartfelt gratitude: 'I thank you for what you tell me about the Whitworth guns and for whatever you can do for us in that way.'[146]

In all this time the question of electoral reform had not been lost sight of but remained an integral part of the radical programme. In the early 1850s Newcastle upon Tyne was one of the few places which still had a viable Chartist membership and strong links to other radical groups.[147] A public meeting of the NFAC in 1855 resolved therefore to demand the restoration of Poland, major reforms of the army *and* a reform of parliament which included universal manhood suffrage. The NFAC called upon all democratic associations to act together and an attempt to put aside the call for universal suffrage because it was 'ill-timed and impolitic' was promptly overruled.[148] According to Margot Finn, '1858 marked a watershed in English radical politics'[149] – a year punctuated by the final collapse of the National Charter Association and a noticeable rapprochement with some sections of the middle classes, and yet this was also a year of regeneration and renewed campaigning. In 1857 reform was once more at the top of the radical agenda on Tyneside, on the grounds that 'if ever it was important to enfranchise the whole of the people it was when that people were called upon to take arms…in the name of liberty abroad'.[150]

These were no idle words. Felice Orsini's attempt to assassinate Louis Napoleon on 14 January 1858 scandalized the international community and prompted Palmerston to introduce repressive legislation. In the mid-1850s Orsini had been a guest at Stella Hall and also briefly spent some time in the Lake District with Adams and Linton. Cowen was implicated by his connection with Orsini's fellow conspirators, Thomas Allsop and Dr Simon Bernard, as well as Holyoake who allegedly was recruited to test the bombs.[151] Neither Holyoake nor Cowen were ever charged, though the risk of prosecution was all to real. As Jane noted afterwards, it was 'a great relief' when the 'not guilty' verdict was declared.

The Northern Reform Union [NRU] was officially launched on 2 January 1858 to demand manhood suffrage, vote by ballot and the abolition of the property qualification; with a council of thirty members and an executive of five, subscriptions were set at 1s per year, payable in quarterly instalments.[152] Local Liberal MPs were canvassed to exert parliamentary pressure and although, initially, none would declare in favour of manhood suffrage, six of the seven agreed to support the secret ballot and the abolition of the property qualification. The NRU rapidly established itself as a political force with a membership of 481 in the first three months.[153] Cowen travelled throughout the North East, addressing meetings almost every night and 2,000 copies of an address setting out the Union's aims were printed and circulated. Rapid regeneration of the suffrage campaign proved remarkably easy, not least because of Cowen's expert leadership and the fact that he could call upon a network of experienced activists. The NRU Council comprised former Chartists and NPU members, trade unionists (especially miners) and new recruits to the radical cause. It is unfortunate that so few branch membership lists survived but those that have suggest that skilled workers were the most active. (see Appendix III)

At the first quarterly meeting on 5 April 1858 handsome tribute was paid to the press in supporting the Union's objectives; fifteen London papers were said to have published the NRU's opening Address 'in extenso' and forty other papers had published extracts. The Council resolved to publish a monthly journal, the *Northern Reform Record*, which would act 'partly as a tract and partly as a record of the proceedings of the Union'.[154] Cowen hoped that the *Record* would help to relieve the enormous burden on the NRU secretary, Richard Bagnall Reed,[155] by acting as a circular letter to the members. Most of all, he intended to provide working people with 'practical political information' about the abuses of taxation and public expenditure.[156] Cowen cultivated the support of the Financial Reform Association and tried to persuade the middle classes to lend their support to the campaign. In an open letter which spoke of previous 'unhappy political differences' he invited the middle classes to join the Union, promising to seek an acceptable compromise 'except on matters of principle'.[157]

He also wrote to the *Nonconformist* journal complaining of their 'decline in political faith and failure to support the union of middle and working classes in reform'.[158] This was earnest courting indeed but his friendly overtures had little impact. Cowen was forced to admit that middle-class voters had 'turned a deaf ear to the cry for enfranchisement'.[159] In a circular address to the 'Radical Reformers of the United Kingdom', Cowen and Bagnall Reed denounced the 'selfishness' of the middle classes: 'Let them know that the means you used to help them to gain their own political rights, you will use against them to win your own. Those who are not for you are against you.'[160]

On the platform and in Chartist meetings Cowen increasingly identified with the working classes. A familiar local figure, in 'rusty black slopclothes and a soft billycock hat', he appealed to the working classes as one of themselves; as one who sympathised with their views, who would champion their interests and rigorously defend their rights.[161] When the NRU was refused the use of Newcastle Town Hall to hold a public meeting in January 1859, Cowen promptly dismissed the imputation that the working classes could not conduct themselves properly:

> Dirty! It was made to be dirtied. Working men agitated their political rights with becoming modesty, and with reason and gentlemanly decorum. It was not a question of whether the Reform Union was to have a meeting in that gilded chamber, but whether the people of Newcastle were to use their own room for their own purposes.[162]

While the clamour for reform was still being made on the traditional grounds of natural right, those rights were now being linked by some to a notional 'proof of prudence'.[163] Some pressed the cause of women's suffrage or of enfranchising paupers while Lord Teynham produced a circular in August 1859 proposing that a reading qualification should determine who should be able to vote.[164] As for Holyoake, he enthused in an article for the *Newcastle Daily Chronicle* that 'the Northern Reform Union does not go like O'Connor for an Irish-brained, fustian-jacketed, stubble-chinned, antagonistic suffrage; but for an English moulded, clear-headed, clean faced, decently attired, self defensive franchise'.[165] Holyoake, it seems, became so carried away by his own rhetoric that he completely lost sight of the Union's express objective to demand *universal* suffrage.

Greater efforts were made to recruit among the working classes. From Berwick upon Tweed, Robert Mathison wrote to say that their committee was to be an 'equal proportion of workies and shoppies'.[166] He also requested some cheap tracts for members who could not afford the *Northern Reform Record*, insisting that such propaganda 'would make the cause march forward'.[167] The

Ayr branch, too, was said to be entirely working class. As the branch secretary explained, Ayr was 'too aristocratic a place' and local workers had been deeply insulted by the Tory candidate, Sir James Ferguson, 'describeing them as unimproveing and irresponsible'.[168] Closer to home, a Newcastle member highlighted the need to recruit the colliers, since 'every intelligent pitman is a Radical, both from education and conviction'.[169] In the event, north-east colliery villages were successfully canvassed for support and became the backbone of the movement. Gradually the working classes began to rally to the fight as this offer of assistance shows:

> I say sir that it is the duty of every Working Man to rally round you…
> there maybe many things that I could do for you Either in the Shape of
> Collecting Name Livering tracts gathering subscriptions Livering notices
> of any king Anything I am willing to Do Either in one capisity ore anothe
> that I can do is am Ready anytime.[170]

Despite the fact that the NRU carried the cause of reform onwards at a time when other districts were relatively inactive, it has not always received the recognition it deserves. All too often it has been dismissed as a short-lived phenomenon or as a 'dismal failure'.[171] Margot Finn has readily acknowledged the initiative invested in this bid to secure radical reform, but she concludes that the NRU was an 'anomaly within the wider middle class reform movement and failed to rally liberal opinion behind manhood suffrage'. What she does highlight, however, is the way that it established a political platform 'upon which the Reform League would capitalize in the mid-sixties'.[172] This view has been further reinforced by Owen Ashton and Paul Pickering's biography of Richard Bagnall Reed which helps to highlight the role of key local individuals.[173] At the beginning of 1858 Newcastle seemed almost alone in agitating for reform. Other localities, such as Birmingham, Norwich and Sunderland, were judged to be 'dull' and 'deficient in public spirit'.[174] In early January 1859, Liverpool was thought to be 'not much of a place for Reform' and Birmingham working men, it was said, 'dare not speak out or attend any meeting because their masters belong to our reform association which goes the whole hog with Mr Bright'.[175] In Doubleday's judgement:

> they are looking to the North for a movement and to Newcastle especially,
> Lord Derby's bill not giving anything to the working man, the fustian jack-
> et being really the bugbear of the aristocracy…We shall have the Whigs
> bidding against the Tories on this occasion but both require to be spurned
> by the popular voice.[176]

Holyoake's assistance was enlisted to publicize NRU activities in London. Writing to request Reed's help to 'stir up the cockneys', Holyoake promised that if his editor would not comply he would 'throw Orsini's shells into the offices and simultaneously with a smashing of all the editors I shall organise an explosion of Gas below and blow up the entire office'.[177] Towns such as Berwick, Sheffield, Bradford and Birmingham all looked to Newcastle to supply the lead for 'if only they gave these places a little help, they should put the whole country in agitation'. By the end of the year the NRU was being dubbed the 'Aurora Borealis of Reform'.[178]

The Union's strategy was strictly constitutional; they lobbied MPs, submitted letters and articles on reform to the radical press nationwide, sent speakers across the country on 'missions' and organised the collection of an enormous petition, bearing some 34,456 signatures (Appendix IV). Despite great organisational difficulties, including North Shields' 'floating population' which made the collecting of signatures seem 'like driving snails to Jerusalem', the commitment of the council members ensured that the petition was filled up within six weeks.[179] John Tennant of Seghill wrote in January 1859 to say that he had secured 'every man's signature in our village excepting two or three solitary conservative devils'.[180] The petition is a remarkable testimony to the enthusiasm for reform which the NRU generated in the North East. An estimated six hundred yards of petition was finally presented to the House of Commons on 29 February 1859 by General T. Perronet Thompson MP, who 'gathered up as many petitions as he could carry between his elbows and his chin and marched up to the table amidst loud laughter'.[181] A press circular calculated that the petition had been signed by more than half the adult male population of the region. Two-thirds of the signatories were said to be working men and non-electors, and the predominant occupations of those who signed were clerks, agents, engineers, smiths, carpenters and miners.

John Bright's 'sham radicalism' was not thought well of in north-east towns and villages, while H. J. Slack, writing in December 1859, blamed the general apathy in London on the 'unpopularity of Mr. Bright who has been foolishly put forward as the Leader and who makes enemies every time he opens his mouth'.[182] Many NRU supporters were less than enthusiastic about Bright's rate-paying franchise proposal. According to one angry correspondent, Bright would 'exclude hundreds of honest and intelligent citizens'; he was 'no democrat...[and] not even a Chartist'.[183] Cowen was asked to press Bright to improve his Bill but, apart from appealing to Bright to reconsider, Cowen advised the NRU Council to oppose no honest measure of Reform…but still firmly and persistently put your programme forward as the only sound one; and make it manifest that while you do not oppose a moderate measure, you only accept it as an instalment of your just rights.[184]

Aside from the campaign for electoral reform, the Union became actively involved in exposing corruption at elections, especially the two elections held in April and August 1859 at Berwick. The Berwick branch, led by Robert Mathison, formally requested the NRU to investigate the last election which they claimed had been corrupt. Reed agreed to conduct an enquiry and his two reports were subsequently sent on to every MP.[185] For Cowen, the sorry affair vindicated his belief in the secret ballot. John McAdam, the Glasgow radical, jokingly expressed his admiration for the 'candour of both bribers and bribed' in that 'rotten borough',[186] but the case was to cost the NRU and Cowen dearly. Even though the NRU finally succeeded in bringing a number of successful cases, and one man was fined £100, he remained convinced that the existing legislation would have to be changed. The NRU had to find surety of close to £2,500 in order to ensure that the case would be pursued as a matter of urgency.[187] The defendants hoped to circumvent matters by bringing a libel case against the NRU first and thus a number of potential backers were reluctant to get involved. On balance, while the pursuit of the case looks foolhardy and drained the Union's precious resources at a critical moment, Cowen and Reed succeeded in bringing electoral corruption into the public domain. It could be argued that such legal challenges did much to ventilate the debate about the secret ballot, though it was to take many years before the necessary legislative changes were secured.

That same year an attempt was made to field an NRU candidate in the Newcastle elections. The Italian sympathiser, P. A. Taylor, was recommended by Cowen largely because he had excellent republican and radical credentials. They had worked together on a number of republican initiatives and Cowen held him in high regard. Unfortunately, Taylor's commitment to disestablishment led him to make a blunt statement attacking the Sabbatarians and this seriously damaged his standing in certain influential quarters.[188] He only managed to raise 463 votes and in the aftermath the NRU Council was forced to concede that strong local and theological prejudices had operated against his selection.[189]

It was to be many years before Cowen finally stood as a parliamentary candidate but it seems clear that his standing in the local community was such that success could have been his had he chosen to put himself forward. He had, in fact, been asked to stand at the 1859 Berwick election on the grounds that 'the only way to recover corrupt boroughs is to field a candidate that will neither bribe nor be bribed'. At that moment in time it seemed to be the last thing on his mind and he declined, claiming that he preferred to work at the popular level.[190] He was a natural leader and a gifted orator who had already proved that he could secure the loyalties of a broad cross-section of society. Through his father's close connections with early radicals he was able to bridge the gap between two generations of radical thought; retaining the best of the old traditional ideas but skilfully modifying tactics to meet the new political climate. The growing clamour for a Radical candidate for Newcastle grew out of his leadership of the Tyneside movement and proved to be the ineluctable challenge with which the Liberals had to contend.

Chapter 3
'Knowledge is Power':
Community politics, associational life
and the press, 1847-1880

By the close of the 1850s Joseph Cowen's political activities on Tyneside had given him a position of influence which he might easily have used to launch his parliamentary career. His role in exposing the corrupt practices of candidates in the 1859 Berwick election had raised his profile and, as already noted, he had been approached to represent the borough. At the time he saw fit to resist the blandishments of his supporters, choosing instead to pursue other projects and, in the process, strengthen his bid for power in 1873 when the Newcastle seat became vacant. In the intervening years, his local standing turned upon much more than his profile as a renowned orator, republican and electoral reformer. Cowen's funeral in February 1900 brought together 'clergymen and coal owners, nonconformist ministers and miners, licensed victuallers and temperance reformers, Quakers and soldiers', in what was justifiably described as a 'democratic gathering'.[1] The strength of his radicalism lay in its broad appeal, effectively cutting across the customary barriers of class, religion and party politics, and stressing above all else the importance of rights, not privileges. In a speech to his constituents in 1883 he sought to explain why he was so committed to democratic rule:

> Aristocracy is class rule, Ochlocracy is mob rule. Timocracy is the rule of the rich, but Democracy is people's rule, the rule of all, rich and poor, lord and labourer, priest and layman. It draws its strength from its universality and its freedom.[2]

Such views were unusual then, to say the least. The concept of universal democracy had few adherents within the Liberal party and even the 'People's William' declared himself to be 'an out and out inequalitarian'.[3] Gladstone's avowed commitment to widen the franchise was strictly limited to the 'capable citizen' – to those whose respectability and virtue would incline them to uphold the status quo.[4] Generally speaking, members of mechanics' institutes, co-operatives, friendly societies and temperance organisations were considered the most suitable recipients of the extended franchise. Historians have made much of the middle-class patronage of such 'agencies of subordination',[5] arguing that social control was the primary purpose – and ultimate reward – of their pater-nalistic endeavours.[6] A scrutiny of Tyneside associational life, however, dem-onstrates that the 'triumph of the entrepreneurial ideal'[7] proved to be a more contested project than was the case elsewhere and, to a large extent, this can be attributed to Cowen's intervention.

Popular radicalism has been viewed as the 'product of the leisure of Saturday night and Sunday morning, the pothouse and the chapel, not of the work-ing week',[8] and Cowen's grip on a plethora of working-class organisations, across the spectrum of both work and leisure, reveals much about the tenor of Tyneside political loyalties. Tyneside's institutional canvass was extremely rich and wide-ranging and, clearly, it would be impossible to give equal considera-tion to all of the organisations with which Cowen was associated. Thus, more attention will be paid to the activities of the major 'improving' organisations such as co-operatives, mechanics' institutes, friendly societies and temperance societies in order to consider whether they were empowering or, as some have claimed, 'instruments of working class amelioration'.[9] A thorough examination of their organisational structure and activities should help to establish whether they diverged from the accepted archetype. Naturally, the creation of a radi-cal heartland could not be achieved single-handedly; the combined efforts of a network of core activists enabled Cowen to proselytize his democratic creed to an ever-widening constituency. Their long term loyalty to Cowen and his reform campaign ensured that an agrarian discourse remained a defining ele-ment of Tyneside radicalism throughout the 1860s and 1870s, and land own-ership schemes found their way on to most, if not all, associational agendas. Arguably, this constitutes a more persuasive case for demonstrating radical continuities than measuring the popular response to single issue causes such as the Tichborne claimant campaign.[10]

As the rapid economic changes associated with industrialisation transformed Victorian towns and cities they became the locus of middle-class power and in-evitably they sought to control vital social and cultural institutions.[11] Mechanics' institutes which served the economic as well as the cultural needs of the busi-ness class are a case in point. In 1853, when James Hole published his critical appraisal of mechanics' institutes, he claimed that the prevalent undemocratic organisation and narrow, discriminatory appeal of most institutes had been prohibitive.[12] As a result, the movement had largely failed to serve the working classes. The problems he identified in Yorkshire were those which had bedevil-led mechanics' institutes in other places, north-east towns included. In the 1840s mechanics' institutes tended to serve only the 'studious few' and the provision of newspapers and novels was frowned upon as 'either useless or dangerous'.[13] In 1848, the Dean of Durham struck a typically cautious note in his address at the opening of the new Mechanics' Hall in Gateshead. An audience composed mainly of the affluent and well-to-do were warned of the 'dangerous combinations' that would arise if the working classes were not appropriately educated. 'Mis-instruction', as well as general ignorance, had to be tackled and he recommended that if mechanics' institutes were 'liberally and judiciously regulated', they might become 'the means of extending to the very humblest classes, the benefits which they need most'.[14] Judicious regulation disposed most executive committees to impose a total ban on the discussion of politics and theology,[15] a rule which was not just designed to create a neutral arena for discussion but reflected the patronage of the local clergy. All too frequently, the lecture programme was delivered by a local minister who, especially in remote rural areas, may have been the only person qualified to argue the finer points of botany or astronomy. On the other hand, discussion of political economy was positively encouraged. In the early years of the century, this was not considered a controversial or party political subject. There was a widespread belief that acceptance of its basic principles would militate against the evils of social unrest and immure the working classes against the evils of trade union agitation.[16]

In January 1847, when Cowen launched the Winlaton Literary and Scientific Society, there was nothing in the proposed rules or statement of principles to suggest that it would differ, in the slightest degree, from the hundreds of other institutes already in existence. The rules that were initially adopted precisely conformed to the established orthodoxy, while the statement of aims ('to promote the moral and intellectual advancement of its members') was probably lifted verbatim from the Handbook of the Newcastle Mechanics' Institute of which his father was an executive member.[17] It is hardly surprising that the young Joseph Cowen should be guided by his father and turn to him for advice, but such deference proved to be short-lived. Cowen must have been aware of the falling membership and mounting debts which threatened the viability of the Newcastle Institute, and drawn his own conclusions. As a committed radical, the promotion of an undemocratic organisation could not be sustained for long.

At the official opening in February, Cowen's Address to the members announced that the Winlaton Institute was to be 'open to all, irrespective of their mark or station, without regard to their religious or political sentiments...a campaign against ignorance, a battle against bigotry and prejudice'.[18] Whereas other institutes aimed to improve the morality of the working classes, Cowen insisted that they would strive for 'mutual moral improvement'.[19] He warned against the dangers of party politics, and expressed the hope that the Institute would protect members from 'the machinations of unprincipled demagogues and aspirants to popular power who might work to mislead them for the promotion of their own sinister and selfish purposes'.[20] This was rather disingenuous, given that Cowen was using the Institute to further his own ambitions, but, as ever, he seems to have had little trouble convincing himself that his motives were altruistic rather than self-serving.

In the new model institute, reconstituted in August as the Winlaton Literary, Scientific and Mechanical Institution, there was no question of limiting the membership to men. From the outset, his open-access policy offered reduced rates for women and their children, although it stopped short of permitting them to stand for office.[21] Partly, this was a reward for those women, including his own mother, who had helped to raise the initial capital, but it was also a bold statement about the egalitarian structure he wanted to put in place. The contradictory rationale which denied women any executive power must be viewed alongside the progressive principle employed in offering men and women the same educational opportunities. Having adjusted the rules to guarantee that at least half the committee would be working class, Cowen declared himself satisfied that they had achieved 'the happy union of rich and poor, great and small'.[22] By July 1848 the Institute had some fifty members and plans were already in hand to establish a similar institute at Blaydon.

Needless to say Cowen's innovations met with significant opposition yet he persisted, regardless of the difficulties of hiring rooms and the wilful sabotage of his attempts to publicize the Institute's activities.[23] A keelman, Thomas Vallance, was elected President of the Blaydon and Stella Institute and it subsequently 'served as a model' for a dozen similar institutions within a twelve mile radius.[24] Cowen's missionary zeal in personally promoting popular education was to pay enormous dividends later on. Charismatic leadership is said to depend upon an ability to demonstrate that he/she can achieve success where others have failed ('if he wants to be a prophet, he must perform miracles') and upon evidence of virtue ('charisma is never a source of private gain').[25] There can be little doubt that popular acclaim for Cowen's leadership owed much to this initial show of strength and to the belief that his activities were expressly designed to benefit the working classes. By 1852, the Blaydon institute was entirely controlled by working men 'who very wisely dispense with the formal patronage of those who do not feel the want and therefore cannot realize the benefit of such a society'.[26]

Cowen's network of radical contacts ensured that the Blaydon Institute was never short of a distinguished speaker. The Chartist orator Henry Vincent and radical press entrepreneur George Dawson[27] were among the first to visit the

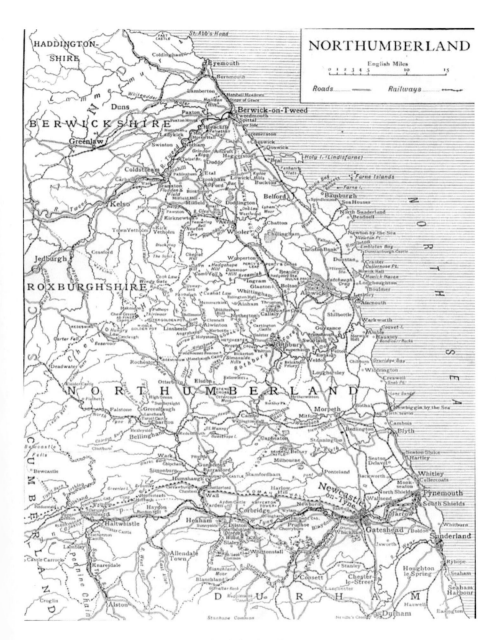

Northumberland, 1921

Joseph Cowen c. 1860

Joseph Cowen c. 1881

PHOTO BY BARRASS, NEWCASTLE   LENT BY JOS. COWEN, ESQ.

JOSEPH COWEN, ESQ.

'Joe', *Vanity Fair*, 27 April 1878

'The Incorruptible Brick'

"The Reason Why" Parliament was dissolved'

'When is he going to stop?'

'Going to Parliament'

The unveiling of the Cowen Memorial, Newcastle upon Tyne, 7 July 1906

Institute in 1848; the Hungarian exile Lajos Kossuth and the conspirator Felice Orsini were both given honorary life membership while even Garibaldi found time to give a lecture during his brief visit to Tyneside in 1854.[28] But aside from the valuable contributions of experienced lecturers, such as Holyoake and Charles Bradlaugh, the members themselves were largely responsible for the delivery of lectures which exhibited a markedly radical tone. The 1848 Revolutions, state education, Italian emancipation and 'The Male vs. the Female Mind' all found their way onto the lecture programme. Thus, while the Alnwick Institute was seemingly content to explore 'The Rise and Progress of Botany'[29] the Winlaton members were being stirred by the abolitionist William Brown.[30] As an active proponent of self-education, Cowen deployed the popular slogan 'knowledge is power' to encourage local institutes to expand the scope of their educational facilities. Nevertheless some institutes, for example North Shields, remained resistant to change. At a time when the Winlaton Institute was receiving two daily and seventeen weekly newspapers, chosen by a ballot of the members, a proposal to introduce newspapers into the North Shields Institute was summarily rejected.[31] Ultimately, these needs had to be met by the opening of a low-subscription 'News Room', prompting a sympathetic editorial from the *Newcastle Guardian* which questioned why two similar institutions were needed in the town.[32]

Under Cowen's guidance, the Blaydon Institute went from strength to strength. In the teeth of strong opposition, sufficient funds had been raised by 1852 to finance a new, purpose-built institute with extensive educational and recreational facilities, including a playground for the children. Local people benefited enormously from the provision of elementary education, much of it being offered without charge and available to non-members.[33] Many of his innovations were a direct response to criticisms he had heard levied at a working men's gathering. With good reason, they claimed that lectures and subscription rates were pitched at a level which discriminated against the unskilled working classes. As Cowen observed, 'the Mob are the very parties we want'[34] and, exerting his considerable influence with the newly-formed Northern Union of Mechanics' Institutes [NUMI], a more relaxed recruitment policy was gradually adopted as standard practice by a large percentage of the affiliated institutes.

Entertainment became a regular feature of the Institute's programme. The Cowen family piano, trundled back and forth between Stella Hall and the Institute, was pressed into service at numerous concerts while Cowen took upon himself the task of providing scenery and hiring musicians. As his daughter Jane recalled:

He took along one of the kid glove and white waistcoat class of reformers, who philosophize about the working classes at a distance but who never go among them…and his feeble nerves were shaken. 'Why', he exclaimed, 'all the rabble of Blaydon are here'![35]

Such recreation, he believed, served a two-fold function: as an attractive alternative to the public house which would discourage intemperance and its ill-effects, and as a way of recruiting those who might otherwise have remained uninterested. Unfortunately, there were frequent clashes with the local clergy and a 'few narrow minded dissenters'.[36] The decision to hold Sunday meetings aroused considerable controversy but Cowen confounded his critics by publicly disputing that one day was any holier than another:

God is omnipresent. It is not the day but ourselves we are to keep holy. The Sabbath was intended for doing good, and in disseminating knowledge…in stirring the people to the practice of virtue, justice, temperance and charity, we are doing good. I object not merely to the Sabbath, but to all formal worship of any kind.[37]

Naturally, such sentiments did not endear him to local churchmen, who were already hostile to him on account of his connections with the Anti-State Church Association. Festering resentment finally came to a head in 1856 over the vexed issue of secular education. The Institute's non-sectarian policy positively encouraged freedom of theological discussion, on the grounds that anything less was discriminatory. But Cowen's plan to provide a neutral meeting space for those with conflicting religious and political views brought forth widespread accusations that he was encouraging atheism. The *Northern Daily Express* roundly condemned the policy, claiming that atheism 'ought to be fenced off wherever young people are moving about'.[38] The Blaydon Institute was even threatened with prosecution under the blasphemy laws but, undaunted, Cowen mounted a vigorous defence in a letter to *The Times*.[39] It is a measure of the independence of the Blaydon Institute that it was able to stand firm against this level of censure when, elsewhere, attempts to overturn the restrictions on religion and politics were effectively blocked.[40] The antagonists were forced to accept that their coercive methods had failed and, in the aftermath, a rival institute was set up which was 'weak in numbers, but strong in rancour'.[41] If anything, the Blaydon Institute was strengthened by the affair and a large crowd of some 1500 people gathered for the 12th Annual Soirée to hear Cowen report that the Institute represented 'full nine tenths of the inhabitants'.[42]

Cowen's reforming zeal was not solely confined to the Blaydon Institute. As secretary of the NUMI he used his influence to inculcate radical ideas and to persuade the younger generation to embrace the demand for 'the Charter and something more'. The *Tyne Tribune* (later published as the *Northern Tribune*) was pressed into service to forward the 'mental, moral and political advancement and regeneration of the People'.[43] The education and welfare provisions of Sir Ambrose Crowley were offered as a model, as was the Blaydon Institute, but the NUMI was heavily criticized for failing to concentrate its efforts where they could be most effective. Ideally Cowen wanted to restrict its sphere of influence to Tyneside where the patronage of large landowners and the clergy was less significant than in the outlying rural areas, for this would have secured his control of the committee and given him a free hand to promote other progressive reforms. Unfortunately, his fellow members were not convinced. His relationship with the NUMI was thereafter rather problematic. He was scathing about the Union's annual dinner which, with its establishment overtones, epitomised everything he was fighting against: 'something about the War, the Ministry all right, the noisy Radicals of Shields all wrong…a good deal of eating and drinking…the sooner it is remodelled, or dead, the better'.[44]

Local mining villages, such as Killingworth, Marley Hill and Bedlington, were often the most receptive to Cowen's radical ideas and, generally speaking, their institutes continued to flourish long after others had been swallowed up by the Free Library movement.[45] By the late 1860s many institutes had foundered, much to the disappointment of those who had expected them to revolutionize society. The NUMI remained an unwieldy organisation, resistant to change, and some members were said to have been lured away by the 'seductive attractions of the beershop'.[46] The introduction of an essay competition in 1879 found the Union still pondering the same old question: 'To what extent will scientific instruction improve the condition of the industrial Classes'? – but unwilling, or unable, to progress beyond any theoretical resolution of the problem.[47] The winners (a clerk and two check-weighmen) perfectly exemplified the originally-targeted artisan class but then, perhaps, they were the only working-class group that might reasonably be expected to respond to such a question. The NUMI executive remained an unhappy combination of radical activists, like Cowen, James McKendrick and John Oxberry, and establishment figures such as Earl Percy. Newcastle did not obtain its Public Library until 1880, some twenty years after the *Northern Tribune* had welcomed the Free Library movement as a 'step in the right direction'.[48] William Brockie compared the Manchester Free Library favourably with the 'petty bickering and cavilling' that typified most mechanics' institutes.[49] On balance, Cowen's intervention might be considered an enabling force. Although his impact was unevenly spread, particularly in rural areas, the Tyneside working classes achieved a level of control over their own mechanics' institutions which was, to say the least, unusual. In the process, members embraced a radical agenda on other fronts too.

It is hardly surprising that there should be a considerable crossover of membership between mechanics' institutes and co-operative societies, given that both organisations were committed to the principle of self-help. In the autumn of 1858 Cowen gave a series of lectures in the Blaydon Institute on co-operation. Reading aloud extracts from Holyoake's book, *Self Help by the People*,[50] which charted the foundation of the Rochdale store, he urged the membership to consider opening their own store.[51] Shortly afterwards, in December 1858, the first co-operative store in the North East was established, initially operating from two hired rooms, but soon sufficiently solvent to finance independent premises.[52] All previous attempts to introduce co-operative principles into the region had failed dismally. Robert Owen's visit to Newcastle in 1843 had precipitated a near riot as local clerics, Sabbatarians and some excitable members of the Irish community combined to denounce his 'godless socialism'.[53] As Cowen observed, Owenite ideas 'were not successful. They were to a great extent connected with political organisations; their management was incapable and not very harmonious; and their death was somewhat disastrous'.[54] Thomas Doubleday, an old Chartist friend of the family, also tried to deter Cowen: 'You will make or help to make these Northumbrian workmen Tories if you try to get them into too good a condition. Try to inculcate good, sound Radical doctrines, and let the material part of the business take care of itself'.[55] Doubleday's fears were not entirely groundless. At first glance, mid-century co-operative traders certainly seemed intent on more immediate goals, namely an improvement in the material and social welfare of their members.[56] However, as Peter Gurney has argued, 'late-nineteenth century co-operation produced its own brand of utopianism'[57] and many Tyneside co-operators were determined that their guiding principle ('each for all and all for each') would not be abandoned in favour of the pursuit of profits.[58] Cowen was quite convinced that the spread of co-operation would provide a unique opportunity for educating the people 'to a better understanding of our principles'.[59] Even when a working man bragged to him that the Blaydon store was 'the best thing going; at the end of the last quarter it made its members a present of £5', he remained confident that such a pragmatic view of the world would eventually give way to more positive co-operative values.[60]

Cowen was always a firm advocate of self-help but his belief in the overarching principle of collective rather than individual action prompted him to direct local co-operative energies into the wider radical sphere. While he was quick to acknowledge the importance of unadulterated food, reasonable prices, and the avoidance of credit and debt, he was far more concerned to promote co-operation's fundamental moral and educational ethos. In his view, too many schemes for reform had failed in the past because of deep divisions within the working classes. He knew that if the working classes were to secure the political and social reforms they needed they would have to be united. They were, Cowen argued, far too suspicious and mistrustful of each other, especially in matters where money was involved. As a businessman, he believed that participation in the commercial and business aspects of co-operatives would foster a greater understanding of the fluctuations of trade and, in turn, this would reduce the likelihood of strikes and disputes; as a politician, he hoped that the unifying experience of co-operative enterprise could be 'brought to bear at the hustings'.[61] It was Cowen's ability to pursue both immediate and long term objectives, realistic and idealistic goals, that singled him out from many other prominent co-operators and which may be said to account for the phenomenal success of the Co-operative movement in the North East.

Of course, in sheer weight of numbers, the North East could not possibly compete with Yorkshire or Lancashire but then societies in those counties had a far longer history and an altogether larger population. It is only when statistics for other 'Radical' centres such as Birmingham and Sheffield are taken into account that the true scale of the regional movement emerges. In 1873, when there were 43,615 members in the two counties of Northumberland and Durham with a combined share capital of £201,800, Birmingham had just 128 registered co-operators in an estimated population of 343,000; Sheffield had a mere 600, although its population stood at 240,000.[62] Cowen's proselytizing efforts were largely responsible for the movement's rapid progress, not least because his role in the NUMI provided an ideal operational framework for his propagandist activities. By April 1862, Cowen was able to call together delegates from twenty-three local societies to consider the viability of forming a Central Co-operative Committee for the North of England.[63] Having undertaken a comprehensive national survey of the larger co-operative societies he was persuaded that access to wholesale trading was essential. While Lancashire co-operators were still debating the issue, plans were already well in hand on Tyneside for the establishment of a central purchasing store and a management committee had been duly elected.[64] Unfortunately, not everyone shared Cowen's enthusiasm for setting up a Northern Co-operative Union. The members of small societies were strongly opposed to any outside interference and proposals to appoint an official accountant and introduce bulk buying were vigorously opposed.[65] As late as 1870, the Cramlington society was still trying to overcome the reservations of its membership, even though the financial advantages of utilising the services of the Co-operative Wholesale Society (CWS) had, by then, become widely accepted.[66] The Blaydon society, needless to say, was one of the first to become a member of the North of England Wholesale Society when it was finally established in Manchester in 1864.[67]

Cowen's Co-operative Union offered a unified central structure for the pursuit of his wider radical aims. It is important to remember that the NRU was gathering momentum at roughly the same time as co-operative trading was being introduced into the region and, inevitably, the two movements were promoted in tandem. After Cowen acquired the *Newcastle Chronicle* in 1859, he was quick to exploit its potential as a vehicle for promoting his political projects, especially the advantages of co-operative activities. He appointed W.E. Adams who had worked on the *English Republic* and the *Northern Tribune* as editor-in-chief of the *Daily*'s stablemate, the *Newcastle Weekly Chronicle*, in 1865 and thereafter he relied heavily upon his judgment and support. It was Adams who took the initiative to publish a detailed survey of individual co-operative societies in the *Newcastle Weekly Chronicle* throughout 1867, demonstrating that co-operation was to be regarded as a vital expression of local radicalism. Cowen's intervention in securing special trains for working men was in no small measure a response to their stated desire to continue to live near their co-operative stores.[68] A good example of the harmonisation of local radicalism is offered below to show the way that two disparate campaigns contributed to the expansion of co-operative enterprises in the North East.

The campaign by the Nine Hours League to reduce the traditional working week of engineering workers on Tyneside had reverberations that extended beyond the immediate interests of those who agitated the dispute in 1871.[69] Two leading working class co-operators, James McKendrick and Matthew Pletts, played a prominent role in the dispute, while Cowen himself acted as principal arbiter. The viability of venturing into the sphere of co-operative production had from time to time exercised the minds of the co-operative leadership who were already persuaded that this should be a primary objective.[70] A number of small productive enterprises had already been established on Tyneside when the engineers' strike raised the whole level of the debate.[71] Addressing a meeting of interested groups in the Newcastle Mechanics' Institute, Dr J. H. Rutherford,[72] who sponsored the venture, said that mediating between the competing claims of capital and labour was 'one of the most serious problems of the time…it was nothing less than social war – industrial war – and it was, or threatened to be, chronic'.[73] The employers, argued Rutherford, would have to recognise that workers had 'a will and a brain as well as a stomach'.[74] Citing the example of Briggs & Co. he urged them to support the establishment of a co-operative engineering works, to be based at Ouseburn in Newcastle.[75]

As the *Chronicle* press was quick to point out, co-operative membership had provided a 'fair proportion' of the strikers with a reserve fund and this had alleviated the strain on League funds.[76] When the Ouseburn Works were officially opened in July 1871 all prospective employees were required to take up a £5 share in the company (paid in instalments) and to sign over an agreed percentage of their income for the purchase of additional shares. A fifty-four hour working week was officially introduced, with an inbuilt proviso that further reductions in working hours would be sought as soon as was practicable. All disputes were to be settled by an appointed arbitration committee and all profits in excess of 10 per cent were to be divided equally among the shareholders.[77]

The success of the Ouseburn project depended upon widening the share ownership so that the initial capital could be raised, and on devising some mechanism for retaining absolute control. An appeal to the entire co-operative membership met with a ready response and, once the legal obstacles had been overcome, there was no shortage of willing investors. Strong links had been forged between local trade unionists and co-operators as a result of their involvement in the Northern Reform Union and Northern Reform League. Essentially, by 1871, many co-operative societies regarded the backing of the Ouseburn Works as little short of a moral obligation. Cowen's newspapers fully endorsed the scheme throughout July and August, assiduously publicising the take up of shares and the numerous promotional meetings at which League members such as McKendrick hailed it as 'the most important movement ever started on Tyneside'.[78] The Wallsend Society became the first of many to respond to McKendrick's promise that the 'strike epidemic' gripping England would disappear if industry was remodelled on cooperative lines.[79] By this time, most societies had accrued substantial revenue and the Blaydon Society required little persuasion to part with £1,000 of its capital. As the Treasurer William Douglas pointed out, they were simply required to risk half the usual dividend for one quarter of the year.[80] Many believed they were 'in honour and duty bound' to contribute.[81] Apart from the pledges of local co-operatives, large sums of money were also forthcoming from Yorkshire and the Co-operative Wholesale Society, and the success of the Ouseburn Works seemed to be assured. With the strike still underway there was no shortage of work, and from a position of unusual confidence the management team declared that an arbitration board was superfluous to an industry with a co-operative structure.[82] In the immediate aftermath of the strike, Cowen applauded their endeavours which he claimed had 'contributed materially to promote that great social victory which had just been achieved'.[83]

Rutherford's popularity as manager of the works was formally affirmed when the entire workforce marched in unison to pledge their votes for him in the municipal elections,[84] and even when the works collapsed in 1875 his popularity with the Tyneside people withstood the bitter recriminations which swiftly followed. Notwithstanding the enormous losses sustained by almost all local co-operative societies, and the two miners' unions which had been encouraged to deposit their funds with the Industrial Bank (floated in 1873 to provide additional financial support), Rutherford was exonerated of blame. He retained the unwavering loyalty that Alex Scorer had pledged at the height of the Ouseburn's success:

> For we think, think, sweat, broil
> Fra buzzor unto bell
> But what gis plishur te wor toil
> Pairt profit's for worsell!
> Say! mun we leev the Doctor oot
> Wivoot a word o' praise,
> That brow't the Yuseburn works aboot,
> That did the Cumpnee raise?
> No! Let us show the foke outside,
> We can his morrits see,
> And t'yek him willin' as wor guide
> Bi geen him three times three.
> For he'll work, think, think, work
> Fra mornin'until neet
> An not a bit o' bother shirk
> Te see the works a' reet.[85]

Undoubtedly, the Ouseburn's ignominious collapse amidst accusations of mismanagement impeded further progress in the sphere of workers' co-operatives. Almost from the outset, the Ouseburn had been beset by industrial disputes, particularly in relation to the employees' compulsory purchase of shares.[86] Nationally, there were two schools of thought. Prominent co-operators, most notably E. O. Greening, wanted employees to be full partners, whereas others believed that their overriding aim should be to provide goods 'at the cheapest possible price'.[87] Many feared that employees would sell their shares to outsiders when they left, and control would no longer be retained by co-operators.[88] Robert Oakeshott claims that the Ouseburn workers were not seriously committed to the project and that 'they never came to think of it as in any genuine way *theirs*'.[89] Locally, the Co-operative movement was damaged by the experience. The loss of capital not only precipitated falling membership in some societies, but those who remained became extremely wary of other capital ventures.[90] It is hardly to Cowen's credit that he so studiously avoided any direct involvement in the Ouseburn's management, especially as Rutherford had no business acumen or relevant experience. Ever the entrepreneur, Cowen was careful not to risk his capital unless the rewards were certain.

On a more positive note, the expansion of co-operative societies received a powerful boost from an unexpected quarter in 1872. A sudden increase in the price of staple foods sparked off a violent agitation in the North Durham coal-field which carried all the hallmarks of early-nineteenth-century food riots.[91] The significance of the dispute does not reside in the fact that it was managed and controlled from the start by local women, even though such activity was a singular occurrence. Rather, it is the immediacy with which a 'co-operative' solution was arrived at that distinguishes this women's campaign from its forerunners. Employing the language of exploitation the women rapidly implemented a boycott of local traders and resolved to establish their own co-operative stores. Women on Tyneside had been politically active throughout the period, participating in all of the local electoral reform initiatives and, more often than not, acting as principal fundraisers for a gamut of radical activities. Their role may have been circumscribed in accordance with the prevailing gender stereotypes and yet the solvency of mechanics' institutes, temperance societies and Cowen's numerous reform campaigns depended largely upon their fund raising efforts, especially the regular soirées, festivals and dinners which they organised with considerable expertise.[92]

On this occasion, however, the colliery women seemed determined to demonstrate that they could conduct their own affairs, without any outside interference or assistance. This proved to be no orderly, polite exchange but an aggressive and violent defence of their right to obtain good quality produce at a fair price. Initially, the campaign was treated with a combination of scorn and patronising good humour by the local press. The *North of England Farmer*, which reported the mass protest meeting at Seaton Colliery, ridiculed the women's unseemly exodus into the nearby public house, the editor's sympathy clearly with the 'hundreds of poor fellows' who 'emerged from the bowels of the earth to find that no dinner was ready for them'.[93] Undaunted, the women organised a collection to pay off their outstanding debts to local butchers and rigorously enforced a total boycott. 'Blacklegs' were summarily punished, often by 'tarring' or being stripped naked, to ensure the effectiveness of their ban. The railings of a house in Seaton Colliery were torn down and an effigy of one offender was burned when she was found to have purchased meat from a blacklisted supplier.[94] Mobile butchers' vans were stoned and lengthy detours had to be made to reach those areas unaffected by the dispute. For all its comic overtones, this was a serious dispute and after the initial hostilities had been declared the women voted to avoid public house meetings – not just to defend themselves from the accusation that they were enjoying 'a drunken spree' but to demonstrate that they regarded publicans as equally exploitative.[95]

The decision by Durham butchers to form a union to protect their threatened trade demonstrates that the women's tactics were having considerable impact. High prices were not the only source of grievance. Resentment also festered over the invidious operation of credit schemes and the adulteration of food supplies, for debtors were not able to complain about either exorbitant prices or poor quality. The Jarrow contingent, who arranged to have the local milk supply analysed in July 1872 were incensed when they discovered that it was 'mostly water'.[96] Co-operative stores offered a solution to all these grievances and, even though many of them were obliged to sell meat at prices the same or higher than those which had caused the dispute, local butchers were forced to adopt a 'ready money policy' in order to compete.[97] The strike was given sympathetic coverage by the *Chronicle* which praised the manner in which the campaign had been fought and applauded the women's decision to set up their own co-operative stores.

The women's agitation in the Northern Coalfield was mirrored by similar disturbances in Lancashire and London throughout the summer months, and the extended publicity served to heighten local interest and instigate a more rigorous analysis of its cause. The London Patriotic Society which met at Clerkenwell Green at the end of August insisted that high meat prices were caused by the existing land and game laws, and the provisions of the Contagious Diseases (Cattle) Act – a view that the *North of England Farmer* swiftly rejected.[98] Although the agitation was relatively short-lived the local Co-operative movement benefited enormously, not least because it brought co-operative trading into isolated colliery villages and raised awareness of its wider potential to improve the living standards of the working classes.

In the early 1870s, Cowen had good reason to believe that the spread of co-operation in the North East would be wholly beneficial. Addressing the annual Co-operative Congress at Newcastle in 1873, he stressed that co-operative trading was primarily aimed at rescuing 'the poorest class of men' who were being ruthlessly exploited by dishonest traders. Temperance and thrift, he insisted, were 'personal and not class values'.[99] It is clear that Tyneside mostly escaped the ameliorating effects of co-operation which, it is often asserted, diverted the working classes away from radical reform.[100] Local co-operators were not expected to choose *either* shop keeping or community building, or identify themselves exclusively with either Owenite or Smilesian philosophy. Cowen offered them an alternative radical philosophy which liberated them from the inherent snares of both ideologies:

We hope that, not by any violent revolution, but by a gradual, yet sure means, we shall effect a better distribution of the wealth of the country, so as to spread comfort more equitably…We mean to preach a higher and better doctrine. We wish the be-all and the end-all of this existence not to be more money or greater material prosperity; we want to make men citizens, we want to preach the doctrine of brotherhood and fellowship – we wish to preach to you a new gospel.[101]

Under Cowen's careful guidance, co-operation on Tyneside pursued the same ideological objectives that had stood at the heart of local radicalism for generations. The importance of extending land ownership was thus a primary objective and many societies introduced mortgage and lending schemes at preferential rates. The allotment scheme introduced to the Winlaton Institute membership in 1849 had proved enormously successful and, through the pages of the 1873 *Co-operative Almanack,* Cowen made his own views on the subject absolutely clear: 'above all, let us unite to be the proprietors of the land in which we live. This is the true end and aim of cooperation. Without it, every other form of union will sooner or later prove a failure.'[102] Wallsend Co-operative Society claimed to be the first to introduce house building and allotment provisions for its members.[103] The Society's founder, Robert Douglass, is credited with being the prime mover in acquiring thirteen acres of freehold land in 1868. Douglass was a working man and it was said that 'no phase of applied co-operation had more interest for Mr Douglass than the development of land and the building of workmen's' dwellings'.[104] Members were able to rent their garden allotments for a nominal sum (1d per sq. yard p.a.) and the Society sold any surplus produce in the store. A large number of houses were built and sold at cost, with the Society advancing up to 80 per cent mortgage and the balance paid off quarterly from the members' dividend. The street names reflected the involvement of the committee who fostered the scheme (*Douglass, Harrington, Blenkinsop* etc), and the members' pride in the movement itself (*Provident, Industrial, Artisan* etc). Colliery districts were a little slower to invest in working-class housing for many of their members were already provided with housing by the coal companies. Even so, similar schemes were gradually introduced during the late 1870s.[105]

Educational initiatives, too, were a major priority and almost all north-east co-operative societies reserved a portion of their working capital to be used as an Education Fund. In most cases the Fund was used to purchase copies of the national journal, the *Co-operator,* for circulation among the membership and for the free distribution of the *North of England Co-operative Almanack.* In addition, some societies introduced penny readings to familiarise their members with 'what co-operation was and what it might become'.[106] Although these initiatives were rather low key and some societies made only a small allocation of capital, they nevertheless contributed to the overall cohesion of the local movement. The *Almanack* in particular, while providing all the usual statistical and social ephemera, was a powerful document for proselytizing Cowen's radical ideas and for pressing home his ambitious plans for the future, a future in which the Co-operative movement was to play a major part:

> Much has been accomplished – much more remains to be done. Not by violence but by the force of the moral situation is this to be accomplished. The race is not always with the swift, nor the battle with the strong. Labour on then, and success will surely crown your efforts; Let your watchword be 'Persevere'.[107]

By 1870, the radicalisation of the Tyneside electorate had reached a self-conscious maturity, not least because of the power wielded by the Northern Co-operative Union. Educated to push co-operation to its ideological limits, a considerable proportion of its vast membership associated themselves with the other major improving organisations, namely temperance and trade unionism. Temperance had an important role to play but the nature of its contribution is somewhat amorphous. For Cowen, who was a lifelong abstainer, the issue was relatively simple. 'Sobriety', he contended, 'must precede all moral, mental and political reformation if that reformation is to be real'.[108] He was in constant demand as a speaker for the local circuit and, convinced that temperance would help to mitigate the evils of pauperisation which kept the working classes in a state of dependence, he gave generously of his services. In essence, it was the liberating opportunities that were created as a result of the efforts of temperance campaigners which yielded the sober and thrifty mass membership so necessary to the success of the mechanics' institutes and Co-operative societies.

Temperance in Newcastle upon Tyne can be traced back to 1830 when the first society was formed and within a few years it had expanded sufficiently to warrant the establishment of a Northern District Union.[109] The emphasis during those early days was firmly on teetotalism and adherents were expected to sign a pledge to abstain from all alcoholic drinks.[110] When the agent of the British Temperance League, Thomas Whittaker, visited Newcastle in 1836 enormous crowds of working men turned out to hear him speak. His working-class background clearly served him well as he argued that their hard earned sixpences would be better spent on steak, potatoes and bread than on a quart of ale.[111] By 1840 there were reputedly 20,000 registered teetotallers in Northumberland and Durham.[112] A massive propaganda programme in which thousands of temperance tracts and pamphlets were circulated had generated much of this support, and the organisers knew only too well that they would need stable financial backing if the momentum was not to be lost. The fundraising problem was tackled by the formation of Ladies Committees, who also organised social gatherings aimed at providing 'rational' alternatives to the public house. In the main, the Temperance movement's vast committee structure enabled women to participate more fully than was usual, although the management remained a male preserve until the British Women's Temperance Association was eventually founded in Newcastle upon Tyne in 1876.[113] Given the generational spread of the Movement's activities, large numbers of women were required to supervise Sunday schools, choral societies and contingents of the Band of Hope. Moreover, the presumed correlation between intemperance and prostitution was an important factor in the decision to include women on visiting committees.

Not everyone supported teetotalism, however, and on Tyneside, as elsewhere, the moderationists fought back by claiming that the detrimental effects of alcohol were unproven. Charles Larkin, the renowned local Chartist and political reformer, denounced his opponents as 'ignoramuses, wretched quacks and downright rascals' and asserted that teetotal doctrine was 'a form of oppression...to reduce the men of England to the water and potato diet of Ireland'.[114] Enforced teetotalism was not a position to which Cowen could or would subscribe. While he acknowledged that the principle 'deserved respect'[115] he had little time for the intolerance with which it became increasingly associated. His *Northern Tribune* was scathing:

> The intolerance and self righteousness of too many temperance apostles and their intemperate exaltation of the pump as the only panacea for the moral, social and political salvation of society, find no favour in our eyes. Those who make a good cause obnoxious, ridiculous to men of understanding, deserve to be scourged with the whip of satire.[116]

Cowen was more interested in promoting a wider vision of 'self help' through co-operative retailing and mechanics' institutes. Questioned pointedly during the 1874 election as to whether he would 'rob a poor man of his beer', he declared that he 'utterly repudiated the doctrine of attempting to make men sober by Act of Parliament...people should have control of their own affairs'.[117] As ever, his concern was to empower the people, to give them the right to manage the licensing laws as they saw fit and, ultimately, to uphold the principle of democracy. New legislation aimed at restricting the licensing hours introduced earlier in 1871 was vigorously opposed by the drink interest who claimed that abolition would cost the Exchequer £500,000 every week if it was carried.[118] The tactics of the Good Templars, too, came under fire when the first prosecutions were made under the 1872 Act and the *North of England Farmer* claimed that the entrapment methods used were little short of 'contemptible'.[119]

In order to trace the connections between temperance societies and other working-class organisations some account must be taken of their religious roots. The religious and moral ethos that underpinned the Movement's activities and organisational structure was primarily an expression of traditional nonconformity, drawing strength from a range of dissenting groups among whom the Methodists might be regarded as the senior partners.[120] *Testimony for the Million* (1847), a pamphlet based on the public testimony of working men, demonstrated that the commitment to temperance often involved a religious as well as a practical conversion.[121] The claims advanced by some historians that Methodism provided an organisational training for working class leaders, and a political language of protest relevant to a range of radical causes, are substantiated by the available local evidence.[122] In the first instance, a powerful case can be made based on the significant crossover of membership and this important point will be addressed below, as it relates to the associational life of the locality as a whole. Accusations that teetotallers were politically active were frequently levied and this gives a certain credence to the general point that Methodism and, by association, temperance were conducive to radicalism. Consider this vituperative attack on teetotallers by a local surgeon during a debate at the Literary and Philosophical Society in 1850:

> They were the ready agents of violence in Ireland; that in the muddiest pools of Chartism, the Teetotallers were down among the dregs – that they incited the pitmen to the great strike which proved so ruinous; that their missionaries were even now stirring up the men to another great strike.[123]

T. P. Barkas, a prominent member of the Newcastle Temperance Society, parried the charge by publishing this cleverly worded rejoinder:

> We rejoice...that Mr. Potter has taken such a dirty job in hand as to go down to the muddiest pools of Chartism...we congratulate him on getting up again to tell us that he found Teetotallers down among the dregs. We accept it as a tribute indicative of success...Hitherto the warrens of political strife have been the beershops, the dark parlours and the dirty taprooms...the nation is no longer to be impelled by pot-valiant, pothouse politicians.

Expressing his pleasure that teetotalism had 'permeated the whole mass of society', Barkas claimed that it was to the movement's credit that 'the pitmen had the good sense to commit the management of their affairs to sober men rather than to beer-muddling drinkers'.[124] The overt republicanism of certain sections of the Temperance movement simply added fuel to the fire. The Cowen press had actively championed the cause of Italian emancipation throughout the 1850s and 1860s and with Garibaldi cast in the role of popular hero considerable capital was made of his temperate habits.[125] The agent for the United Kingdom Alliance, Revd James Wilson, was promoted as the 'Garibaldi of Prohibition' when he attended a Permissive Bill demonstration at Wallsend in 1860,[126] and the support he attracted suggests that this was an extremely effective tactic. Even temperance band competitions, it would seem, proved susceptible to the tide of republican fervour that had captured the Tyneside imagination, for all entrants were required to play 'The Garibaldi March' as a competition piece at the Brancepeth Grand Gala in July 1860.[127]

Expressions of radicalism, such as those described above, point towards the connections that were being forged with other local organisations. The emphasis upon rational recreation naturally underpinned the close relationship with the mechanics' institute movement. Cowen actively promoted reciprocity in numerous speeches and through the pages of his journals, arguing that mechanics' institutes were 'fitting adjuncts to *all* temperance societies'.[128] At the same time, the Newcastle Temperance Society exerted its own considerable influence to persuade the Town Council to help finance the Newcastle Mechanics' Institute, instead of spending public money on the annual Race Week festivities which they claimed would merely encourage intemperate behaviour.[129] On a practical level, temperance insurance schemes and building societies encouraged the working classes to be thrifty. In 1844, the Newcastle Life Insurance Society offered a retirement package of £40 per annum for the price of a daily pint of beer. The Society's slogan was 'Keep your pledge whate'er you do, For if you keep it, Your pledge will keep you.'[130] By 1862, temperance insurance and building societies had large registered incomes and the influence of the Movement had grown proportionately greater.[131] Public outcry against drink-related corruption helped to fuel the call for legislation and, by 1872, the *Chronicle* was drawing attention to the power of the Good Templars who were predicted to have 'a great impact upon the national and local elections'.[132]

Co-operative stores benefited most from the spread of temperance, not least because they operated an embargo on the sale of intoxicating liquor.[133] In colliery villages, temperance was the vitalizing connection which facilitated the close relationship between the Methodist chapel and co-operative store so often remarked upon. A scan of the constituent branches of the North of England Temperance League and the Northern Co-operative Union reveals that a large proportion of them were located in the same small mining communities, thus demonstrating the overlapping interests between them.[134] These links were not confined to the collieries but were also detectable throughout the region. Nationally, Brian Harrison's analytical table of the reforming activities of prominent teetotallers places co-operation high on the list of ancillary interests.[135] Equally, the groundswell of popular affection for abstainers such as Thomas Burt and Dr. Rutherford, who played such a prominent role in the Tyneside Co-operative movement, clearly prompted large numbers of the working classes to emulate the example of those who had so conspicuously served their interests. Burt's involvement in the anti-vaccination agitation of the early 1870s was spearheaded by the Co-operative movement,[136] and well supported by local temperance campaigners. Sympathy with the underlying issue of civil liberty served to reinforce the common ground between the two groups.

Since the Temperance movement was expressly committed to encouraging sobriety by providing rational recreation, this, initially, brought them into conflict with the friendly societies whose meetings were invariably held in public houses. With an estimated four million members, and revenue of more than £11 million in 1874, the friendly societies could claim a far larger working-class membership than either trade unions or even the Co-operative movement,[137] and yet our knowledge of their activities remains somewhat superficial.[138] The origins of friendly societies has been traced back to the early guilds but their later expansion in the nineteenth century was, in some measure, almost certainly a reaction to the threat of pauperisation and the fear of the workhouse generated by the Anatomy Act (1832) and the Poor Law Amendment Act (1834). The main function of such societies was to provide insurance against sickness, accident and death, and the proliferation of registered Burial Societies suggests that the desire to secure a respectable funeral for their families loomed very large in the working-class consciousness.[139] There are notable difficulties in precisely distinguishing between friendly societies and freemasonry orders, both of which fulfilled a similar social welfare function. Working men's societies seem to have been mainly, though not exclusively, freemasonry orders, such as the Oddfellows and the Foresters, and greater stress seems to have been placed upon brotherhood and union.[140]

Surviving evidence of Tyneside friendly society activities is very sketchy indeed, being almost entirely dependent upon brief press reports of their annual celebrations and the occasional Rule Book. Interestingly enough, much of what survives of the earlier period relates to the proliferation of women's societies. However, it is worth noting that many female societies had a discriminatory membership policy which excluded the old (i.e. those aged over forty) and those who were judged immoral ('must be of good character').[141] Entry fees, some of which were as high as 3s 4d, and the monthly subscriptions which were bolstered by a complicated system of fines for non-attendance, were clearly prohibitive. The subscription fees of societies invariably included a levy for the consumption of ale at the regular meeting and its supply, in large quantities, as part of the death benefit provisions. The Friendly Society of Women, North Shields, for example, provided £7 burial expenses and four gallons of ale for the wake.[142]

Peter Bailey has highlighted their social function, particularly the annual feasts where large quantities of strong ale were consumed 'as part of the birth-right of the freeborn Englishman'.[143] In the event, it is hardly surprising that they should become a primary target for the temperance lobby's reforming zeal and, by mid-century, middle-class patronage brought many of them into line with the self-improving ethos of the mechanics' institutes. The Cowen family had strong links with the working men's orders. A freemasonry order, The Lodge of Industry, had been established at Winlaton from as early as 1700 and a large percentage of the Crowley workforce were members.[144] Cowen's brother, John, was also a member, representing the Lodge at the funeral of the renowned local oarsman James Renforth in 1871. Sir Joseph Cowen was Grand Master of the Sunderland branch of the United Order of Nottingham Oddfellows in 1865 when some 5,000 members attended a celebratory picnic in the grounds of Stella Hall.[145] The gymnastics and games that dominated the proceedings locate this squarely in the arena of rational recreation and contemporary commentators were eager to stress the self help, thrifty and sober principles that Oddfellows and Foresters espoused.[146] In 1850, the *Newcastle Chronicle* was at pains to point out that with over 15,000 members in Northumberland and Durham Oddfellows and Foresters were saving the country two million every year in poor rates.[147] Notably, Cowen Jnr is listed alongside other prominent politicians such as Mundella and Gladstone as an honorary member of the Loyal Order of Ancient Shepherds.[148] As a numerically influential section of the local community it is not too surprising that he should have taken an interest in their activities or that he should have exerted considerable effort to ensure their participation in his radical campaigns. Although he acknowledged their welfare provisions, he was much more interested in encouraging them to function as part of the self-help network of organisations which were intended to make the working classes independent.[149] Cowen and other radical activists provided the vital linkage between temperance and friendly societies, especially after the mid century when 'alternative' meeting places became more widely accessible.

Historians including Harold Perkin and Paul Johnson have stressed the 'political neutrality' of friendly societies.[150] While it would be difficult to challenge this view on a general basis, the evidence for Tyneside suggests that an alternative reading is possible. Cowen's honorary membership might be considered immaterial but his advocacy of friendly societies is not. The prestigious role allotted to friendly/ freemasonry societies during the Northern Reform League demonstrations in 1867 indicates that their presence was not token. The major freemasonry orders were all fully represented: Oddfellows, Free Gardeners, Foresters and Druids.[151] Moreover, a number of friendly society delegates were known radical activists, involved in republicanism, electoral reform and the Co-operative movement. Jonathan Rayne (Free Gardener) and Josiah Thomas (Sons of Temperance Order), for instance, were both former Chartists who were also members of Cowen's Foreign Affairs Committee. Other close friends and fellow radicals who worked closely with Cowen on a number of projects include Thomas Gregson (Ancient Order of Druids) and Richard Bagnall Reed who was secretary of the Northern Reform Union and manager of the *Newcastle Daily Chronicle*.[152] These men were not ordinary members but held executive positions and it is their influence over a large working-class membership that is at issue here. Reed, for example, subsequently went on to become Deputy Provincial Grand Mark Master of Northumberland and Durham Lodge of Industry. Their radical affiliations were widely known and there are good reasons for assuming that they were not likely to secure election if their political views were unacceptable to the 'brotherhood'. Such 'webs of affiliation' as Roger Burt and others have noted were formalised in the initiation rituals which created 'strong trust relationships.[153] Tyneside activists who held an executive position in their lodges were thus uniquely well positioned to recruit their fellow members to the radical cause.

The links between friendly societies and trade unions require little elaboration. During the period following the Combination Acts friendly societies enabled early trade unionists to continue to meet and support each other without falling foul of the law, and it was not unusual for such societies to offer financial assistance when their members were involved in a strike.[154] In the North East radical trade unionism was something of a tradition, particularly as it related to mining and heavy engineering. From the heady days of the Miners' Association[155] the miners had stood in the vanguard of every political campaign:

> A class of men have taken the lead in the new movement who have ever been ready to give earnest and valuable assistance in the work of popular progress. I mean the miners of the North. The services they have at all times rendered to the cause of the people is well known to those who have had charge in this district of former agitations for the enlargement of the franchise.[156]

The individual self-reliance that Cowen prized so highly may be said to have found its ultimate expression in the confident local trade unionism which emerged in the 1870s. Trade unionism was demonstrably not an isolated activity but one which had a reciprocal relationship with co-operation, temperance and mechanics' institutes. Their aims were not wholly confined to improving working conditions and practices. Tyneside trade unionism also embraced the need to improve the condition of the working classes as a whole, to press for more leisure time, wider access to education and more equitable political representation. The complexity of trade union activity cannot be traced in any detail here. Rather, specific examples will be used to demonstrate their growing confidence in pursuit of unusually ambitious objectives.

The pivotal importance of the 1871 Nine Hours Strike has already been referred to as the context in which co-operative production was developed. This dispute, however, exerted an impact far beyond the immediate locality and that of the engineering trades. With somewhat exaggerated enthusiasm, Cowen congratulated the engineers for their struggle had been 'a great social conflict' in which ' the moral, social and political welfare, not only of themselves, but of the artisans of the whole world, was advanced'.[157] From the outset, the dispute was publicised as an important test case, not just of the legitimacy of their claim to shorter hours but of the right to have that claim adjudicated by impartial arbitration. As Matthew Gillender told the Hartlepool working men, they could easily obtain similar working conditions if the Tyneside strike was successful. The League, he said, would have the satisfaction of leaving the world 'in a vastly better condition than that which they found it'.[158]

Arbitration had been mooted in the *Northern Tribune* as early as 1854 as a solution to the endemic disputes and strikes which caused so much hardship. Samuel Kydd, the author of an article entitled 'Strikes and Arbitration Considered', argued that it was wrong 'to suppose that the employer and labourer can have, reasonably, opposing interests' and, calling upon parliament to legislate for Courts of Arbitration, he challenged the Liberal *laissez faire* dogma: 'Every session proves that parliament cannot reduce to practice the abstract dogma of universal non-interference'.[159] An Arbitration Court set up to resolve a shipbuilding dispute in Sunderland that same year, with equal representation of the Shipbuilders' Society and the Shipwrights' Union and chaired by three impartial adjudicators, was cited as a model that might be successfully adopted by other trades.[160] By the end of the 1850s the local press was moved to comment upon the sea change in labour relations which accepted the need for equity. In 1859 for example, the *Newcastle Guardian* asserted that employers and workers had equal rights.[161] Change was, however, slow and piecemeal, notwithstanding the conciliatory stance adopted by many enlightened employers, including A. J. Mundella, whose settlement of the Nottingham hosiery dispute in the early

1860s had done so much to legitimize the wider use of arbitration boards.[162]

From the outset, Cowen was actively involved in the management of the strike. His newspapers provided ample coverage which helped to mobilise local opinion and he gave financial support in the latter stages of the strike when funds began to run perilously low. But Cowen's most crucial intervention was conducted privately as he attempted several times to mediate on the Nine Hours League's behalf. The employers refused to negotiate and instead attempted to break the strike by importing foreign workers from Germany, France and Belgium. Cowen intervened by explaining the cause of the dispute and offering foreign workers an assisted passage home. By September 1871, attitudes had noticeably hardened and the *Chronicle* denounced those employers who had 'set class against class and created a bitter spirit among workmen which we are afraid will not easily be assuaged'.[163] As reports of widespread intimidation began to filter through, and Black, Hawthorn and Company prosecuted twelve men for breach of contract, the *Chronicle* claimed that the employers were 'precipitating social war... These are days in which neither gold nor caste is any longer omnipotent. The people of England will never permit a petted and pampered plutocracy to rob labour of its rights'.[164] Largely as a result of the League's fundraising efforts, the campaign had by this stage attracted considerable outside interest. Cowen enlisted the help of his old Chartist friend, Thomas Cooper, and persuaded him to prevail upon Mundella to assist.

Cooper wrote to Mundella and urged him to travel to Newcastle as an independent arbitrator under the pretext of investigating the practicability of arbitration measures. Cowen, it seems, had already warned Cooper that the employers would not negotiate with anyone who was acting on the League's behalf.[165] Cowen acted as principal tactician, facilitating Mundella's negotiations with Sir William Armstrong by suggesting the terms most likely to succeed, and preparing the workers in advance for the proposals that might be made. Mundella was urged to rely on Cowen's judgement throughout for he 'is the best friend the men have... he is the most popular man in canny Newcastle and is always the same man. You may confide in him thoroughly'.[166] Mundella was shocked by the prevailing hostility and concluded privately that the employers were 'all in the wrong'.[167] He was less than sanguine that a settlement could be reached and so it proved. The employers rejected his proposed board of arbitration. It was left to Cowen and Ralph Philipson, the Newcastle Town Clerk, to build upon the negotiations begun by Mundella and broker a settlement that was satisfactory to all concerned.[168]

The strike prompted similar demands to be made and conceded elsewhere in the country, and the Amalgamated Society of Engineers subsequently paid tribute to the League 'and the manly, honourable and disinterested part played by Joseph Cowen and the *Newcastle Chronicle*.[169] At the demonstration and soirée held to celebrate their success John Burnett urged upon the audience the importance of encouraging trade unionism. Cowen, as ever, grasped the opportunity to press home his political agenda. They had, he said, 'learned the value and necessity of organisation', now they must combine 'not just for trade but for social and political purposes'.[170] The clamour for the nine hour working day became the clarion call of virtually all trades but in the North East, unpredictably, it prompted a swift response from the Northumberland agricultural workers.

With average wages among agricultural labourers in the Northern Counties significantly higher (over 50 per cent) than those in other rural areas, the primary impetus of the dispute was not economic but focused sharply on the bondage system and the demand for equitable working conditions.[171] Beginning at the Northumberland village of Earsdon in early February 1872, the agitation quickly swept through the surrounding areas. Coincidentally, a similar agitation had begun in south Warwickshire by Joseph Arch.[172] The *North of England Farmer* deplored the way that the agricultural labourers had 'become infected' by the Nine Hours agitation when they had so little cause to complain, although it was prepared to concede that the bondage system was anomalous and should be given up.[173] The *Newcastle Daily Chronicle*, however, insisted that

> No one with an English heart in his bosom can refrain from giving Godspeed to the effort now being put forward by and on behalf of men who spend their whole lives in semi-starvation, in practical serfdom and on the verge of utter destitution. If only for the sake of furthering the laudable endeavours of poverty stricken farm servants in the South, the Northern Peasantry should persevere in their attempts to improve their own condition.[174]

Once again, it seems, north-east workers were being asked to lead the fight for reform. The labourers' claims were vigorously resisted amidst accusations that they were idle and intemperate, prompting the *Chronicle* to warn that the agricultural workers had public opinion on their side.[175] The Cowenite press highlighted the plight of female agricultural workers and conducted a rigorous analysis of the bondage system during the weeks leading up to the annual hirings when the labourers hoped to press their case. Moreover, the strength of Arch's campaign was relentlessly exploited as the *Chronicle* sought to buttress their bargaining position. The new Union, claimed the editorial, had 'noble work to do which nothing else could do so well'; it would be a 'school of self help'.[176] In the event, the agricultural labourers were able to wrest considerable improvements from their employers on pay, hours and holidays at the Hexham and Longbenton hirings.[177]

As the above examples show, trade unionists on Tyneside were able to bargain effectively and confidently by the 1870s. Their ability to stand firm and obtain significant concessions is directly related to the political cohesion that had been fostered across a plethora of working-class organisations, encouraging greater individual self esteem and collective responsibility. Thomas Burt's election as MP for Morpeth in 1874 marked a significant turning point, not just for the miners whom he represented but for the Tyneside working classes as a whole; with militant democracy as the ultimate aim of radical politics, this was a reaffirmation of the 'rights of man'. Cowen had, in no small measure, provided the means; the rest, he said, was up to them:

> I am sorry that, as matters now stand, the only body of men that are not represented in Parliament are the artisan class; but if the working men want that changed, they know how to do it. You have the power, gentlemen; you can soon settle the business for yourselves.[178]

Cowen's own bid for political office would scarcely have been possible if he had not been able to draw upon such a large network of committed supporters. He worked very closely with Adams in promoting radical and republican causes through the pages of the *Chronicle* newspapers and their intellectual partnership was the key to many successful campaigns. Cowen's network of radical activists were mostly working men and they connected him to a myriad of diverse associations, providing intimate knowledge of their needs and concerns. Cowen's ability to juggle his business commitments with an active involvement in local, national and international politics depended heavily upon the careful selection and placement of key personnel. Every member of Cowen's inner circle were involved in the reform campaigns of 1867 and/or 1873 and, apart from James Birkett, they all had a leading role in at least one of the identified 'improving' organisations. More than 50 per cent served as co-operative delegates and almost the same number were members of freemasonry orders. The percentage that was identified with temperance and mechanics' institutes was comparatively less but still sufficient to maintain a strong radical voice within those movements. Appendix VI provides only a partial glimpse into the activities of the core radicals. Several of them (Gregson, Hunter, Rayne, Reed, Thomas and Watson) were members of the Newcastle Foreign Affairs Committee, the Newcastle and Gateshead Republican Club (Hunter, Rutherford and Thompson), the Northern Reform Union (Curry, Cook, Gregson, Hunter, Rayne, Reed, Sutherland, Thompson, Thomas and Watson) and the abolition movement (Rutherford, Gregson, Watson, Thomas, Curry and Herdman). The precision with which radical demonstrations were coordinated was greatly facilitated by the existence of the core network and their ability to mobilise key members of other sympathetic organisations. The Northern Reform Union offices in Grainger Street acted as operational headquarters for the Northern Co-operative Union [NCU] and, in the circumstances, it is not surprising that so many NRU Council members also served as delegates for the NCU.

Identifying core members of Cowen's radical network was relatively straightforward. They were all active over a considerable period and became well known on their own account. Tracing the ancillary interests of lesser-known activists across such large organisations, on the other hand, was more problematic. Incorrect spellings of surnames, the use of familiar rather than given forenames, *and* the prevalence of common surnames (Robson, Ramsey, Thompson etc.) all make it difficult to provide definitive statistical data. No account can be given of co-operative delegates who may well have been 'ordinary' members of any or all of the organisations analysed by the study. The appended membership lists identify ancillary interests only where the member concerned acted in an executive capacity, and does not claim to offer more than a very rudimentary appraisal of the network. A scrutiny of the lives of individual members can often provide a better illustration of how these relationships worked in practice. Elijah Copland, for example, who was the Labour Representation Committee's candidate in 1883, began life as an apprentice wood carver. In time he was a prominent member of the NRU, secretary of the Alnwick Co-operative Society, President of the Cabinetmakers' Union, secretary of Alnwick Workingmen's Club, and Chief Ranger of the Ancient Order of Foresters.[179]

In 1873, as Cowen stood on the brink of political office, the cohesiveness of Tyneside associational life was a tangible force, demonstrable through the effectiveness of the reform movement and the growing solidarity and strength of local trade unionism. Cowen's radicalism was the gravitational pull which unified the disparate organisations, giving them a common cause and providing an irresistible moral imperative for the 'militant democracy' he sought to establish. His was an intensely personal campaign and it would be difficult to overstate the extent to which he involved himself in local organisations – social, educational and political. He was already an energetic member of the local council, and coupled with his newspapers and other business interests, it is all the more remarkable that he should still commit himself at every level to so many organisations and campaigns. The 'Popular Lectures for all Classes', which he introduced in 1872, is a case in point. Aimed specifically at 'people who were working from day to day for their daily bread', charges were pegged at a nominal rate and lecturers gave their services free. Any profits were pledged to the mechanics' institute, the working men's club and the two temperance public houses. As if this were not enough, he undertook to deliver some of the lectures himself.[180]

Cowen's political ambitions were, of course, a powerful incentive. He knew that success depended upon his ability to capture the allegiance of the working classes and that public speeches alone, however stirring they might be, would not suffice. He had to prove himself on their terms, and convince the Tyneside people that in backing his election they were empowering themselves. If Cowen's leadership can be defined as charismatic,[181] and all the indications are that it should be, then this is its source. His father's sudden death in December 1873 prompted an election for which Cowen was more than ready. There was scarcely any need for him to canvass in the usual way or to elaborate unduly upon his political philosophy. By then, he had repeatedly proven his worth and the required Weberian 'act of recognition' had already taken place.[182] His newspaper empire enabled him to extend that influence, in a personal way, far beyond what normally would have been possible and, perhaps most crucially of all, he had secured the unwavering allegiance of the Tyneside Irish.

Chapter 4
'The Wearing of the Green':
Irish nationalists and Tyneside radicals, 1819-1884

Nineteenth-century Tyneside politics cannot be fully understood or indeed adequately explained without due reference to its Irish roots and influences. The number of Irish-born migrants in the North East of England in the nineteenth century has been judged small in comparison to those who settled elsewhere, in Lancashire, London, West Yorkshire or lowland Scotland. Nevertheless, in 1851 Northumberland and Durham reputedly had 'the fourth highest ratio of Irish to English in England and Wales'.[1] On the basis of numerical strength alone, the Irish were bound to have an impact upon local politics. Add to this the relatively good relations which the Irish had with their host community and that influence becomes even more impressive.[2] The Irish who settled in such large numbers in Lancashire, for example, encountered considerable antagonism and hostility.[3] In varying degrees, sectarian attitudes undermined the assimilation of the Irish in most, if not all, of the major centres in which they settled.[4] The comparative work undertaken by Donald MacRaild and Frank Neal has thrown the spotlight on the prevalence of inter-communal conflict in some parts of the region.[5] Nonetheless, as Neal notes, only 'a minority' were involved in violent activity.[6] It remains the case that the Tyneside Irish population were not nearly as embattled as their fellow countrymen elsewhere and, most significantly for this study, radical politics became an important bridge between the host community and its Irish citizens.

Tyneside Radicalism, as already shown, rested upon a political tradition which was underpinned by a strong agrarian and internationalist critique. The currency of these ideas undoubtedly contributed to the emergence of a workable political alliance, capable of serving the interests of both Irish nationalists and local radicals. In essence, the Irish represented a highly visible test case; a graphic example of the corruption of the political system. This 'fusion of loyalty' has been identified in radical Glasgow where the publisher John Ferguson proved to be the catalyst for collective action.[7] On Tyneside, the special factor was the mediation by three generations of the Cowen family[8] who applied their considerable influence to the fostering of good Anglo-Irish relations. During their terms of office, both Sir Joseph Cowen and his son adopted a distinctively

pro-Irish stance, and consistently opposed a succession of Irish coercion legislation.[9] Most crucially, Cowen championed the Irish cause through the pages
of his newspapers and gave Ireland's affairs extensive coverage. Events such as
the nationalist uprisings in the late 1860s, which elsewhere provoked a widespread sectarian backlash, were sensitively reported to ensure that no blame
or charge of complicity was lodged against the local Irish.[10] For their part, the
Tyneside Irish embraced Cowen's radical agenda. His intervention on their behalf protected local radicalism from the fractures that bedevilled other Irish
strongholds. And, as the usual gulf between Irish and English issues virtually
disappeared, the cohesiveness of Tyneside radical politics and its immediate future was assured.

Given that much of what follows has been driven by the need to explore the
workings of nineteenth-century Tyneside politics, any assertions as to the harmonious nature of Anglo-Irish should not be misconstrued. There is certainly
no intention here to gloss over the social and religious tensions which erupted
from time to time, or to claim that this remarkable political détente was secured in other parts of the region. Evidence suggests that the Irish vote in towns
such as Middlesbrough could be extremely unpredictable.[11] By the same token,
however, Tyneside radical politics was not a discrete activity but one which impacted upon other areas of working-class life. Part of the explanation for the
low level of sectarian hostility must surely reside in the political consensus that
prevailed.

Before moving on to consider the Irish dimension of Tyneside radicalism,
it must be noted that this analysis presented some intractable methodologi-
cal challenges. The surviving records of reform groups or trade unions, for instance, often revealed little or nothing about the ethnic origin of their members,
and even newspaper reports and court records rarely gave any detailed ethnic
data unless it was judged relevant. Some assumptions can be made where names
are recognisably 'Irish' but, at best, any conclusions drawn must be extremely
tentative. Fortunately, other avenues of research proved more fruitful, especially where consistency and cumulative effect could be demonstrated. Thus,
while it has been impossible to give any hard statistical data, the scale of Irish
involvement in Chartism and successive reform movements has been deduced
from the inclusion of Irish songs and banners, the deployment of Irish speakers
and the centrality of Irish issues on the agenda of radical meetings.

Most historians accept that the available statistics for nineteenth century
Irish immigration have 'severe limitations'.[12] The 1851 and 1871 censuses, from
which most of the information has been derived, are widely acknowledged to
be incomplete. While an extensive survey of the Irish-born in the larger towns
is available, data for newer urban areas (e.g. Blackburn) is noticeably lacking.

Additionally, the narrow focus upon 'Irish-born' residents took no account of second or third generation Irish immigrants. These distortions have to be borne in mind when assessments of Tyneside's Irish community are considered. According to the 1851 census Newcastle had 7,124 Irish-born residents or 8.1 per cent of the population, and Gateshead just slightly more with 8.6 per cent. Whilst these figures scarcely compare to those for Liverpool (22.3 per cent) and Glasgow (18.2 per cent), residential clustering produced substantial concentrations.[13] It is worth noting, too, that for a sizeable proportion of Irish migrants, Liverpool and Glasgow served only as a temporary refuge; they frequently moved on to other areas where they had family connections and work was readily available.[14] Inevitably, this type of 'floating population' was unlikely to have the same political impact as a more settled community which, over the course of three generations, could build up a network of contacts via an array of religious, social and work-related organisations. In this context the stability of the Tyneside Irish community is a critical factor.

Roger Cooter's study of the Irish in Newcastle and County Durham traced a large majority of Tyneside's Irish population back to the same few counties: Mayo and Sligo,[15] while Felix Lavery noted the 'strong County Down leavening' of the Newcastle Irish and attributed this to the intervention of Monsignor William McCartan.[16] These older ties of kith and kin undoubtedly contributed to the creation of new community solidarities, especially as residential clustering was as much a feature of Tyneside as it was of Manchester, with its 'Little Ireland' ghetto.[17] However, the issue of segregation, implicit in the use of the term ghetto, needs to be carefully examined. While the vast majority of Irish immigrants were housed in the most impoverished areas, poverty and kinship were the key determining factors.[18] On Tyneside, for example, the Sandgate and All Saints wards were predominantly Irish. Residential clusters in Gateshead gave the town a ratio of 1:4 in 1872, and Hebburn and Jarrow a ratio of 1:3.[19] As the Northern Coalfield expanded after 1850 many colliery villages assumed recognisably Irish characteristics, prompting the *Newcastle Daily Chronicle* to comment in its survey of Ryhope that 'you cannot help the result reminding you of Connemara or Tipperary, or other centres of Irish cabin life'.[20] According to Tom Gallagher, these 'Little Ireland's constituted a 'Victorian form of apartheid' and in both Glasgow and Liverpool the Irish became scapegoats for a panoply of social ills: disease, squalor, drunkenness and violent crime.[21] Even cholera was popularly dubbed 'Irish fever'.[22] Anti-Irish hostility in Liverpool was further compounded by the prevalent sectarian divisions which largely dictated settlement patterns.[23] By comparison, the Tyneside Irish fared rather better. Even though the Sandgate area was ravaged by cholera, in 1847 and 1853 the Newcastle Medical Report did not attach any blame to the Irish but instead

stressed the need for measures to alleviate the overcrowded, insanitary conditions.[24] It was external bodies, such as the Board of Health, which reiterated
the prejudicial conclusions reached in Leeds and Manchester.[25] Moreover, the
Tyneside Irish was given access to poor relief even though, strictly speaking,
they did not satisfy the residential qualifications.[26]

Clearly any analysis of Anglo-Irish relations must look beyond the *Newcastle
Chronicle*'s pronouncement that Tyneside was simply 'famous for its hospitality'.[27] To begin with, Tyneside did not experience the massive influx of Irish im-
migrants after 1847 which produced a sectarian backlash in other British towns.
Scarcity of work in some areas was a major source of antagonism between the
Irish and their host communities. This was particularly the case in cities such as
Liverpool which had a greater dependence on unskilled labour. On Tyneside,
as in Glasgow, the indigenous population were mostly able to monopolise the
skilled jobs and there was comparatively less friction in the labouring sector.[28]
Rapid industrial expansion in the North East provided more room for employment growth and, as a result, the Irish were less likely to be regarded as an
economic threat by the local workforce. Apart from the usual unskilled jobs in
agriculture and building, the Irish found work in the burgeoning iron industry,
where working opportunities were not unduly restricted by established traditions and working practices. Shipbuilding and railway construction became a
major source of Irish employment, as did coal mining after mid century. Since
many of these jobs could be described as 'high risk' this has implications for
the creation of working-class solidarities. As for the issue of using Irish labour
as strike breakers, this has probably been greatly exaggerated. Scottish and
Lancashire employers do not seem to have been averse to using Irish labour
to discipline and control their workforces, whether in terms of wages, conditions or for the settlement of disputes.[29] On Tyneside, though, the use of Irish
strike breakers is said to have been 'unusual'. According to Roger Cooter, the
1844 mining strike was an 'exceptional instance'.[30] He argues that the number
of workers Lord Londonderry transferred from his estates in County Down was
far too small to have had a decisive impact upon the dispute. Without the requi-
site skills, they hardly constituted a viable substitute workforce and, as Dorothy
Thompson observes, there is a critical distinction to be made between the use of
'local' Irish and 'foreign' Irish labour.[31] The *threatened* use of immigrant labour
was another matter entirely and this seems to have been a fairly regular, and effective, disciplinary ploy.

Although Irish workers were active members of early trade union organisations, especially in the textile industry, in the 1830s the Roman Catholic Church
sought to outlaw membership by denying the sacraments to those who did not
comply.[32] Even so, the world of work afforded plenty of opportunities for the

Irish to associate with the local community. A brief scan of national radical newspapers and journals reveals a demonstrable commitment to a union of the working classes during the Chartist period. Publicity material was deliberately targeted to reach the Irish people, whose support was considered to be vital if the campaign was to be successful. Political circulars and addresses were explicitly worded to inculcate a strong sense of solidarity between all workers and rule out any possibility that the Irish might feel excluded.[33] The pages of Henry Hetherington's *Poor Man's Guardian* gave Irish grievances a thorough airing, particularly through the reports of the National Union of Working Classes (NUWC) which exhibited a marked preoccupation with Irish matters and their relevance to the cause of reform. The general view, as expressed by an Irish working man in 1832 to the NUWC, was that 'the union of the population of England and Ireland would restore the liberties of both'.[34]

Public displays of solidarity with the Irish at Tyneside radical demonstrations were something of an established tradition. For example, at the Spital Fields meeting in 1819, the Tyneside reformers carried a distinctive banner bearing a wreath of entwined roses, thistles and shamrock. The Spenceans had already used the emblem to great effect in their journal, *The Shamrock, The Thistle and The Rose*, as part of their bid to establish a 'radical mass platform'.[35] Given the Tyneside connection with Spence, such initiatives were bound to be influential. The same banner was pressed into service by the Brassfounders and Brassfinishers Union at the Tyneside Reform League demonstration in January 1867. More commonly, a red, blue and green tricolour proclaimed the sense of unity which Tyneside radicals were so determined to encourage.[36] While it is impossible to state with any accuracy how many Irish people attended such demonstrations, the consistent use of such emblematic devices indicates that they were a recognised and valued constituency. It is important to appreciate that political demonstrations were always carefully orchestrated and rhetoric was not the sole mechanism for expressing solidarity. Banners, songs, poetry – even clothing – all worked by cumulative effect to convey the collective concerns and aspirations of the meeting. In this context, the regular inclusion of Irish songs and airs embodied a profound political message far beyond their apparently innocuous lyrics. The massed crowds who gathered to hear Harney speak on Christmas Day in 1838 were not only treated to an impassioned rendition of 'Scots wha hae' but also 'Sprig of Shillelagh' and a telling quotation from 'their sainted Emmett'.[37] Harney, who introduced himself as 'the friend and brother of Irishmen', reassured the crowd that the Irish would not be duped by 'sham patriots and hireling philanthropists':

Let them put arms into the hands of Irishmen. Let them land them in

England, and the moment they set foot on the soil of England, that moment would they desert the cause of despotism, and Daniel O'Connell and his little Queen, and join the real cause of liberty and the Radical Reformers of England.[38]

Feargus O'Connor was a familiar figure at north-east radical demonstrations and it is certain that his appearances attracted a large body of Irish support. For his part, he clearly relished his visits to Tyneside, marching at the head of the Hibernian Society of Newcastle, Irish nationalist banner aloft, 'to the old air of Garry Owen'.[39] The Tyneside Irish were also well served by local radical leaders such as Charles Larkin and Thomas Ainge Devyr, whose eloquent defence of the Irish cause did so much to engender a climate of friendly cooperation. And it was Irishmen, more often than not, who were to be found at the forefront of the press for physical force Chartism.[40] Should any further evidence be required, a sizable Irish participation in demonstrations can be deduced from the prominent role played by Irish working men. Speakers such as Mr. McKinney, a sail-cloth weaver from Londonderry who had encountered hostility in a number of places, including Sunderland, shared a platform with O'Connor.[41] And, of course, for every speaker identified as Irish there must have been many others whose Irish roots are indicated by their names and the partisan sentiments they expressed, but who, nevertheless, cannot be formally identified as such without an exhaustive survey of the census returns.

Irish grievances were given equal prominence on the radical agenda, for as the North Shields branch of the WMA argued

Long had we groaned beneath the intolerant tyranny of a Tory faction... and Ireland has equal cause for lament and indignation when she considers their first measure, after being firmly seated in power, was a bill for her coercion.[42]

The general consensus was that both communities were suffering at the hands of an unrepresentative government, which had passed a 'Murderous New Poor Law of England' and 'a Coercion Bill to famishing Ireland'.[43] 'Justice', said William Thomason, 'never would, never could be done to Ireland or England till Universal Suffrage became the law of the land'.[44] The Whigs, he argued, had conspicuously failed to settle the vexed question of Irish tithes or to reform the Irish Church. In a determined bid to secure Irish support the NPU authorized a sub-committee to distribute their pamphlets throughout Ireland.[45] The willingness to sanction such expenditure when resources were so limited is a measure of the importance they attached to Irish initiatives. In 1838 Irish women, too,

were actively encouraged to join the new Female Political Union. Their influence, especially among the young, was readily acknowledged and local radicals
such as William Parker and James Ayre were quick to offer their assistance.[46]
Ultimately, efforts to unite the radicals of both communities proved so successful that, as far as the local Tory press was concerned, Chartists and Irish nationalists were regarded in the same light.[47] John Saville's emphasis upon the new,
closer relationship between Chartists and Irish Radicals in 1848 is borne out
by the evidence from Tyneside, though it is notable that this reflected a steady
strengthening of solidarity rather than any new development in community relationships.[48] According to the *Gateshead Observer*, the Chartist Movement was
'half Irish' while the *Newcastle Journal* insisted that the 'traitors' of the 1848
Chartist Trials were 'not English. . . some of the others are Irishmen'.[49]

The involvement of north-east miners in Chartism has already been established and considering the numbers of Irish employed in the coalfield their
contribution must be a given. Their unskilled minority status and their limited
involvement in trade unionism at this stage might suggest that they contributed
more to the mass following than to the leadership of Chartism. It is, however,
interesting to note the prominent role played by the St Lawrence colliery. This
colliery, located as it was in an Irish enclave in the All Saints area of Newcastle,
almost certainly drew heavily upon Irish labour.[50] The establishment of a reading room in 1838, in connection with the Newcastle WMA, suggests that the
St Lawrence colliers' support for the Charter had a rational basis and was not,
as was so often claimed, just another expression of Irish excitability. Thomas
Devyr's Joint Stock Company was aimed mainly at the colliers. With weekly
sales in excess of £2,000 his advocacy of O'Connor's Land Plan must have carried considerable weight among his own countrymen.[51]

The problem of tracking Irish involvement in trade union activity becomes
less formidable after 1850 when their occupational spread becomes even more
closely identified with mining and other heavy industries. Later reform movements increasingly relied upon the support of mining communities to provide
the necessary numerical strength. In 1859, Cowen sought the backing of the
Northumberland and Durham collieries for his Northern Reform Union. The
NRU petition, presented that same year, was signed by 'more than half the adult
male population' with 'Engineers, Smiths, Carpenters and Miners' identified
as the 'most numerous designations'.[52] And in 1866, when the reform campaign began to gather new momentum, it was Cowen's *Chronicle* newspaper,
the 'Pitman's Bible',[53] which stressed the vital link between the Irish cause and
the need for electoral reform. At the national level, it is clear that some of the
Reform League's leaders were intent upon securing the support of the Fenians.[54]
Inevitably, this coalition of Irish and English radical forces was viewed with

considerable alarm in some quarters. After a period of relative quiescence, Fenian activity had resurfaced at the end of 1865 and at that point *The Times* was inclined to attribute this to the malign influence of America.[55] Thereafter the attitude of the British press hardened and the violent activities which followed raised fears among the reformers that an alliance would critically damage the Reform League's credibility. Memories of 1848 were, it seems, still too painful.[56]

The rise of Fenianism fuelled popular prejudices, particularly in areas where the Irish presence was so pronounced.[57] In the North East, the Fenians had an unusually large following and, although large numbers were subsequently wooed by the constitutionalists, regional membership of its 'front' organisation, the Irish Republican Brotherhood, was an estimated 6,000 in 1884, as compared with 3,000 for Scotland and 2,500 for south-east England.[58] Tyneside is said to have been 'honeycombed with Fenians. . . men spent half the night in dark cellars, planning, organising and getting the stuff – rifles, revolvers, ammunition – all aboard harmless looking boats'.[59] Throughout the mid–to–late 1860s the Cowen press protested that the Irish were sorely provoked, and called upon the government to abandon their repressive policies and institute effective reform of the Church and land ownership.[60] Unflinching condemnations of Fenian violence were always supplemented by a rigorous analysis of the roots of Irish grievances:

> About two grievances no man in this age can be ignorant – the Church and the Land… Fenianism is no more than the sign and fruit of existing wrongs…Whoever would deal successfully with Ireland must grapple with the land question. The condition of Ireland, say what else we like of it, is a disgrace to English Statesmanship.[61]

Despite Tyneside's reputation as a centre of Fenianism, there were no major incidents in the locality, and this undoubtedly helped to maintain political harmony. One of the few notable incidents, a riot of three hundred Irishmen on the Town Moor during Race Week in 1866, was denounced as Fenian but it has been suggested that this was mostly scaremongering on the part of the police and the courts.[62] Race goers were, it seems, challenged to declare their allegiance to 'Garibaldi or the Pope', and violently assaulted with a shillelagh if they gave the wrong answer.[63] The rioters could hardly have chosen a more contentious issue upon which to make their stand. Garibaldi was something of a folk hero on Tyneside, especially following his visit in 1854 and, prompted by Cowen and Adams, the Italian cause had assumed central importance in local radical circles. The Garibaldi Testimonial Committee, originally formed to coordinate the Italian patriot's visit in 1864 had, by then, begun to devote some of their energies to the Northern Reform League.[64] In the event, an attack on Garibaldi could easily be misconstrued. It is important to note that the Tyneside Irish were overwhelmingly Roman Catholic and, as such, their loyalties were bound to be sharply divided. [65] It is, then, all the more intriguing that the *Newcastle Chronicle* should continue to exhibit a markedly partisan stance in their reporting of the event. In 1860, the *Chronicle* had actually coordinated a recruitment drive for a volunteer force to assist Garibaldi's campaign, and yet it still questioned whether the sixteen accused were actually Fenians at all. The evidence, they claimed, was 'rather circumstantial'.[66] Even the *Newcastle Courant*, who had described the rioters as 'fools from America', were prepared to exonerate the local Irish from blame.[67] The *Chronicle*'s sympathetic editorial argued that the 'unfortunate men' who 'presented a peculiarly forlorn and woeworn spectacle' had been 'nearly quite as much sinned against as sinning'.[68] Lack of education (sic) was judged to be the root cause of their intemperate behaviour. As ever, Cowen's guiding hand is clearly detectable in the *Chronicle*'s pro-Irish policy. At a crucial juncture, when Anglo-Irish relations could so easily have been permanently soured, positive intervention by the Cowenite Press ensured that the unity of Tyneside Radicalism was not breached.

In other 'Irish areas' outbreaks of anti-Catholic violence occurred with seemingly monotonous regularity throughout the 1850s and 1860s. In Lancashire, where membership of the Orange Order was particularly high, sectarian tensions reached a high point during the Murphy Riots of 1867-71.[69] In his role as agent for the Protestant Electoral Union, William Murphy toured a number of English towns, lecturing provocatively upon the evils of Popery and the sexual depravity of Catholic nuns and priests. Strictly speaking, underlying religious tensions were not solely responsible for the virulent Murphyism which divided communities as far afield as Birmingham, Wolverhampton, Plymouth and Merthyr Tydfil. As Roger Swift observes, the riots reflected 'deeper ethnic, economic and political strains'.[70] It was towns such as Birmingham, Ashton-Under-Lyne, and Oldham, where active Fenianism seemed to pose a serious threat to public order, which proved to be the ideal breeding grounds for Murphy's distinctive brand of bigotry.[71] Tyneside was, though, singularly unaffected by Murphyism save for an isolated disturbance. The *Chronicle*, which carried full reports of Murphy's activities, was moved to declare that it was 'fortunate for the public peace that there is only one Murphy in England. The brutality and ferocity of that man are something extraordinary.'[72] When he lectured in North Shields in August 1872 the meeting was violently terminated as incensed local Irishmen stormed the hall. Tyneside Irish Catholics had a staunch defender in Charles Larkin, the old stalwart of the NPU who had published a famous refutation to

The Awful Disclosures of Maria Monk (A Letter to the Protestants of Newcastle) in 1836.[73] Larkin also actively denounced Fenianism in his regular column in the *Newcastle Weekly Chronicle*: 'Fenianism must be put down. Fenianism will be put down. . . and its destruction will be the triumph neither of the dungeon nor the gibbet, but of justice alone.'[74] It would seem that, while Tyneside did not escape the attentions of Murphy altogether, there were none of the aftershocks that heightened sectarian tensions in the Midlands and Lancashire.[75]

In part, this may also be attributed to the predominantly Catholic confession of the Tyneside Irish. Notwithstanding the difficulties of documenting Orange Lodge activity, in the 1870s when Orangeism revived on Tyneside membership levels were still comparably low.[76] There were some important branches of the Order, most notably at Gateshead, Felling, North Shields and South Shields, but far more were located in the west of the region, in the Consett and Hartlepool area where there was a much higher percentage of Ulstermen.[77] South of the Tyne, sectarian skirmishes were regular, though not serious occurrences, whereas the reported confrontation between Tyneside Ribbonmen and Orangemen in 1856 was unusual. Numerically weak, Orangeism on Tyneside was effectively marginalised – so much so that in 1871 the Tyne True Blue Loyal Orangemen of England complained with some justification at their meeting in Gateshead that 'their processions were interfered with, while Fenians might do as they liked'.[78]

As the Fenian campaign was stepped up throughout 1867, antagonism towards the Irish grew apace. The abortive raid on Chester Castle, the rescue of Fenian prisoners at Manchester and the explosion at Clerkenwell prison, prompted the authorities to arm the police and recruit large numbers of special constables.[79] In the ensuing panic, there were numerous rumoured 'sightings' of the Manchester escapees, Kelly and Deasy, and a number of false arrests were made in Durham, Weardale and Hartlepool.[80] The *Chronicle* roundly condemned the violence of the Fenians but tempered their criticism with a barbed comment that the upper classes were taking advantage of the situation:

> We are hearing just a little too much of what is called Fenianism… Fenianism is the scapegoat of every villain in England…even the Manchester crime could not have been committed if the authorities there had attended to their duties… Advantage is taken of the prevailing trepidation to procure the arming of the police.[81]

At one level, this diatribe was aimed at the *Newcastle Journal* whose editorial policy, as Neal notes, was persistently hostile to the Irish and in line with many other provincial newspapers in the North.[82] As a noted centre of organised

Fenianism, Newcastle was one of the areas in which special precautionary measures were thought to be necessary. In October 1867 the Newcastle police force was armed and several hundred special constables sworn in at North Shields. Fifty revolvers and 1,000 rounds of ammunition were sent to Sunderland, prompting widespread unrest until the local Council finally conceded that 'severe measures are not needed in the North' and returned the unwanted weaponry.[83] The proposal to station the headquarters of the Second Battalion of Foot Soldiers in Newcastle was opposed on similar grounds.[84] This show of force proved to be counter-productive for it irritated those who regarded it as a threat to civil liberty. While a 'rival mob' of several hundred held a meeting in favour of hanging the Manchester prisoners in Birmingham, the *Chronicle* relentlessly campaigned for clemency and sought to establish the unquestionable loyalty of the local Irish.[85] A special edition of the *Chronicle* gave a graphic and lurid account of the executions and called for the abolition of capital punishment to prevent any further miscarriages of justice.[86] In an unusually provocative editorial, the *Chronicle* insisted that 'the people at all times have the right to revolt against its rulers' and suggested that English Radicals and Irish Catholics could effect constitutional change by peaceful means, if they worked together.[87]

Political solidarities were severely tested when the loss of life caused by the Clerkenwell explosion was revealed. The *Newcastle Journal* claimed that the working classes – 'those who work, that is, not those who attend Reform meetings' – were against the Irish.[88] For once, even the *Chronicle* could offer no satisfactory defence and warned that 'unless Irishmen are prepared to renounce tactics which are rather the tactics of savagery than civilization, then they must combat alone'.[89] A planned procession, in memory of the 'Manchester Martyrs', was abandoned after the Bishop of Hexham and Newcastle issued a directive that Catholics should avoid any public display.[90] Similar 'funerals' arranged in Glasgow, Liverpool and Leeds were prohibited by local magistrates, who feared that violent confrontation would result. In a bid to restore public confidence in the legitimacy of the Irish cause, the Cowenite press published a series of sympathetic articles. The exemplary behaviour of the local Irish was repeatedly stressed amidst demands that the majority should not be made to suffer for the folly of the few: 'That there are some members of the Fenian brotherhood in Newcastle upon Tyne does not admit of doubt. But…we cannot believe that there are amongst us any Irishmen with sympathy for the Clerkenwell atrocity'.[91] In London, some Irish working men lost their jobs in the wave of reprisals that followed. The *Chronicle* called upon the Tyneside Irish to publicly demonstrate their abhorrence of the tragedy and so escape becoming an easy target for unsympathetic employers. Sir Joseph Cowen lent his considerable weight to the Irish cause at a public meeting convened by the Mayor of Newcastle. 'English

Protestants', he insisted, would never put up with the intolerant religious leg-islation to which Irish Catholics had been subjected and arguing forcefully that reform was urgently needed, he said that 'the people of England do not wish to govern Ireland as a conquered province but desire, I maintain, to govern it in a spirit of equality'.[92] Cowen's press campaign to protect the local Irish was enormously effective. Elsewhere, the Clerkenwell disaster had alienated the Irish from their natural supporters and violent clashes became the norm in places such as Birmingham, Wolverhampton and the Lancashire towns. Even the *Newcastle Journal*, which insisted throughout that Ireland had always been 'as well and fairly governed, and more lightly taxed than Great Britain itself', was forced to admit that there was no fear of any local unrest.[93]

The Fenian disturbances coincided with the resurgence of electoral reform and, from the outset, the Northern Reform League made Irish reform a cen-tral focus of their campaign. At a large open air demonstration, James Watson promised that while the government had consistently failed to alleviate Irish distress, 'the vote would change that'.[94] As the campaign gathered pace, Dr Rutherford reiterated Watson's pledge in March 1867 when he told the massed crowds at Durham that 'If working men were admitted to the franchise...they would remedy the wrongs of Ireland (*Cheers*) – and make the sister country a source of greatness to England'.[95] The solidarity of the Tyneside radicals was made manifest by the enormous attendance at rallies and demonstrations. An estimated 50,000 people took part in a procession in January 1867, marching be-hind the official NRL banner which proclaimed its fraternity with Irish reform-ers.[96] Meanwhile, Benjamin Lucraft's statement that the 'Fenians were justified in using physical force' had brought to a head the ideological split within the National Reform League.[97] The *Newcastle Journal* was stung to enquire 'What next? Physical force for the radicals?'[98] But, while the Fenian episode caused a good deal of rancour among the national executive, it was never a contentious issue on Tyneside. The case for Irish reform had been argued too eloquently; the loyalties of the Irish firmly established, not least through their participation in radical activities. By the late 1860s, Irish trade unionism had moved on to another level as they began to take up key positions as delegates of the powerful mining, engineering and shipbuilding trades.[99] As representatives of large num-bers of Irish workers, they could, and did, exert considerable influence.

With the passing of the 1867 Reform Act, the Irish vote assumed great signifi-cance.[100] For the first time, politicians had to take account of the 'Celtic fringe' at election time. In Newcastle, for example, the All Saints ward went to the polls with an electorate increased by 215 per cent.[101] Sir Joseph Cowen had nothing to fear from an increased Irish vote. As an outspoken defender of Irish interests who had consistently voted with the Irish lobby in parliament he was bound to be the preferred candidate of the newly enfranchised Irish. The Irish Church Disestablishment issue which dominated the 1868 Election was, in any case, one with which he had been associated for some time.[102] Fenianism created sufficient alarm to concentrate political minds upon the Irish problem and in some areas, notably the Lancashire towns, the Tory Party clearly gained from the inevitable upsurge in sectarianism.[103] Later, divisions over education reform, which greatly undermined the Liberal's popularity in Lancashire between 1873 and 1874, and could so easily have had the same impact on Tyneside, were cleverly sidestepped by Cowen's decision to play the 'non-sectarian' card. Liberal education policy was thus able to appeal to the widest possible electorate and most, if not all, Irish Catholics were kept within the radical fold.[104]

As it turned out, miners, who had fought hard for electoral reform, were anomalously excluded from the franchise by the provisions of the 1867 Act because of a distinction made between the borough and county qualifications. The Northern Reform League was subsequently resurrected in 1873 to press the miners' case, with the *Chronicle* newspapers playing a key role in coordinating the campaign. A series of articles entitled *Our Colliery Villages* was published by Adams in the *Weekly Chronicle* between September 1872 and February 1874 in order to generate local support.[105] Contemporary historians, such as Richard Fynes, have documented the solidarity of the Northumberland and Durham miners, particularly after the formation of the Durham Miners' Association (DMA) and the Northumbrian Miners' Association (NMA).[106] By 1873, membership of both unions was virtually comprehensive and obviously this included a large Irish contingent. Union membership on this scale was a distinct advantage as the campaign for franchise reform began to gather momentum. When the Manhood Suffrage Committee met to plan a mass demonstration on 12 April the importance of encouraging 'all workmen, whether members of trade societies or not', was unanimously agreed.[107] With Cowen acting as Chairman of the Committee and Adams's unstinting efforts the demonstration was given unprecedented coverage in the *Chronicle* press: the timetable of special trains reserved for demonstrators, the order of procession, and declarations of support were all prominently publicised in both the weekly and daily editions. In addition, Newcastle and Gateshead Trades Council helped to coordinate participation by other organised trades and circulated ballot slips to determine the 'pecking order' of the different groups.[108] On the day, more than 110 collieries were represented by some 70,000 men and a further 10,000 trade unionists, co-operators and friendly society members brought up the rear in a procession which took some three hours to reach the Town Moor. Two hundred thousand people thronged to the Moor to hear fifty speakers declare that the existing electoral provisions were 'irritating, perplexing and unjust'. In his key role as

Chairman of the event, Cowen insisted that

> When the Hyde Park railings went down before the uprisen democracy of
> the metropolis, reform was inevitable – and the combined influence and
> power of 10,000 Tories was unable to stay it. The Bill that they introduced
> was a most mongrel measure – it was neither fish nor fowl, flesh nor good
> red herring... The qualification ought to consist, not in the house or the
> property, but in the man...with an extended Reform Bill we would see the
> last remnant of feudalism in the shape of the Game Laws swept from the
> statute book.[109]

A new reform banner of intertwined 'oak leaves, rose, shamrock and thistle' was
specially commissioned for the occasion to affirm the unity and strength of the
campaign.[110] Victory, when it came, was made all the sweeter by Thomas Burt's
election in 1874 as the first working-class MP.[111] That same year the local Irish,
too, were also setting a new precedent with the election of Bernard McAnulty as
Town Councillor for All Saints ward.[112]

By the early 1870s the new Home Rule movement founded by Isaac Butt was
beginning to have a significant impact, redirecting Irish energies towards constitutional initiatives and away from Fenian aggression.[113] John Barry, a prominent Fenian who had lived in the North East from his childhood, played a key
role in promoting the establishment of Home Rule Associations in numerous
industrial towns throughout Britain.[114] Although Manchester, Birmingham and
Glasgow are often regarded as the principal centres of Home Rule activity, much
of the organisational initiative emanated from Newcastle and Gateshead.[115]
Many leading Irish Nationalists were close friends of Cowen. Apart from Barry,
Timothy Healy MP, John Walsh and Joseph Biggar all had local connections
which ensured that Tynesiders remained at the forefront of any reform movement. Thriving branches were established in Glasgow as a result of the pioneer-
ing activity of John Ferguson, and in Manchester, with Barry acting as secretary of the local association. It is clear that both centres provided England and
Scotland with organizational headquarters.[116] However, there are also strong
indications that activities on Tyneside were pivotal. A large public meeting
in Newcastle Town Hall was convened on 6 January 1872 and addressed by
Professor Galbraith of Dublin and Alex M Sullivan, editor of the *Nation*.[117]
Sharing a platform with eighteen Tyneside activists, Sullivan expressed his faith
in the people of Newcastle and Gateshead:

> already he noted signs abroad throughout England of a better, a wiser,
> and a brighter spirit towards his countrymen. He need go no further than

the pages of one of the journals of this town, containing an article upon the Irish question – an article worthy of the pen and intellect of a scholar – worthy of the heart of a christian and a patriot.[118]

The first conference of the Home Rule Confederation was held in Newcastle in August 1873 to appoint an executive council and to confirm Butt's presidency. Both Manchester and Birmingham had hosted executive meetings prior to the Newcastle Conference but while they managed to agree upon an organizational framework for the Confederation, unity between the Fenians and the Home Rulers remained fragile.[119] The Supreme Council of the Irish Republican Brotherhood (IRB) were far from convinced that Butt's constitutional initiative would have the desired effect, and therefore Fenian participation was agreed on a conditional basis only, for a period of three years. After that time, support was to be withdrawn if Ireland had not been granted control of her own domestic affairs.[120] Two hundred delegates attended the Newcastle Conference and sanctioned Butt's proposal to apply electoral pressure during the forthcoming contest. Afterwards, Butt was able to write confidently to Mitchell Henry MP: 'we are wielding a tremendous power here in the North of England and I feel it will tell immensely at an election'.[121]

Although the primary aim of the Tyneside Home Rule Associations was to secure autonomy for Ireland, their appeal was not narrowly restricted to the local Irish. A large percentage of the branches were located in the collieries of Northumberland and Durham, at Bedlington, Hexham, Wylam and Prudhoe, for instance. Supporters were active trade unionists as well as Irish nationalists. The Bedlington branch held their meetings in the Cooperative Hall while the Gateshead Association used the Temperance Hall for their gatherings.[122] This crossover between groups ensured that the Home Rule campaign was not a fringe activity but remained relevant to the wider radical movement. If any further sanction was needed, Cowen's commitment to Irish reform ensured its place on the radical agenda. According to T. P. O'Connor, few Englishmen were prepared 'to say a word for the Irish cause' at that time. Cowen was held to be unique in possessing the 'political genius' and 'reckless courage' required

to advocate a cause that was regarded with aversion as disloyal, impractical, visionary and perilous. But in Newcastle there happened to be such a man. He was a man who could alone perhaps at the time venture on a course so daring, apparently so quixotic and so impossible – But fortunately Joseph Cowen, who proved to be the man for this great mission, had already begun to work the spell of his eloquence on his own people and on his own city.[123]

The Cowen Press was the primary instrument of this eloquence. To all intents and purposes, his newspapers functioned as *bona fide* Irish journals, proving so effective that the *United Ireland* claimed that 'not even the Irish press could have given the Irish cause so strong a sounding board'.[124] Irish elections, political meetings, eviction statistics and parliamentary divisions were given such extensive coverage as to obviate circulation of a local Irish journal. Charles Diamond's[125] journal, the *Irish Tribune*, was not published in Newcastle until 1884, and even then Diamond made a point of approaching Cowen to obtain his backing for the venture.[126]

Sharing the same radical newspaper was bound to have a beneficial effect. All too frequently, in other areas, an unbridgeable 'cultural distance' was created as the Irish sought to establish their own group identity.[127] Separate clubs, social groups and especially newspapers were usually perceived by exiles as offering the best means by which they could retain a grip upon their cultural heritage.[128] On Tyneside, the boundaries between Irish and English social activities were in place but were regularly breached whenever it was politically expedient. St Patrick's Day celebrations were held in the Town Hall, and as they became increasingly politicised they attracted a broad cross section of Tyneside society. After 1871, the Newcastle Irish Literary Institute provided facilities for a range of political meetings in addition to supporting Irish cultural activities. For their part, the Irish could enjoy an Irish play just as easily at Cowen's Tyne Theatre as anywhere else.

In 1881, the government clearly considered Cowen's *Chronicle* newspapers to be just as seditious as the rest of the Irish nationalist press. Circulation of the *Chronicle* to Irish political prisoners inside Kilmainham and elsewhere was firmly vetoed, despite an official protest in the Commons by Tim Healey MP.[129] It has been suggested that the *Weekly Chronicle* was targeted primarily at the unskilled working class[130] but, arguably, the two papers were complementary. While the *Daily Chronicle* concentrated on providing coverage of news and events, the *Weekly Chronicle* fulfilled the need for a more rigorous analysis of the underlying issues. Popular understanding of Irish affairs was thus significantly enhanced by such items as the biography of Wolfe Tone, published in 1875, sympathetic Editorials written by W. E. Adams under his pseudonym 'Ironside', and the inclusion of regular articles by the veteran radical, Lloyd Jones.[131] Undoubtedly, Cowen's newspapers acted as a vital unifying force upon the Tyneside community. Their radical critique of society diagnosed a common solution to the preoccupations of English and Irish radicals alike. By stressing collective rather than ethnic goals, local politics acted as a unique rallying point around which all sections of the community could, and did, converge.

Land reform and religious liberty were primary goals of the Tyneside radical movement. As already noted, at an early age Cowen was convinced that 'all have the right to worship God according to their own conscience, which is the common inalienable right of men'.[132] His commitment to land reform was just as firm and throughout his political career both principles were resolutely advocated through the pages of the *Chronicle* press and from numerous political platforms. Civil and religious liberty, observed Cowen, had been the 'watchword for English Liberals for more than a century'.[133] Nationally, discussion of Church questions had come to the fore in the late 1850s, prompted mainly by the religious revival which followed publication of the 1851 census.[134] Although campaigns to reform church rates, qualifications for office, marriages and burials had all been successful, full religious liberty remained as elusive as ever.[135] The abuses of the Irish Church, commonly identified as a primary cause of the troubles in Ireland, acted as an additional spur to Tyneside radicals interested in Church reform. The Liberation Society became ever more influential as it aligned with other radical groups such as the Ballot Society. Consequently, its members were able to exert considerable pressure over electoral candidates and Liberal success at the polls, to some extent, came to depend upon placating the insurgent dissenting lobby.[136]

In the 1860s Tyneside proved to be fertile ground for the work of the Liberation Society. The debate over Church reform had assumed a greater profile during the Fenian troubles as the *Chronicle* actively sought to shift the blame from the Irish nationalists to what it saw as the root cause of the problem: 'the Church and the Land'. The President of the Liberation Society, Carvell Williams, addressed a large meeting in Newcastle on 31 October 1867, and it was the Newcastle branch, with representatives of all dissenting groups, which first considered the possibility of holding a meeting in Ireland. As Williams declared, the time was now ripe to 'transfer their action from English to Irish soil. . . Ireland would become the first great battlefield on the Church Establishment Question'.[137] Both Cowen and his father were active members of the Liberation Society and it is not surprising that the *Chronicle* was pressed into service to praise this initiative, and to insist that the district was 'comparatively free from those ecclesiastical annoyances and irritations which our countrymen in less fortunate districts are compelled to endure'.[138] As the debate over disendowment of the Irish Church gathered momentum, the *Newcastle Journal* adopted a patronising stance, advising Irish people to put 'their faith in the bounty of Providence and the wisdom of Parliament'.[139] Supporters of disestablishment persisted nevertheless and successive elections became a testimony to their growing strength.

Cowen vowed to 'vote and speak for religious freedom' during his election campaign in 1873, and 'Civil and Religious Liberty' was adopted as the first principle of the Newcastle Liberal Association.[140] An invitation to Joseph Biggar

MP to address a Newcastle Liberal demonstration in 1875 on the subject of disestablishment is indicative of the close working relationship between English and Irish radicals.[141] As Cowen pointed out, both Catholics and Nonconformists were excluded from the judiciary and the Cabinet, and it was to the credit of the Irish that they had 'not been as narrow as Englishmen and Scotchmen in their political leanings'. He praised the willingness of some Roman Catholic constituencies to elect Protestants as their representatives and claimed that, if Dissenters could convincingly demonstrate their determination to remove religious inequalities, 'this would be accomplished with less hesitation than most people imagined'.[142]

Cowen cited the relatively low level of Orangeism on Tyneside as one of the reasons why there was no comparable Tory reaction in the 1874 elections.[143] Reviewing the political scene in 1877, he claimed that there was only one way to beat the Tories and that was for 'Liberal Churchmen, Nonconformists and working men to make common cause in favour of the nation, and against the interests of either sects or classes.[144] Unfortunately, as Cowen was forced to admit, the Liberals were 'divided, dispirited and demoralised'. The Liberal Party, he warned, could no longer depend upon Irish votes, as they 'viewed questions submitted to them, not from an English or a Liberal point of view, but from an Irish aspect'.[145] Only a concerted campaign for religious equality, he believed, would reunite them and resurrect popular support.

Irish involvement in Temperance provided another vital link with the Nonconformist lobby. Blue Ribbon Lodges flourished on Tyneside and attracted praise from Cowen who was invited to address their annual conference in 1882:

> The Tories have a plaster and the Liberals have a pill – many pills indeed for curing all the ills that flesh is heir to. (*Laughter and Cheers*) The Democrats want structural, and the Socialists, functional alterations. There is something to be said for all their plans…but neither franchise nor education, nor social transformation will, of themselves, keep people sober – sobriety must precede all moral, mental and political reformation if that reformation is to be real.[146]

Ultimately, political activity aimed at securing Church reform had vital social advantages for the Tyneside Irish. It gave them an entrée into other voluntary organisations – temperance, cooperatives, mechanics' institutes etc. which Joan Smith argues were so significant a barometer for measuring levels of Irish assimilation.[147] In Glasgow and Edinburgh the Irish were well represented in local temperance groups, whereas in Liverpool their involvement in such organisations was considerably less. Inevitably, this had a negative impact upon their ability to integrate successfully with the host community. Politics was the key and, on Tyneside, the politics of religion was only one side of the coin. The 'land question', which had proved so enduring a feature of Tyneside radicalism, was a central preoccupation of both groups and it was this issue, more than any other, which gave them a common goal.

Cowen, who vociferously denounced the laws of primogeniture and entail, regarded the custom as 'not only mischievous but, in certain respects, unnatural'.[148] Every venture aimed at encouraging a wider distribution of the land received his firm support. The Freehold Land Association, for instance, was warmly welcomed and he derived particular satisfaction from the achievements of the working men of his own village. In 1848, a number of Winlaton men purchased four acres of good land, 'California', which they divided into eighteen allotments. They also secured some additional ground which was 'laid out as gardens for the workmen'.[149] Providing similar opportunities for the wider Tyneside community was an intrinsic part of Cowen's commitment to co-operative principles: 'above all, let us unite to be the proprietors of the land in which we live. This is the true end and aim of co-operation. Without it, every other form of union will sooner or later prove a failure.'[150] He accepted that the agrarian system could not be democratized easily or quickly but he urged reformers to press for change:

> Every dispassionate observer must detect grave political danger in the locking up of so large a portion of the soil of the country in the hands of a section of the population – relatively small and progressively dwindling – who have profited so enormously, and with so little effort of their own, by the national prosperity.

And, calling for a repeal of all laws which made land transactions 'tedious, uncertain or costly,' he concluded that he 'would link past tradition with future hope, and subordinate the interest of party to that of nation, the interest of classes to that of justice, the interests of section to that of liberty, and the interests of all to the elevation of man'.[151]

Land reform became the radical issue *par excellence* in the latter half of the nineteenth century.[152] John Stuart Mill and Karl Marx, Henry George and Joseph Chamberlain, all put forward their own strategy for change and, while some initiatives were more successful than others, collectively they influenced the orientation of British radicalism. Economic depression in the early 1870s drew attention to the plight of the agricultural labourers and this added fuel to the debate.[153] Joseph Arch, leader of the National Agricultural Labourer's Union

(NALU), presented the situation as a stark choice: 'Union or No Union, Serfdom or Manhood, Bondage or Liberty, Feudalism or Fraternity for the Labourers of Our Nation', in his appeal to the Trade Unionists of Great Britain and Ireland.[154] Arch insisted that an increase in wages of two or three shillings per week was not the primary aim of the movement. He wanted 'to educate the labourers'.[155] As a devout Methodist, Arch linked the issues of land and church reform together and, as he later explained to a gathering of the Liberation Society, a good deal of suffering and poverty could have been avoided 'if the Christian ministers in the villages of England had spoken out fearlessly...and done their duty as they ought to have done'.[156] Cowen gave firm backing to Arch's efforts, and played a key role in the formation of local branches of the NALU.[157]

By the time that Cowen entered parliament in 1874, his interest in land reform was increasingly inflected by his reading of Irish affairs. His appointment to the Royal Agricultural Commission consumed all of his energies. In a letter to his friend Richard Reed, he described how he was 'absorbed in the Irish Land Question, with the Commission meeting four times a week and the Bill going on in the House of Commons, I hear and think about little else'.[158] Frequent visits to Ireland served only to confirm his resolve to press for reform, winning him the warm approval and gratitude of the Tyneside Irish. As John Martin MP (Meath) told the Irish gathered in the Town Hall for their Annual St. Patrick's Day celebration, 'Cowen was the most valuable friend that Ireland had among Englishmen':

> English Members of Parliament had all been educated to be ignorant of the truth about Irish matters...he only knew one English Member who not only desired to remove the injustice that had already been done, who not only desired that Irishmen should be as free as Englishmen, one who not only sympathised with the Irish...but who actually knew their case, and had taken the trouble to make himself well acquainted with it.[159]

Cowen had little patience with campaigns such as the Tichborne question which might take popular interest away from the more pressing matter of Irish reform. Consequently, the *Chronicle* press took up cudgels against the Tichborne Claimant who Cowen described as a 'very vulgar hero'.[160] The trial of Arthur Orton, which lasted 102 days, aroused great public interest and attracted massive press coverage. Adams's Editorial was aggressively derogatory: 'What a nefarious business' , he complained, 'the whole network of villainy reeks with foulness and stench'.[161] The Magna Charta Association spawned in the wake of the Claimant's imprisonment attracted plenty of followers, particularly in South Shields, following a series of lectures in Newcastle by Dr. Kenealy.[162]

Despite dogged attempts by Cowen and Adams to expose the Tichborne movement's 'preposterous quackery and immoral system of agitation', not everyone was convinced that Orton and Kenealy were 'impostors'.[163] When the Northumberland miners decided to invite Kenealy to address their annual Picnic, Cowen expressed his disgust by declining to attend. Other speakers – Charles Bradlaugh and Alexander MacDonald – also refused to share a platform with him. Burt, on the other hand, could hardly absent himself and, fortunately for him, Kenealy withdrew, sparing Burt considerable discomfiture.[164] Adams deplored the 'wasted energies' to effect the 'substitution of one landed proprietor for another', arguing that the time might have been better spent 'agitating for land tenure reform'.[165] Elsewhere, the agitation appears to have been much more resilient. The movement's tenth annual demonstration attracted deputations from Nottingham, Sheffield, Leeds, Manchester and Liverpool, though noticeably there was no Tyneside contingent.[166]

Irish affairs returned to public prominence in the wake of the 1880 Election. The agricultural crisis in Ireland, and the upsurge of disorder that accompanied it, caused increasing concern in government circles and prompted a wave of coercive legislation. Cowen was one of the few 'maverick' MPs to oppose the Liberal's policy, earning him the support and loyalty of the Tyneside Irish – and the vituperative animosity of the local Liberal Association executive.[167] The publication of division lists, which singled out politicians who voted for Irish coercion, did not endear Cowen to those Liberals who felt that he should have upheld the party line. With ample justification they complained that his *Chronicle* press conspicuously failed to represent Liberal policy; eviction statistics, not Gladstonian eulogies, filled its pages.[168] By November 1880, the number of recorded evictions stood at 10,657 and, on Tyneside, recruitment to the Irish Land League gathered pace. Once again, mining communities proved to be the most active: Wallsend, Walker, Houghton, Murton and Ashington were but a few of the branches whose regular meetings were given prominent publicity.[169] Not surprisingly, when Cowen decided to send a delegation to Ireland on a fact-finding mission, he selected two prominent mining leaders (Bryson, NMA and Paterson, DMA) to make up the group.[170] An account of the visit was subsequently published in series of articles in the *Chronicle*. The Ladies Land League was no less successful in finding willing recruits and the first meeting of the Newcastle branch was held in the Irish Literary Institute in March 1881.[171]

Cowen's undaunted defence of Irish interests, at a time when other renowned radicals such as Chamberlain were trimming their sails to suit the weather,[172] so impressed the Nationalists that they offered Cowen an Irish seat: 'He might have his pick of twenty!'[173] In the circumstances, Newcastle was the obvious choice when the National Land League of Great Britain planned their first convention in August 1881. Healy spoke warmly of the Tyneside people: 'he had learned to love the people by whose side he had worked, and he thanked Cowen for enduring 'prejudice, aye, and obloquy for the sake of what he knew was right and true'.[174] Seven local radicals were elected alongside Cowen to serve on the national executive.[175] It is some measure of the esteem in which local radicals were held that they should be accorded the same status in the League as Parnell, Biggar and T. P. O'Connor.

On Tyneside, radical interests had become so interwoven with that of the Irish people as to be scarcely distinguishable. In 1881, the advent of Henry George's best-selling book *Poverty and Progress* was initially welcomed as a valuable contribution to the land nationalization debate.[176] Michael Davitt, founder of the Irish Land League, had met George in New York in 1880 and was so impressed by his land scheme that he agreed to help promote the book on his return to Britain.[177] Henry Hyndman, whose brainchild the Social Democratic Federation had adopted 'land nationalization' and 'legislative independence for Ireland' as key objectives, subsequently invited George to stay at his London home during his visit to Britain in 1882.[178] For a time, their shared interests in land and Irish reform enabled them to collaborate but, eventually, the clear divide between George's capitalist doctrine and Hyndman's socialist beliefs proved insurmountable. Equally, it would seem that George aroused more controversy than support on Tyneside. As the *Chronicle* was at pains to point out, his ideas were said to have been 'borrowed' from the Tyneside radicals Spence and Devyr.[179]

Events in Ireland quickened public interest and this helped to publicise George's ideas. 'Notes From The Farm', a column in the *Weekly* which ostensibly offered farming tips and weather forecasts, but was actually a shrewd piece of political journalism, argued that 'we have a land question to settle in England as well as in Ireland'.[180] As another regular contributor facetiously remarked, this should not prove too difficult given that the government all too 'frequently legislates on the land in India and Ireland'.[181] Devyr, who was planning a visit to Newcastle to promote his own book in 1884, was scathing and complained that George had 'mixed up nonsense with his methods'.[182] Although George promoted a 'single tax' scheme after 1888 as the optimum method of land reform, prior to that date he was advocating a nationalisation programme by confiscation.[183] The correspondence pages of the *Chronicle* were inundated with letters from readers such as W. Smith of Wallsend who claimed George's scheme of 'nationalization without compensation' would be disastrous to ordinary working people: it would

> ruin thousands of small landowners...the wage earning classes who, by their own industry and the help of the Building Societies of which they are

members, possess or hope to possess, at some future time, a house they may call their own.[184]

As William Trotter observed, the Newcastle Industrial Land and Building Society, established in 1873, was flourishing and the amount of money invested was 'not without important significance...to the land question'.[185] Parnell's intervention effectively killed off popular support for George on Tyneside when he drew attention to the 'absurd and preposterous proposition' of encouraging tenants to become the owners of their own holding and then expecting them to 'turn around, retrace their steps and commence anew'.[186]

Just as in Birmingham and Sheffield, where Chamberlain and Mundella shaped the direction of local politics, so Tyneside embraced the pro-Irish sympathies of Cowen. The land issue from which Chamberlain made so much political capital was framed as an English reform, to assist the agricultural labourers.[187] Roland Quinault maintains that Chamberlain's opposition to Home Rule largely turned upon his frustration that Irish issues were squeezing out his agrarian reforms.[188] For Cowen, Irish Home Rule was the central plank of his radical programme. He had been its advocate for many years, long before Gladstone's supposed conversion, and it had even brought him into headlong collision with his constituency party. Cowen's radicalism, which explicitly promoted civil liberty, agrarian reform and religious equality, had profound meaning for both English and Irish radicals. Legislative freedom for the Irish, as embodied in the Home Rule campaign, could not be denied by those who held such principles. Cowen sought to persuade his opponents that Home Rule was not a divisive measure which threatened to destroy the Empire. It was, he said, 'a decentralising but not a disuniting Bill'. The aim was to achieve:

> national union – union, mark – not centralization. These two things are not only dissimilar, but antagonistic. Destroy the Empire! Why I would grapple it together with hooks of steel – make it as lasting as the granite which underlies the island. . . We seek to show that the Empire is not a noun of multitude, but a moral personality and that its benignity is its strength.[189]

The unity which Cowen had nurtured so carefully among the Tyneside radicals entirely eluded the parliamentary Liberal Party. The Irish question, which had strengthened Tyneside Radicalism, served only to expose the inherent contradictions and weaknesses of nineteenth- century Liberalism and, in so doing, proved to be a fatally disruptive force.

Chapter 5
Power and Responsibility:
The workings of the Radical-Liberal alliance, 1873-1883

The entrenched Liberal loyalties of Tynesiders in the nineteenth century has been well documented, their faith apparently unshakable, even in 1874, when the Liberal Party suffered their worst defeat since 1832.[1] As Cowen himself recalled, 'there was no Tory reaction in the North of England'. Northern Liberals, he claimed, had not only increased in number but 'compared with any other district in the country' their views were altogether more progressive. Carefully sidestepping his key role in that victory, he applauded the electorate's 'intelligence'[2] in resisting the general disaffection which had gathered pace during the course of the previous administration.[3] The problem here is that Tyneside thereby acquired a Liberal profile for this period which virtually negates the prevailing radical culture. While post-Chartist radicalism has benefited from recent revisionist studies there is little indication that the deeper implications of that reconstruction are being actively pursued. Conspicuously lacking an official party structure and a designated leadership, radicalism is invariably relegated to the realms of faction and any redefinition of the political landscape seems remote.[4] Antony Taylor has helpfully advanced a new reading of the period which identifies a 'fault-line in the relationship between Liberalism and radicalism' but his analysis turns upon the unique features of metropolitan politics.[5] In keeping with the dynamics of provincial political life, the confidence of Tyneside radicalism was shaped by markedly different factors and yet the outcome was the same. The relationship between Tyneside radicals and those who embraced Gladstonian Liberalism was highly problematic and this must call into question the supposedly 'untroubled unity' of Liberal politics.[6] What follows will argue that Tyneside radicalism retained its traditional roots; it remained 'the politics of opposition', not the politics of compromise.

As the Senior Member for Newcastle between 1874 and 1886, Cowen's affirmation of his political affiliation must carry some weight here, as should McCalmont's *Parliamentary Poll Book*,[7] which has been described as 'the irrefutable corrective of received ideas'.[8] Cowen rarely, if ever, referred to himself as a Liberal, other than in its broadest sense. His official listing in McCalmont's as a 'Radical' in 1879, when other famous radicals such as Mundella, Chamberlain and even Ernest Jones, the former Chartist, are registered as 'Liberals', raises some important questions. If it can be demonstrated that the strength of the Liberal vote on Tyneside largely turned upon Cowen's personal standing and leadership, this must also undermine those explanations which credit that success to Gladstone and his 'vitalizing connection' with the rank and file.[9]

Before 1886 the prevailing Liberal colours of the Tyneside electorate appear to have had relatively little to do with either official party policy or Gladstone's charismatic personality. In reality, this was a personal vote for Cowen and his radicalism: a far more progressive, individualistic political vision than that ever envisaged by Gladstone. Eugenio Biagini has made much of Gladstone's visit to Tyneside in October 1862 and views this as an early indicator of the powerful hold he was to have upon the affections of the British working class.[10] The occasion was certainly extraordinary, marked as it was by a ceremonial trip on the river and lavish civic receptions in several north east towns.[11] However, as Holyoake noted afterwards, the success of the event turned upon the promotional efforts of the Cowen press and its owner who 'was really responsible for the wonderful warmth of the reception'.[12] At this point in time, relations between Gladstone and the Cowen family were extremely cordial. Sir Joseph Cowen was making his mark as chairman of the River Tyne Commission and the economic benefits which flowed from these improvements were of no little significance to the Treasury. Added to this, Gladstone's apparent enthusiasm for the Italian cause lent him pseudo-republican credentials which were bound to endear him to Cowen Jnr.[13] Gladstone's reception on Tyneside thus owed more to his hosts' influential endorsement than to his own personal following.

Cowen's rise to power was undoubtedly facilitated by his family's wealth, local stature and political connections, but the secret of his success (if indeed his turbulent career can be described in such terms) rested upon his unerring cultivation of the working-class vote. Cowen's close involvement in a range of working-class organisations and causes earned their lasting respect, and this greatly extended his sphere of influence. As the proprietor of the *Chronicle* newspapers he had a unique platform for disseminating his radical views. So much more than just a provincial newspaper with a healthy circulation, it was a political manifesto which reached an international readership – avidly read by his supporters and carefully monitored by his rivals.[14] Arguably, Cowen's political strength rested upon his ability to traverse the class barriers by encompassing traditional and non-traditional spheres of influence. His hold on the affections and loyalties of the working classes, especially the Tyneside Irish, freed him from the usual restraints of party politics, enabling him to pursue the independent stance that was to be, curiously enough, both glorious vindication and damning indictment.

In 1873, when his father died and the seat fell vacant, Cowen was not the Liberals' chosen representative but a compromise candidate. Born out of the recognition that he was the people's choice, they perceived him to be their passport to electoral success. Or, as Cowen put it, they simply 'believed his candidature would create the least division'.[15] The aim of the executive was to harness his high-profile popularity securely to the Liberal bandwagon. In 1873 Cowen comfortably beat off his Conservative opponent, Charles Hamond, but when Gladstone dissolved parliament a few weeks later his second election victory was even more convincing; he defeated Hamond 8,464 votes to 6,479 and, controversially, the long-serving Whig Thomas Headlam lost his seat.[16] If the Liberals calculated that his revolutionary impulses could be curtailed or at least contained they were destined to be disappointed. It was from such inauspicious beginnings that relations with the Liberals at national and constituency level steadily deteriorated as Cowen doggedly refused to toe the party line. Given that his uncompromising views on the caucus system, the Eastern Question and Irish Home Rule created the unbreachable rift which culminated in his withdrawal from national politics in 1886, these are the issues upon which the subsequent analysis will concentrate.

The 1870s heralded the dawn of a new era in British politics as the greatly expanded electorate produced by the Second Reform Act presented an ineluctable challenge to the parties of the day.[17] Concessions embodied in the Act did not, however, embrace a genuine commitment to widen the basis of power beyond the traditionally privileged elite. As John Vincent notes, 'the Liberals were not democrats'[18] and, on both sides of the political divide, electoral reform sprang from a recognition that it had become 'safe to concede enfranchisement and dangerous to withhold it'.[19] With class alliances firmly to the fore, the passing of the Reform Act does not appear to have unduly disturbed the customary ebb and flow of parliamentary life.[20] But, even if power sharing had no place on the political agenda, the general consensus was that new tactics would have to be employed to maintain the status quo. This 'modernization' process, according to Dunbabin, led to a 'refinement of party organisation' and a 'proliferation of public speaking' in an attempt to sway an electorate 'too large to be influenced in the old ways but which had come to follow politics as a spectator sport'.[21] While few would quarrel with this general rationale, the persistent representation of late Victorian politics as entertainment or sport has dubious validity.[22] Biagini has since argued that working-class involvement was far more rational than previously supposed.[23] The question has some resonance for those interpretations which stress the symbolic importance of the vote to the working man, while denying its potential as a 'lever of power'.[24] The polarity of the debate, with the protagonists irreconcilably divided as to whether parliamentary pragmatism or pressure politics was the most decisive factor, ignores the more salient issue of how events were actually perceived, at the time, by the newly enfranchised electorate.[25] For, if the reformers believed their popular campaign had, in any way, forced the hand of parliament this was bound to be empowering. On balance, the adoption of new electoral tactics would seem to suggest that, in the eyes of the political strategists, the new electorate was indeed a reckonable force.

The requirement to find a new strategy for the age of mass politics flew in the face of the existing tradition. Whereas electoral qualifications could be amended by legislation, the cultural practices governing the attainment of political office remained firmly in place. Traditionally, the holders of power were expected to display wealth, status, education, respectability and any number of other attributes, individually dictated by local circumstances. In 1868 Members of Parliament were still predominantly drawn from the landed class.[26] Since electoral and parliamentary costs constituted a major financial burden, only those of independent means could contemplate a political career.[27] In the North East, electoral costs could be as high as £18-20,000, and candidates were vetted accordingly. Cowen parodied the dilemma by relating the way that one Lancashire nominee candidly addressed the electorate: 'I canna speak. I know now't o'politics. But I stink o'Brass and if you send me to the Big House I'll vote for the Party.'[28]

At municipal level, Councillors received neither salary nor expenses, once again restricting the social group from which they were drawn and, given that political office had an inbuilt hierarchy, progression through the ranks was expected before a candidate might be considered suitable. Conspicuous involvement in the various judicial, charitable, cultural and political institutions was the accepted means of demonstrating both a talent and a commitment for public service. The point can be illustrated by Sir Joseph Cowen's presentation to the electorate in 1865. His agent, Mr Mawson, deliberately stressed his local stature and connections, rather than his political convictions, in the belief that this would best commend him to the voters:

> It is a firm and solemn conviction of my mind…that a great trading and commercial and manufacturing community like this, demands that at least one of its Members ought to be identified with its interests and personally acquainted with all its wants and requirements. Such a gentleman we find in my friend Mr Alderman Cowen. He has been born and brought up amongst us. He has filled every office of trust and responsibility which has been imposed upon him by his fellow townsmen and he has discharged the duties incumbent upon him with credit, satisfaction and honour.[29]

These local connections were very important, especially in Northern towns. In Whitby, for instance, even W. H. Gladstone's matchless lineage failed to endear him to the local electorate, or adequately compensate for his want of local stature – and this at the height of Gladstone's popularity.[30] His father's active intervention availed him very little and his majority remained perilously slim. He was persistently regarded as an outsider, not least because he failed to display the expected level of 'generosity'. In 1878, when he eventually vacated the seat in favour of the Flint constituency, the local man, Arthur Pease, romped home comfortably.[31] Similarly, it was the lack of local roots, not funds, which cost George Howell the Aylesbury seat in 1868. Howell's trade union credentials ought to have commended him to the constituency but, according to his financial backer, Walter Morrison, the local people 'distrust a stranger be he who he may'.[32] More than just mutual trust and obligation was at stake here, though this was a significant element; in fielding their own candidates, local elites were able to publicly express their own 'distinct identity and powerful sense of civic pride and independence'.[33]

Cowen's claim to power rested firmly within this established tradition. His dynastic claims were impeccable for his father had already served the Tyneside community as Poor Law Guardian, Town Councillor, Alderman and Mayor. In addition, Sir Joseph's chairmanship of the prestigious River Tyne Commission attracted national recognition in the form of a life peerage.[34] It was a commonplace for sons to follow their fathers into politics and so it was that in 1873 Cowen was held to be his natural successor. The Cowens' entrepreneurial success reflected well on the town, contributing to the general prosperity and providing much needed employment for the local workforce.[35] More importantly, the display of conspicuous generosity was 'an essential attribute' of those seeking power.[36] It was not just a question of general philanthropy, although the Cowens gave both time and money to the city's many charitable institutions. Their involvement in town improvement, both fabric and facilities, was of crucial importance, demonstrating as it did that the successful progress of both city and citizens were inextricably bound together.

As a Councillor, Cowen served on a number of committees, including Trade and Commerce, Water, and Schools and Charities, but the Town Improvement Committee, to which he was appointed in 1865, was undoubtedly the powerhouse of city politics and his stature grew accordingly.[37] Through his involvement in the provision of education and leisure facilities, as well as structural and functional improvements, he demonstrated his commitment to the cultural vitality of the city and the welfare of its people. Yet, as many have noted,[38] such philanthropic effort invariably served double duty, bringing financial and commercial rewards and, crucially, for a businessman with his range of interests, the opportunity to influence planning applications in his favour. Undoubtedly, Cowen's position on the Town Council was as politically advantageous as it was personally satisfying.

His role in local politics prompts the obvious comparison with Joseph Chamberlain, whose 'Municipal Socialism' is widely held to have transformed Birmingham, securing its place in the annals of Liberalism and ensuring his own impregnable powerbase.[39] Roland Quinault's reappraisal has helped to temper the somewhat idealized view that Chamberlain was a popular provincial politician, fiercely protective of Birmingham interests and his own deeply held radical convictions. He contends that Chamberlain's roots lay in London and his first concern was always for national rather than local issues.[40]As for Chamberlain's contribution to local affairs, this was short-lived, lasting a mere six years.[41] His political success is attributed much more to his Unitarian connections, 'reflecting the dominant influence which Nonconformist Liberalism exerted over the city' and rather less to his much vaunted municipal reforms.[42] By definition, Cowen's local standing was of a different calibre and closer scrutiny serves only to point up the fundamental differences between them.

Prior to 1876, when they disagreed publicly over the Eastern Question, relations appear to have been cordial, though not close. It was Cowen, in fact, who introduced Chamberlain to the House of Commons. His willingness to address the Birmingham Conference of the National Education League in 1871 at Chamberlain's request suggests a certain accord but, interestingly enough, the accompanying offer of hospitality was politely but firmly declined.[43] Chamberlain was on rather closer terms with Robert Spence Watson, a wealthy Quaker solicitor who acted as Cowen's electoral agent in 1873 and subsequently presided over the National Liberal Federation (NLF). Spence Watson had a large circle of influential friends, including John Bright, a fellow Quaker, who first mooted the idea of creating a Federation.[44] Chamberlain became a regular visitor at the Spence Watson home in Newcastle as they collaborated over the formation of the NLF and, according to T. A. Jenkins, he moved to strengthen his bid for a cabinet position.[45] Cowen's profound dislike of the caucus system, which the Federation introduced, placed him at odds with both politicians, especially Chamberlain, whom he reputedly dubbed a 'bedizened place-man'.[46] 'Party', argued Cowen, was 'the madness of the many for the gain of the few'.[47]

In the circumstances, it seems somewhat ironic that Chamberlain should have emerged as the archetypal Radical of his day whereas Cowen is scarcely remembered, even in his native city.[48] Unlike Cowen, Chamberlain 'did not make the weather, but dressed to suit it. . . he was a product rather than the progenitor of urban radicalism'.[49] While Chamberlain openly sought parliamentary power and ministerial office, Cowen's political ambitions are shrouded in ambiguity. It has been suggested by E.I. Waitt that Cowen deliberately sought office and that even as he feigned disinterest he employed devious and manipulative methods to secure his election.[50] The hindsight testimony of Thomas Headlam and Spence Watson, upon which Waitt's analysis largely depends, is unhelpful as the objectivity of both men must be considered questionable.[51]

Cowen was politically ambitious, of that there can be no doubt. What is less certain is whether political office as a Liberal candidate was the path he would have chosen for himself. Waitt overlooks the fact that Cowen had been repeatedly urged to stand but until 1873 he had always declined.[52] For a man of such eclectic interests and activities, political office had definite disadvantages, not least because it would interfere with his business and keep him away from Tyneside for the greater part of the year. And, the covert activities he relished so much could only be threatened if he became the focus of too much official scrutiny. Equally, by 1873 Cowen's reputation as a 'sort of political missionary in the North East' was firmly established. He could embark upon an electoral campaign with confidence, knowing that he could secure a large share of the poll.[53] It was his father's death and the unsuitability of the proposed candidates that produced the 'peculiar circumstance'[54] which finally forced his hand:

> I would have been glad if this had been otherwise. I have had no ambition for Parliamentary honours. I have been actively engaged in political warfare since I was a lad...I would rather live outside its walls, simply because I believe I could there lead a more useful life.[55]

And, by his own criteria, he was an ideal candidate, easily satisfying the conditions necessary for successfully contesting the city:

'A man should be known'
'A man should be identified with the local, industrial and commercial operations of the district'
'A man should have definite and decided opinions'.[56]

Having decided to contest the seat, pride dictated that he should do everything in his power to win. He was already a practised tactician; conspiracy and subterfuge were, arguably, second nature given his long experience of gun-running for the Italians and other republicans. In the circumstances, it is no surprise that he should make secret preparations to secure his selection, stealing a march on the Liberals and thereby strengthening his negotiating position. He had grown accustomed to being in absolute control. The Liberal colours, if he accepted them, would have to be on his own terms.

Effectively then, Cowen's rise to power was greatly facilitated by his smart middle-class credentials and his noteworthy contribution to local government. His eligibility for office under the usual preconditions was all that could be desired and yet his extreme republican views worried some senior Newcastle Liberals. In 1871 Newcastle had attracted high profile scrutiny following Charles Dilke's unprecedented attack upon the profligacy of the monarchy at a local meeting of the Republican Club.[57] Chaired by Cowen, it was reputedly his introductory remarks that galvanised Dilke into saying more than he intended.[58] Dilke's speech caused an absolute furore and in the aftermath some Liberals sought to distance themselves from his remarks.[59] On Tyneside, even the restored popularity of the monarchy did little to stem the tide of republican fervour that gripped the locality in early 1872. Although republicanism has been regarded as a declining, if not moribund, force by 1872,[60] Tyneside branches continued to proliferate and large open-air meetings remained a prominent feature of local politics for at least another twelve months.[61]On balance, however, Cowen's extraordinary influence over the working classes was held to outweigh the political capital their opponents, or even their own supporters, might make of his republicanism.[62] His popular leadership simply could not be ignored, especially at a time when wooing the newly-enfranchised electors was at the top of every political agenda. The other Liberal candidate, T. E. Headlam, was patently inept, railed by his opponents as a closet Tory with no demonstrable commitment to Tyneside or its inhabitants. In Cowen, they had a candidate who could secure the allegiances of more than just a faction or a class; his nomination, they believed, might effectively forestall the growing clamour for a working class candidate.

It is hardly a coincidence that one of the first working-class MPs should be a Northumbrian, Thomas Burt, the miners' leader elected to represent Morpeth in 1874.[63] Cowen and Adams gave unstinting support to Burt's campaign through the pages of the *Chronicle* [64] and in numerous speeches. The Morpeth electorate, Cowen noted, were mainly working men 'determined to send one of their own body'. Criticising the vested interests of many candidates, he argued that Burt would represent 'not just a party or a section but the entire constituency'; he was unlikely to be 'beguiled by the blandishments and brilliancy of power'.[65] Keith Robbins'comment that 'from the 1870s onwards, 'Lib-Lab' MPs appeared in a number of constituencies' masks the tortuously slow progress of political change.[66] Burt's election was exceptional, indicative only of the power of the Northumberland miners and their union, and the strength of local opinion. As a rule, working men encountered formidable opposition.[67] At the turn of the century, as George Bernstein's detailed survey shows, less than 5 per cent of Liberal MPs could be described as having 'no obvious profession'.[68] In practice, working class candidates were all too often dissuaded from standing, on the grounds that doing so would split the Liberal vote – a ploy used to great effect by Gladstone in 1880, when Hyndman relinquished his interest in the Marylebone seat.[69] Other hopefuls were recruited as paid agents 'thus preventing anything like united action'.[70] Cowen, though, identified widespread prejudicial attitudes as the primary obstacle to progress:

> the social usages and the customs of the Country, and, to a large extent, the prejudices of the English people who dearly, too dearly love a lord, have been the chief causes that kept political power in the hands of its present holders.[71]

On Tyneside, the activities of the Gateshead Representation League exposed the incipient vulnerability of the Liberal executive. Formed to secure a 'bona fide representative of labour for Gateshead', the League urged the working classes to select 'a man of their own choosing, and one who will speak manfully, honestly and wisely on their behalf'.[72] Ultimately, Cowen's candidacy offered a satisfactory solution to the dilemma: Tyneside Liberals were satisfied that they had staved off the pressure to elect outside of the usual ranks while, for their part, the lobby for working-class representation were perfectly content to back Cowen who had promised to accelerate the pace of political reform.

Cowen's political power, as it derived from this other, non-traditional sphere of influence, can only be understood in the context of Tyneside radicalism. Its resilience in the 1870s was in no small measure due to Cowen's activism and dynamic leadership. For him, keeping a radical tradition alive and in the forefront of the public mind remained an overarching priority. As we have already observed, Cowen was, first and foremost, an 'English Radical' who was 'more concerned for liberal principles than for the Liberal Party' – joining the ranks of the latter was simply an electoral necessity.[73] As he explained,

> The original English Radicals were a school of politicians who went to the root of things, and fought for principle, irrespective of faction. They were in general sympathy with the Liberals, but in advance of and independent of them.[74]

He was determined to resist at all costs the rising tide of 'elastic and accommodating Liberalism which may mean this, that or t'other thing or anything or nothing' and which threatened, he thought, to swamp radicalism.[75] Exasperated by the 'political effeminacy and cowardice' of the rising middle classes,[76] he cautioned the working classes to be on their guard against complacency:

It is a very common practice for a man to be an earnest Radical when he is at the bottom of the ladder, but when he gets up in the world, procures a good shop and is able to live in an excellent house, he very often quits the Methodist meeting in order to attend church and gradually emerges a comfortable Whig. Let us not follow such a course.[77]

Cowen lost no opportunity to press home his radical agenda or to promote radicalism as a far superior creed with an absolute commitment to progress and change.

His emergence as a formidable contender for power in 1873 cannot be ascribed simply to good timing, municipal largesse or the advantages of a partisan constituency – though clearly all three worked in his favour. His oratorical skills were a singular asset; his stirring speeches and distinctive accent[78] drew plaudits from even the most hostile audience. As Mr Grant, a leading member of the Liberal executive, complained 'his ability was such that, whenever he appeared, any opposition that might be brought against him would melt and be as nothing'.[79] His reputation as a powerful orator extended far beyond the boundaries of the locality. The *Pall Mall Gazette* followed Cowen's interventions in the Commons with great interest and were quick to recognise his leadership qualities:

Turn a man like Mr Cowen loose for a single month in the most 'advanced' constituency thus misled, and we should see at the end of that period what had become of the malignancies that distracted it.[80]

As *The Times* leader observed, 'He lifts politics...contrasting sharply with the second and third hand opinions which make up the staple of ordinary speeches.'[81] As for the Birmingham radicals, an 1893 retrospective in the *St. James Gazette* was scathing:

At a time when machine made rhetoricians and political contractors hold their heads so high, it is well that the speeches of an Independent Radical, who has done more to maintain a high standard of political integrity in St Stephens than all the Birmingham manipulators put together, should be collected and published.[82]

The *Lancashire Evening Press* claimed that his speeches 'woke the country as if they had been a modern example of the Cross of Fire'.[83] Not only was he an accomplished orator, but he had effectively mastered the art of mass media. Even his opponents acknowledged that

He is a man of far more than average ability…his fervid eloquence is well calculated to bewitch the natives, and the powerful newspaper he has at his back more than doubles his personal influence, considerable as that is.[84]

Historians have increasingly recognised the importance of newspapers in defining the polity of urban Britain.[85] Cowen's astute proprietorship of the *Chronicle* newspapers enabled him to achieve that which was physically impossible: to be a daily presence in the lives of the population, to drip feed his ideas about society and democracy in countless ways and to win over those who, in the normal scheme of things, were unlikely to attend a political meeting or join a radical organisation. As W. E. Adams observed in 1863, 'the press became the adjunct of the platform'.[86] No expense was spared as technical expertise was married to innovative journalistic methods. Sports reports, serialised literature, domestic anecdotes and local gossip were all offered as sweeteners to advance the *Chronicle*'s more serious intent: that of giving the people a radical education. Special features, such as the series of articles on local co-operative societies in 1867,[87] and the weekly portraits of mining villages in 1873,[88] promoted the view that mechanics' institutes, trades unions and co-op stores were the appropriate associations for those who espoused radical beliefs. For their part, these small isolated villages were encouraged to regard themselves as a valued section of the Tyneside community.

In Cowen's capable hands, the *Newcastle Daily Chronicle* became a powerful political weapon:

It is read by opponents as well as friends. It influences all readers. It is powerful because dogmatic. If it changes politics, it changes the politics of a city and a district. It is the most powerful leader in the Northern Counties, men or newspaper.[89]

Political and social reform groups were all assured of generous and sympathetic coverage. The positive intervention of the Cowen press was particularly significant during the Nine Hours Strike in 1871 and the 1873 campaign to extend the vote to local miners anomalously excluded from the franchise. Moreover, as already shown, Irish issues and news were given exceptionally generous coverage. While other Liberal newspapers assiduously trod the party line, Cowen's newspapers adopted a singularly independent editorial policy. With Adams at the helm of the *Weekly Chronicle,* Cowen had an editor whom he trusted implicitly and upon whose judgement he completely relied, not just because of his abilities as a journalist but because intellectually they were evenly matched. As a former Chartist, radical reformer and intrepid republican author Adams had powerful credentials.[90] Other contributors, such as Harney, Holyoake and Bradlaugh brought the talents of a wider network of first rank radicals to bear and enabled the debate on civil liberty, democracy and republicanism to be thoroughly ventilated. For example, Harney's regular column, 'Letters from America', which was published between 1864 and 1883, helped to familiarise readers with the working of American democracy and encourage them to espouse this as the ideal form of government.[91] Inevitably, the Cowen press attracted the hostility of the local party faithful. They attempted to engineer a partnership between the Liberal Association and the Cowen press but he would have none of it. He knew that ownership of the *Chronicle* newspapers was a vital factor in his continuing political authority and he was not about to give the Liberals any opportunity to undermine his independence. By 1882, the anti-Cowen lobby was finally forced into financing another newspaper in a desperate bid to secure more favourable coverage of Liberal policy.[92]

The Liberals' failure to harness Cowen's popularity to their cause accentuated his claim to be an independent politician and strengthened the belief that his radicalism was not empty rhetoric. The moral convictions which underpinned his speeches were given vivid realisation through all of his activities, political and social, and the voters responded by giving him their unstinting support and loyalty. Spanning two generations, he had been involved in every campaign and movement of local importance; through his family connections he could legitimately claim over fifty years commitment to the struggle for reform. Dynastic claims to power, in this way, operated just as effectively in the new sphere of influence as they had in the old. Cowen's personal involvement in the organisational life of the Tyneside working-class community demonstrably had a cumulative effect in building up his extraordinary power base.

Vincent, quite rightly, focuses on leadership as the key to explaining Liberal popularity. 'The ordinary MP', he insists, had little influence on public opinion, 'he simply gave the picture of a very rich man addressing poor men on subjects not of burning interest to either side'.[93] 'Tribunes', such as Bright, Chamberlain and Mill are said to have been the true leaders of opinion; winning over the radical lobby and taming the working-class movement, they successfully allied both to the parliamentary Liberal Party. Cowen, though, was no 'ordinary politician'. His appeal was broad and direct, both speech and clothing unequivocally signalled his identification with the working-class electorate. His informal attire and dialect-laden speech hardly commended him to his fellow members of parliament where ostentation, not informality, was a given. While Burt immediately adopted the customary top hat and tails, Cowen persisted in wearing his soft 'billy cock hat' and an ordinary suit. On Tyneside, such 'eccentricity' translated into a large share of the vote by those who were persuaded that he was, as he claimed, one of themselves.[94] Bright, whom Vincent singles out as the most important 'tribune', had only minimal influence in the North East.[95] He never spoke publicly in Newcastle where his radical credentials were considered extremely suspect, as this extract from the *Daily Chronicle* shows:

> Bright is no democrat. He is not even a Chartist…he asks for a rate paying franchise which would exclude hundreds of honest and intelligent citizens from the electoral register.[96]

Cowen did invite Bright to address the Northern Reform Union in 1859 but their correspondence shows that this was purely a matter of courtesy.[97] Since north-east radicals regarded Bright as a 'cuckoo in the nest' in 1859, Cowen was not disposed to press the issue.[98] As for Bright, working-class audiences were never truly his forte and he appears to have studiously avoided them whenever possible.[99]

Cowen's well established reputation as the 'Tribune of the North' should have earned him a place on Vincent's list of leaders who generated the 'goodwill' from which Gladstone's administration benefited.[100] As demonstrated, his leading role in associational life helped to 'translate urban individualism into social solidarities' which, in turn, dictated political loyalties.[101] Unusually for the times, Cowen gave politics a human face, effectively breaking through the old traditional barriers between politicians and voting public. He was a familiar figure in their midst; affectionately referred to as 'The Blaydon Brick' or 'Radical Joe'.[102] He was instantly recognisable, not just in Blaydon or Newcastle but throughout the North East. This was personality politics on a powerfully intimate level, made even more meaningful by Cowen's aggressive promotion of Tyneside at every opportunity. His politics were given an unashamedly local colouration and, in return, his radical reputation became the flagship of regional pride. Employing the emotive language of radical patriotism, Tyneside, not Britain, was cited as the 'birthplace of liberty'.[103] And, given such local emphasis, patriotism could remain the ideological property of the Tyneside radicals long after 1870, when Cunningham detects the disintegration of the patriotic left.[104]

All of this begs the question whether Cowen can legitimately be defined as a charismatic leader. Max Weber's criteria require charismatic leaders to be sufficiently free from economic restraint to develop independent judgement, based on their own 'freely chosen' convictions. Independence, according to this definition, is essential: the leader 'is an individualist; the source of his actions lies in himself, in his own personal convictions and not in his following or associates'.[105] On these grounds the definition can certainly be applied to Cowen. Moreover, if we accept the argument that the extension of the franchise brought with it personalisation of politics, and weighted the scales in favour of the outstanding individual who was capable of securing the mass vote by force of personality and demagogic appeal,[106]

it can be asserted that Cowen, no less than Gladstone, met the challenge posed. Biagini's study of nineteenth century Liberalism views Cowen as 'much more than a provincial demagogue' and highlights his 'exasperating spirit of independence'.[107] In doing so, however, he draws a sharp contrast between the phenomenon of 'being Gladstonized' by the Liberal leader's hypnotic rhetoric,[108] and the charismatic impact of Cowen's 'didactic nationalism' which is said to have been wholly appropriate to the 'Puritan mass intellectualism of the Northern counties'.[109] Cowen, as we have noted, was a masterly tactician and while it is clearly understood that charisma was bestowed, not possessed, he was more than capable of deliberately engaging in the sort of activity most likely to produce the required act of recognition. Thus, albeit on a far lesser scale, his 'missionary' tours of mining villages is not so far removed from the ritual journeys made by kings in early times in a bid to confirm their sphere of authority: 'making appearances, attending fetes, conferring honours, exchanging gifts or defying rivals, they mark it, like some wolf or tiger spreading his scent through his territory'.[110] Most crucially, as Clifford Geertz has suggested, the most 'flamboyant' charismatic figures are often heretics, who challenge the strength of the existing leadership or social order – who are 'at some distance from the center' and 'want very much to be closer'.[111] If Geertz is correct, and there is a central paradox within charisma embodying both orthodoxy and heresy, then it is the latter, more extreme form that can most usefully be applied to Cowen and his leadership of local radicalism.[112]

To attribute Cowen's popularity to any specific reform campaigns might be considered somewhat specious, and yet there are good grounds for doing so. His involvement in the Co-operative movement and education reform were both vitally important. By 1873, the Co-operative movement could boast a membership of 36,354 in Northumberland and Durham,[113] and its success reflected well on Cowen's leadership qualities. The crossover of membership between co-operatives, mechanics institutes and temperance groups has obvious implications for the extent of Cowen's leadership, as he provided the focal point around which all of these diverse interests could converge. His presidency of the 1873 Co-operative Congress gave him a powerful platform from which to promote his vision of creating a 'militant democracy'. His ambitious idealism proved enormously attractive.

Education had always been a pivotal principle of Cowen's political strategy. He believed that the best way to help people was 'to teach them to help themselves' and he roundly condemned the sort of charity which 'generates a sense of arrogance on the one hand, and a sense of subservience on the other'.[114] Disraeli, he complained, aspired only to keep the people in 'a sort of well fed slavery'.[115] Prior to 1868, Cowen's educational initiatives had been more or less confined to the voluntary sphere, reflecting his belief that mechanics' institutes and the provision of free public libraries 'would contribute as much, if not more, to the promotion of popular education'.[116] But, by the autumn of 1869, interest in education reform began to gather considerable momentum. This was hardly surprising for, as Cowen noted

> It had always been a cardinal point of Radical doctrine that whenever the people got the extension of the suffrage, the first use they would make of it would be to establish a system of education.[117]

Drawing upon his network of radical contacts, he compiled a valuable register of known sympathisers to whom appeals for money and support could most profitably be made.[118] Once again, Newcastle became the focus of radical activity when the first Education Conference was convened at the Literary and Philosophical Society in November 1869. A heated debate ensued. The National Education Union, dominated by the clergy, was enraged by the Education League's proposal for secular education.[119] Notwithstanding the notable decline in church attendance, public opinion was still markedly hostile to secular ideas.[120] Although Cowen was sympathetic to the Secularist's position, he had to tread warily. In the event, the education issue provided him with a golden opportunity to demonstrate his political mettle. In contesting the School Board elections as an advocate of 'non-sectarian' education, he emerged as remarkably even-handed, and this went some way towards placating the opposing factions. Under the School Board provisions of the 1870 Act, Cowen and his four colleagues (George Luckley, Isaac Lowthian Bell, Dr Rutherford and Robert Spence Watson) formally identified themselves as 'Unsectarian' candidates.[121] Cowen defended his stance on the grounds that

> We cannot establish schools in this country that will be universally acceptable until they are made absolutely unsectarian. In schools supported by the rates there should be no doctrine peculiar to any church taught, and the unsectarian candidates go for the Bible being read, with any rational explanation of its contents...The attempt to establish denominational schools is an attempt to buttress up the National Church and establish half a dozen more. The same principle applied to this country would have to be

applied to Ireland. They have abolished the Protestant State Church there, but would be called upon to re-establish the Roman Catholic Church…In selecting candidates, they should not get on this sectarian tack at all. We have been trying to get rid of sectarian feeling for a long time, and by mingling together, to rub off the corners of prejudice, but this Education Act, which has many advantages but great defects, simply propagates those sectarian feelings which we endeavour to destroy…I and the gentlemen associated with me appeal to you as brother citizens, acquainted with your wants and wishes. If elected, we will not go to the Education Board as the representatives of any denomination, but to represent what we believe to be the interests of the town at large. While others battle for special sects, we will battle for the common good.[122]

With its stress on egalitarianism, Cowen's speech was a tremendous tour de force. The Birmingham Radicals requested his assistance in setting up the National Education League, and he accepted an executive position in January 1870.[123] As far afield as London, Derby and Birmingham, Cowen became much sought after as a guest speaker.[124] The Manchester and Salford League pleaded with Cowen to address a branch meeting: 'we require the names of men who are popular with the working people. Among such, none is more so than yourself'.[125] Similar appeals were made by the Middlesbrough branch, who encountered strenuous opposition from the clergy. The working men, they said were 'warming up to take a deep interest in this question'.[126]

Liberal unity was deeply fractured by the education furore and this was further exacerbated by the entrenched militancy of Chamberlain and the League. In the run up to the 1873 election, and with one eye on pleasing the Liberal premier, Cowen gave firm backing to Gladstone and his ministry: 'I know no man who ever guided the councils of this country who was more worthy of our admiration and confidence'. He acknowledged that there had been 'blunders' but compared the Liberals' efforts favourably with the 'stand-still proceedings of previous Governments'. He concluded his address to the electors by promising to 'go in advance of him [Gladstone] when I believe it is necessary; encourage him, if possible, to further progress, and sustain him in all liberal acts'. [127] Gratitude for his father's knighthood was bound to have influenced his attitude to Gladstone, whose leadership had been given sterling defence in 1870 by the *Chronicle*.[128] Relations between Cowen and the Education League had quickly cooled and throughout the election campaign Cowen speeches were not just pro-Gladstone but stressed the importance of party loyalty. The education controversy, which proved to be a major factor in the Liberal rout of 1874,[129] served Cowen very well, providing him with an impressive domestic campaign from which to launch his parliamentary career. Cowen's militant republican-ism attracted some negative press comment but fortunately this never became a decisive issue. Mindful of the need to distance himself from Fenian activity, and the renewed popularity of the monarchy he fudged the issue by claiming that he 'never took part in any of its [The Republican club] proceedings'.[130] It is ironic that the education campaign which so positively assisted his rise to power should also carry with it the seeds of his downfall. The caucus system, which set Cowen on a collision course with the Liberal Party, was actually spawned in the aftermath of 1874, by the very oligarchy which rapidly assumed control of the Newcastle School Board.[131]

In 1874, as Cowen finally took centre stage as Liberal member for Newcastle, he was well positioned to make his mark at Westminster. The question was how long could he sustain this uneasy alliance? He believed that he had a mandate to express his own political judgement and that 'his views were in consonance with those of the people...no man shall say he voted for me under a misappre-hension'.[132] There was no question, in his mind, of relinquishing the right to act independently. 'An MP', he insisted 'is a representative, not a delegate'.

> He has to exercise and express his judgement on many conflicting topics. He is not chosen to vote on a single subject, or set of subjects, in a speci-fied manner...A member of the House of Commons cannot be a delegate; in the course of a session, sudden and unexpected emergencies are con-stantly arising, scores of issues are being started on most diverse projects, upon which no man could, however willing he may be to do so, collect the opinion of his constituents. The work of a member, therefore, is different from and more elastic than that of a delegate. If he is only to vote to order, a machine could do as good, black and white balls would be as good and a great deal less costly than living Whig or Tory members.[133]

Cowen's determination to resist party discipline merits careful consideration. Samuel Beer has argued that 'the golden age of the private MP' was over by 1868, implying that, by then, independence was not a realistic option.[134] Yet some would argue that the truly independent member was 'not unconformable, but incorruptible; virtuous rather than free'.[135] Declarations of independence were often an integral part of electoral formalities: the expected affirmation of the member's integrity and social standing. As Michael Rush notes, the imposi-tion of party discipline through the use of 'whips' was on an upward trajectory from 1871 onwards.[136] In the final analysis retaining power was a restraining influence and this was a strong incentive to vote along party lines.

Nonetheless, it was not until after 1880 that party replaced status as the essential prerequisite of attaining political office.[137] In Newcastle, Cowen was not shackled by the usual constraints for his source of power did not depend upon Liberal largesse or sponsorship. Any obligation, such as it was, rested with the Liberal Association. A man of inordinate (some might say intemperate) pride, Cowen categorically refused to canvass for support. Addressing a School Board meeting in 1871, he explained:

> I never have canvassed for anything for myself, and never intend to do so. I am sufficiently well known in Newcastle and therefore offer my services if they are appreciated. But if the electors can find better men, I will bow to their decision. Indeed, as a matter of personal feeling I would rather have been out of the election, but having been selected to stand with the others, I felt I could not decline the responsibility. Canvassing, however, I regard as a humiliating position, and whatever the consequences may be, I will not adopt such a course.[138]

Even in 1885, when his position had become virtually untenable, he remained obdurate. Having had power 'thrust upon him', as it were, he felt justified in wielding it according to his lights. For the vast majority, however, who were entirely dependent upon their local party, independence was never truly a viable position. The autonomy of even the most ardent radicals seems to have been severely circumscribed. Writing to Josephine Butler in 1882, Cowen expressly attributed the failures of Gladstone's Second Ministry to the undue pressure placed on Liberal members to vote with their party

> If there had been a band of independent Liberals in the House, however numerically small, they might have done something to arrest or restrain the course of the Ministry...as it is, the majority follow the Government blindly and without question.[139]

As for the hated Cloture proposal, a guillotine measure aimed at preventing obstruction tactics, there were, he claimed, at least fifty members who would have voted against it 'if they had been free'.[140]

Cowen's subsequent collision with mainstream Liberalism can be located in the inability of either side to negotiate a satisfactory compromise on the vital question of independence. The Newcastle Liberal Association mistakenly assumed that in accepting the candidacy Cowen would thereafter put the party's best interests first. For his part, Cowen fatally miscalculated the extent to which the Association had been won over to his extreme radicalism. Cultivating the Tyneside electorate was one thing, converting the party faithful to his strident militant democracy was quite another. Cowen's avowed aim to

link past tradition with future hope and subordinate the interest of party
to that of nation, the interest of classes to that of justice, the interest of section to that of liberty, and the interest of all to the elevation of man[141]

was unlikely to appeal to the executive, dominated as they were by a small clique
of wealthy, ambitious manufacturers, who were

all close acquaintances, members of the same club, and...the same radical
school of politics, and, for the most part, the same radical school of theology and the same clan of closely allied families...An independent Liberal
was more objectionable than a Tory, for free thinking in politics was of all
sins, the most unpardonable.[142]

As it turned out, a punishing schedule of business and political commitments
served to undermine his health and in the crucial aftermath of the election he
fell prey to a chronic debilitating illness. His recovery was so protracted that he
did not take his seat until the closing months of the parliamentary session, and
despite a long holiday during the recess he did little more that attend to routine
business in the second session.[143] The evidence suggests that he was suffering
from severe nervous exhaustion and his doctors advised him to retire.[144] The
Liberal Executive, dominated by the ambitious and influential Spence Watson,
took full advantage of the power vacuum created by Cowen's long illness.

After 1874 Spence Watson's control of the Liberal Association noticeably
tightened, helped on by his close working relationship with Chamberlain
and Bright.[145] The ad-hoc informality which had epitomised the local Liberal
Association for so many years was rapidly replaced by a more formalised, dis-
ciplined structure – sarcastically dubbed 'the Caucus' by its opponents, who
rejected it as an unwanted American import. Speaking at the Manchester Free
Trade Hall, Cowen readily acknowledged the need for change but he recommended caution, arguing that if pushed too far the new party machinery would
prove 'despotic'.[146] His worst fears were realised, as he observed in 1885; the
Caucus and the imposition of the cloture had effectively muzzled any voices of
dissent. Cowen deplored what he regarded as its retrogressive effects:

those who support the caucus system will effectively organise all sponta-
neity, intrepidity and initiative out of the people...This stereotyping men
into systems is a prostitution of national aspiration, a violation of human
liberty, an encroachment on individual life and a barrier to progress.[147]

Biagini has argued that opposition to the Caucus emanated from an 'old fash-ioned plebeian radicalism',[148] and that many workers and radicals were actu-ally in favour of a reformed party organisation. Moreover, he claims that its critics, especially Cowen, were motivated by personal animus directed at the Federation's personnel 'rather than the organisation itself'.[149] The problem with this analysis is that Cowen did not recognise any such distinction. He was im-placably opposed to the caucus *and* those who actively promoted it.

In 1876 Cowen's oppositional independence brought him into sharp divi-sion with both sides of the House. In March he delivered his first major speech on the Royal Titles Bill, by which Queen Victoria would assume the additional title, 'Empress of India'.[150] At the time, Disraeli cited the growing crises in the Eastern provinces and advocated the new imperial title as an essentially tactical manoeuvre, aimed at deterring Russia from any further expansionist encroach-ments.[151] Recklessly flouting parliamentary procedure by intervening after both Gladstone and Disraeli had delivered their concluding remarks, Cowen made an impassioned plea for the Bill to be rejected. He poured scorn upon Disraeli's 'frivolous' speech, arguing that the despotic, imperialist connotations of the word 'Empress', posed a serious threat to constitutional liberty:

> In changing the name, I fear they may change the character of Government…we cannot be too jealous of regal and despotic encroach-ments upon popular power and influence…they would be taking the first step, but a substantial step, towards abolishing the time-honoured and historic title of Queen of England, and supplanting it by the tawdry, com-monplace and vulgar designation of Empress…if there is any attempt to establish a species of socialistic empire, to drag into our constitution the forms and principles of Imperialism, the honourable gentlemen opposite would soon find that the superstition of Royalty has no real hold on the people of this land.[152]

Cowen's intervention 'electrified' the House[153] and confirmed his reputation as a powerful orator. The provincial press praised his 'incisive logic'[154] and af-terwards copies of his speech were widely circulated at meetings supporting his anti-imperialist stance.[155] Victoria's new title was duly conferred but with the conciliatory proviso that it would not be used in the United Kingdom. Ironically enough, it was his views on the Eastern Crisis which subsequently brought him into sharp conflict with Gladstone and the Liberal Party.

The brutal massacre of 15,000 Bulgarians in May 1876 at the hands of Muslim irregulars acting on Turkish orders provoked unprecedented public outrage.[156] Mass demonstrations protesting against the pro-Turkish policy of the Disraeli government rapidly gathered momentum in an agitation which, with its sectarian and moral overtones, divided even as it consumed popular opinion. There is little doubt that popular outrage was fuelled by graphic and ghoulish newspaper reports, especially in the North of England, where W. T. Stead, editor of the *Northern Echo*, mounted a relentless campaign.[157] According to Richard Shannon, it was Stead, recognising the need for a 'mighty name' to endorse the movement, who petitioned Gladstone to emerge from his self-imposed retirement and personally intervene.[158] Other evidence, however, suggests that A. J. Mundella's influence was far greater and in some quarters he was 'widely blamed for stirring up Our Chief to this insubordinate act'.[159] In any event, Shannon is right to insist that Gladstone was 'practically carried into the agitation by others'.[160] Political opportunism, not altruism, is said to have inspired his pamphlet, *The Bulgarian Horrors and the Question of the East*, in a bid to 'restore the rapport between himself and the masses which the defeat of 1874 had snapped'.[161]

At the start of the crisis, with parliament in recess, Cowen was still trying to regain his strength by holidaying in the Vosges and this possibly accounts for Newcastle's unusually slow response to Stead's rallying cry.[162] On his return, he promptly endorsed Gladstone's proposal for Bulgarian independence which would 'best commend itself to intelligent Englishmen'.[163] And in his constituency speech in January 1877 he was unstinting in his praise: 'History', he said, would be the final judge: 'then will the work of that great Englishman, who is at once the animating and directing spirit of that assembly, be appreciated and the petty detractions of pygmy politicians will be consigned to oblivion'.[164]

Within three months, however, the Russian invasion of Turkey caused Cowen to radically reappraise the situation and, significantly, to reverse his opinion of Gladstone. Whereas, in September 1876, he believed that Russian expansionism was 'an exploded illusion', by mid-1877 the tone of the *Chronicle*'s 'London Letter' had become increasingly alarmist.[165] As that year drew to a close, the pacifist lobby was increasingly challenged by meetings of 'the war-party', who were distinguished by a good deal of rowdy flag-waving, and patriotic singing, particularly *Rule Britannia* and other jingoistic music hall favourites.[166] Nationalist sentiment was bolstered by the proliferation of special shows and exhibitions which dramatically reprised the principal events of the conflict. For instance, in London, the Russo-Turkish War Exhibition provided a vivid exposition of the campaign, reportedly attracting an enthusiastic audience of more than 100,000 visitors before touring the provinces.[167] On Tyneside, the Exhibition was held in the Town Hall and thousands flocked to view its much-publicised 'novel effects'. Cowen's Tyne Theatre and Opera House in Westgate Road fanned the flames of nationalist fervour by showing a dramatic recreation of the Russian defeat at the Battle of Plevna. The latter displays all of the hallmarks of an orchestrated campaign, aimed at resurrecting older animosities, namely anti-Tsarism, which had been so abiding a feature of Tyneside radicalism and a perennial theme of Cowen's speeches.[168]

Cowen became estranged, not just from most of his Liberal colleagues but also from a sizeable section of the Tyneside working classes. In early 1878, influential sections of the working classes all publicly declared themselves in favour of 'neutrality'. Freethinkers, led by Cowen's old friend Charles Bradlaugh, condemned the religious bigotry which they claimed lay at the root of the conflict and adopted a strictly pacifist line.[169] Close links between republican and secularist groups was an important factor and local branches of the National Secular Society, notably at Bedlington and Seghill, strongly backed the official line.[170] As a key member of the Workmen's Peace Association, Thomas Burt addressed countless rallies in support of Gladstone and his influence over the Northumberland miners can scarcely be overstated. The miners were readily persuaded that war was a 'great waste of men and resources' for they had other preoccupations which deepened their anti-war position.[171] Following a prolonged and bitter strike brought on by the generally depressed nature of the coal trade, some 8,000 miners were 'locked out' in January 1878 and reliant upon the financial support of fellow trade unionists and co-operative societies.[172]

The miners were not the only group affected by the slump in trade. The North of England Iron Trade, for instance, had reluctantly agreed to a 10 per cent wage decrease, reducing incomes to a lower level than that reached during the 1867 depression.[173] As the war party and the peace party collided, 1,200 pints of soup were being distributed to the unemployed in Newcastle every day, and it is hardly surprising that the Newcastle and District Trades Council called for 'strict neutrality'.[174] Agricultural workers, too, were bound to find the economic arguments persuasive, especially when they were delivered by Joseph Arch. In a speech to the Exeter labourers in May 1878, Arch reminded NALU members that they had gained nothing from the Crimean War: 'If the country has money to spare', he declared, 'it should be spent on resuscitating the trade'.[175] Meanwhile, W. E. Adams kept up the pressure in his weekly editorials by asserting that there was little working-class support for the war:

Watch, brothers, watch, the war-dogs are growling,
The great make war, the poor have to fight.
Let your watchword be peace; trade is declining,
As the demons on swift pinions fly.
While the rich and the great in ease are reclining
'Tis we that suffer, struggle and die.[176]

Inevitably, economic tensions were a key factor on both sides of the argument. As the *Chronicle*'s London correspondent observed, Tyneside workers, especially shipbuilders, would benefit from increased spending on armaments:

> No inconsiderable amount of the money recently voted by Parliament would be expended at the shipyards and ironworks at Jarrow and other places on the Tyne…at Jarrow especially…hopes were entertained that an influx of orders would lead to a revival of trade.[177]

Given that only a handful of letters supporting Cowen were printed in the Cowen Press it can be assumed that, apart from the Foreign Affairs Committee, anti-Russian feeling was something of a spent force in the region. With the Quakers in the vanguard, the Nonconformists spearheaded much of the peace campaign. Robert Spence Watson's peace lobby was particularly effective, not just in marginalising the anti-Tzarist faction but in persuading the working-class electorate to endorse Gladstone's challenge to Hartington's leadership. The plaudits of the Newcastle Conservative Association were no consolation to Cowen as he was besieged by a torrent of censorious mail.[178] The excuse that he had 'never set up for a political prophet' availed him little. When Spence Watson took him to task for his aggressive Russophobia, Cowen feigned all innocence, disingenuously claiming that he had not seen the *Chronicle* for three months.[179] Everyone knew that Cowen exerted a tight control over his newspapers, and Spence Watson would not have been fooled by his unconvincing disclaimer. As Cowen refused to back down, relations between the two long-standing friends became increasingly strained.[180] Meanwhile, at the *Chronicle* offices, Cowen found himself equally at odds with his editors, James Annand and W. E. Adams. As ever, Adams commanded Cowen's respect, if not his agreement, and he allowed him to uphold the official Gladstonian line unhindered. Annand was not nearly so fortunate. The *Daily Chronicle* was widely regarded as Cowen's political signature and the kind of latitude Adams enjoyed was never likely to be extended to others. When Annand became ill, Cowen seized the opportunity to force his resignation, claiming that the editorship of the *Daily Chronicle* was too demanding.[181]

As the crisis deepened, Cowen pig-headedly refused to modify his position, and denounced Russia as 'an aggressive, military, ecclesiastical autocracy… dangerous to human freedom, peace and progress'.[182] When Cowen proposed that party considerations be laid aside in the interests of national unity, he and Gladstone clashed angrily in the Commons. Gladstone emphatically denied that Liberals were required 'to prefer party to country', as to do so would be a great and gross mistake, but not a greater mistake than that made by my Hon. Friend himself when he said that in a question of foreign policy we are to surrender to their opinion and judgement, and simply to support that which might be proposed by Ministers…that in questions of foreign policy we are to have no regard to right and wrong; that we are all to be Englishmen and that whatever proposal is made in the name of England we are to support. Such a proposal as that is most shallow in philosophy and most unwise in policy.[183]

In reply, Cowen protested that his words had been gravely misinterpreted and insisted that 'A man speaking under strong emotions ought not to be made an offender for a word. If that rule were applied to the right hon. gentleman, he would have a good deal to answer for.' Defending his stance, he maintained that

when national interests were imperilled – national existence possibly at stake – then we should close our ranks and forget that we are Whigs, Tories and Radicals; remember only that we are Englishmen and present a united front to the world…. The general principles of national action – whether we are to put up a monarchy in one country or destroy a Republic in another – whether we are to be partisans in a strife or neutrals – must be decided by the people, and by them alone. But the policy having been assented to, its execution must be left to the executive. If they blunder, you may censure them, dismiss them or impeach them; but in a moment of national peril, do not paralyse their movements by unnecessary complications.[184]

According to Jane Cowen, 'the Old Man never forgave him, and after his speech in the Commons in February 1878, he practically cut him off'.[185] From that time onwards, Cowen was deeply critical of Gladstone, insisting that the Bulgarian Atrocities had been 'turned to party purposes'.[186] Writing to C. H. de Bille MP in June 1880, he reiterated his belief that Gladstone's Eastern policy had been dangerously unwise:

I am more than ever satisfied that the course Mr Gladstone advocated was fraught with much danger, not only to England but to European liberty. He is a perfectly sincere man, but on this subject his judgement is warped by a bias, partly ecclesiastical and partly personal.[187]

For both politicians, the Eastern crisis proved to be something of a watershed. In Gladstone's case, its effects may be said to have been wholly beneficial, enabling him to capture the high moral ground from Beaconsfield, which, in turn, effected his successful return to national politics as Liberal premier.[188] For Cowen, though, the failure to compromise or even moderate his views had disastrous consequences. In distancing himself so decisively from his fellow radicals, any possibility of his becoming their leading spokesperson was destroyed.[189] This was particularly foolhardy for, in the aftermath of the 1880 election victory, there were strong signs that that the political initiative was about to pass to the radical left. As ever, Chamberlain, who had played his hand more skilfully, was the ultimate beneficiary.

In the main, the Newcastle Liberals favoured Gladstone's return to politics, sending him a loyal address at the start of his crucial Midlothian campaign.[190] Cowen's antagonism was a source of acute embarrassment to his local party, who were deeply disappointed that he had failed to ingratiate himself at Westminster. Unfortunately, the strength of his popularity meant that they could neither discipline nor replace him. Cowen acknowledged, willingly enough, that his behaviour had been 'a source of trouble and annoyance', and on several occasions he offered to resign but this was repeatedly declined.[191] In view of the widening chasm between Cowen and Spence Watson this, more than anything else, demonstrates the degree to which Liberal success on Tyneside, even in 1880, rested upon Cowen's local standing. The decision to field Ashton Dilke (brother of the radical MP, Sir Charles Dilke) in 1880 was part of Spence Watson's long term strategy to secure a more malleable representative. However, Dilke's candidature was compromised when a plot to select him as the 'senior' member was discovered. The Liberals were desperate to return to power and Cowen's threat to retire brought the Newcastle caucus swiftly to heel; even Gladstone was brought to Newcastle to exert a calming influence.[192] Supremely confident, Cowen scorned the suggestion that he should share a platform with Dilke.[193] On election day, Cowen was badly crushed in the mêlée but with the inimitable backing of the *Chronicle* he was returned at the head of the poll (11,766: 10,404).[194] As soon as he recovered his strength, Cowen's outspoken criticism of the Government's Irish policy was causing further furore. His election victory finally liberated him of any lingering sense of obligation to the Newcastle Liberals and he withdrew from the Association the following September.

According to Shannon, who believes that the Bulgarian Atrocities kindled Gladstone's awareness of the plight of the Irish, 1876, not 1886, was the crucial year for the Liberal Party.[195] The radical destiny of the Liberal Party was, he argues, fatally subverted by Gladstone's triumphant return; by championing the Irish cause in preference to the 'standing interests of Liberal politics', Gladstone alienated Chamberlain and 'radicalism was wounded mortally'.[196] The issue was, though, rather more complex. Gladstone's newly discovered obsession with Irish reform was not as altruistic as it appeared for, as Michael Bentley points out, unifying the Whig and radical factions was a primary consideration, particularly in the light of the growing threat posed by the ascendant NLF.[197] And there was also the key issue of Irish votes which had been pledged to secure the election victory, on the unwritten understanding that Irish affairs would be dealt with sympathetically and generously. There can be no quarrel with Bentley's assessment that 'the Ministry began with Ireland, it became, at least publicly, obsessed with Ireland; it destroyed itself over Ireland'.[198] That being said, the tendency to put Gladstone into the driving seat over Home Rule assumes a sympathy with Irish affairs that was, in fact, noticeably lacking. Compared with Cowen he appears to have been an extremely reluctant crusader.

Gladstone's visit to Ireland in October 1877 has been frequently cited as evidence of his growing commitment to Irish reform but the underlying stimulus was essentially negative.[199] The unwelcome opposition of Irish nationalists to his Eastern policy ultimately forced Irish affairs onto his political agenda. Undoubtedly, as Shannon says, the Eastern Question 'helped him on to what was later done' but the attempt to gloss over Gladstone's disinclination to act positively, until events forced his hand, is far from convincing.[200] While Gladstone, it seems, shrank from the idea that there could be a close correlation between the plight of the Bulgarians and that of the Irish, Cowen had no such qualms.[201] In his usual forthright style, he addressed the Commons in February 1878 and argued that

> When we recall the ferocity – for no other word will express it – with which Ireland was, and with which Poland is ruled, we should manifest some moderation in our denunciation of the Turks. I repeat that Governments as venal, as tyrannical, as lawless and as lazy as our allies, and with our own record in Ireland in the past, and in India more recently, English politicians should not be so ready to rush into hysterics over Turkish delinquencies.[202]

Cowen's blunt criticism of Irish oppression reflected his long standing sympathy for the Irish people and this manifested itself in his close friendships with Irish Nationalists, his unprecedented coverage of Irish affairs in his newspapers and his determination to secure beneficial reforms. Whether Cowen was personally involved in Fenian activity would be difficult to prove; as with all his clandestine dealings, he covered his tracks very well. Cowen's vigorous campaign to secure the release of the Fenian prisoners is, in itself, revealing. The very manner in which he expressed himself would seem to betray the direction in which his sympathies lay. He made no attempt to condemn the Fenians when he addressed the Commons in August 1876, rather he accused the government of inconsistency. How was it possible, he enquired,

> to patronise and pension rebellious Russian soldiers and, at the same time, punish with such merciless severity a handful of Irish soldiers who had done exactly the same thing as their brother rebels from Poland? If the Home Secretary can explain the difference of it, it is more than I can do.[203]

The sheer determination of the Irish nationalists drew Cowen's admiration: 'United Irishmen, Young Irelanders and Fenians; Repealers, Home Rulers and Nationalists – what are they all but the collective intuition of the people under emotion.'[204]

Cowen visited Ireland on a number of occasions, most notably in 1876 when he was invited to sit on a Royal Commission on the state of British Agriculture.[205] It was this kind of first-hand knowledge that enabled Cowen to speak so authoritatively on Irish affairs.[206] Following his return from one such visit in August 1880, he urged other members to go and see for themselves the intolerable misery and suffering which, he claimed, lay at the root of Irish violent rebellion. He had, he said, 'witnessed in the West of Ireland scenes of wretchedness and squalor such as it would be difficult to match in any country in the North of Europe'.[207]

The Democratic Federation, of which Cowen was a founder member, aimed at its inception in June 1881 to oppose 'the monstrous tyranny of Mr Gladstone and his Whigs in Ireland'.[208] In collaboration with the Federation, Cowen organised a deputation of working men from Newcastle to visit the south and west of Ireland and 'report on the state of the peasantry'.[209] Land ownership was a key issue around which Irish nationalists and members of the Democratic Federation could rally.[210] For a short time, the two groups worked harmoniously together, holding joint meetings until, under Hyndman's direction, the Federation became more explicitly socialist.[211] Cowen was one of the first to quit the group. He was completely opposed to Hyndman's socialist agenda and had even less time for Communism, as these comments show:

> Society regulated in detail and petrified in form, as Communism would make it, would reduce man to a cypher, or to a machine. His free will, his personal merit, his never ceasing aspirations towards new modes of progress would disappear. It would be the serfdom of the Middle Ages without the hope of Manumission. All that the state can do, all that it is

desirable it should do, is to secure to everyone fair ground for equal effort and leave the rest to the individual, to his application and his aptitudes.[212]

The period of collaboration was not wasted and both Hyndman and Cowen were appointed as executives of the National Land League of Great Britain, alongside Parnell, Biggar, Barry, Healy and Justin McCarthy. Newcastle, which had proved so successful a host for the first convention of the Home Rule Federation in 1873, was chosen as the venue to launch the National Land League.[213] Addressing the massed crowds, Healy praised Cowen and told them that 'so long as one Englishman had not bowed the knee to Baal, there was still trust and confidence and hope in the Irish people for the people of England'.[214]

Cowen's relentless attacks on Gladstone's coercion policy throughout 1881 earned him the support of John Morley who had just taken over as editor of the *Pall Mall Gazette*. Morley poked fun at the 'alliterative jingle of his rhetoric' but predicted that the question would 'rehabilitate' his political reputation and secure his leadership of the progressive radicals.[215] In the event, the anti-coercion consensus that so distinguished north-east Liberals from their colleagues in Sheffield, and elsewhere, melted away by the end of January when the Bill was rushed through with a virtually unanimous mandate.[216] The *Northern Echo* insisted that the decision of the government should be upheld and Thomas Burt declined all invitations to attend public meetings on the subject.[217] Although Cowen found himself in 'a helpless, hopeless minority', he remained unrepentant, undaunted even by the flood of abusive and threatening mail which he received:

> I have deemed it to be my duty to differ from the leader of the Liberal Party on great questions of public policy, and a set of silly, weak minded persons have imagined that they could threaten me or coerce me into abandoning my convictions, or changing my course of action. Possibly by this time, they have discovered that that is not practicable...The government are too fond of coercion. They are coercing the Turk, coercing the Basulo, and now they want to coerce the Irish. They have coerced the constituencies by their Caucuses and coerced parliament by their cloture...The present Ministry, if they do not alter their course, will be known as 'The Ministry of Coercion'.[218]

Countless appeals by the Newcastle Liberals for a compromise position were all met by the same flat refusal from Cowen:

> I mean to oppose the Coercion Bill on every occasion, at every point, by all

the resources in my power. When all opportunity of defeating the principle of the Bill has gone, I will strive to delay its operation by every honourable, fair and legitimate process. When that resource is exhausted, I will assist in mitigating the harshness of its clauses and minimising the despotic powers that the Government are seeking to obtain.[219]

Nonetheless, Lord Roseberry insisted that 'the arguments of 50 Cowens' would not alter the government's course of action.[220]

In resisting Irish coercion, Cowen claimed to have done 'nothing more than sustain the honoured traditions of English radicalism'.[221] He railed against the Liberals who had proved to be nothing more than fair weather friends of the Irish people: 'I leave these honourable gentlemen to justify with their consciences and their constituents, these wholesale breaches of their solemnly recorded pledges.'[222] Convinced that the Government's failure to deal with the underlying cause of the Irish problem would produce difficulties that future generations would have to grapple with, Cowen warned that the Ministry were 'laying up for themselves such a store of popular odium on this subject, as some day will astonish them'.[223] As the *Pall Mall Gazette* commented, Cowen's speeches evoked 'wild applause from the Irish members, sympathetic bursts from the Conservatives and bitter interruptions from his own political associates'.[224] When the nationalists Michael Davitt and John Dillon were imprisoned, Cowen sprang to their defence, arguing that 'you cannot kill ideas by chains and prisons, and the attempt to annihilate them by pains and penalties will fail'.[225] It was obstruction tactics by the Parnellites, ably abetted by Cowen and a handful of radicals, which precipitated the enactment of the cloture. Cowen insisted upon his right to speak as 'one of that section of members that the rule was designed to put to silence', and asked pointedly: 'Whose opinions are to be the expression of public will? The political lotus-eaters who dose away their days in sleepy Pall Mall clubs, or the opinion of the militant democracy in the North of England?'[226] P. A. Taylor, the member for Leicester, gave strong backing to Cowen, stating that 'nothing could have made me vote for the cloture – not if every voter in Leicester wished it'. His critics, he said, were not ordinary working men who were more likely to 'to stand by their principles'.[227]

The Newcastle Liberal Association, roundly condemning the 'relentless, merciless, pitiless savagery' of Cowen's press campaign against Gladstone, sent a formal declaration of support to the Premier, applauding both his coercion policy and the adoption of the cloture.[228] By 1881, divisions in the Liberal ranks had spawned an Anti-Cowen Association, grimly determined to oppose his return at the next General Election'.[229] When Ashton Dilke was forced to retire through ill-health in 1883, John Morley (whom Cowen had recommended as a possible candidate some years earlier) was invited by Spence Watson 'in some haste and secrecy' to contest the seat.[230] Cowen foolishly underestimated Morley and refused to support him, assuming that this would undermine his chances of election. He also fatally misjudged Spence Watson's commanding influence in the region. It is a measure of how out of touch Cowen had become that, when Morley won his seat with a comfortable majority, he was so completely taken aback. He could hardly understand how 'a stranger to Newcastle would ever be elected in that way'.[231] As for Morley, who was already a close confident of Gladstone, Chamberlain and Mundella, he became a great favourite with the Newcastle Liberals.

Morley's election marked a key transition in radical politics on Tyneside. The Newcastle Liberals were confident that Morley's brand of Gladstonian Liberalism would win over the Tyneside electorate and effectively detach Cowen from his previously impregnable power base. Two years later, they finally achieved their objective when Cowen resigned his seat. However, his withdrawal from political office was not nearly as easy as they expected, nor were Morley's machinations the only determining factor.

Chapter 6
Tyneside politics at the fin de siècle:
Irish identity, cultural nationalism and the new radicalism,
1884-1900

The 1880s were a testing time for the Liberal party as it struggled to cope with insurrection in Ireland and the equally troublesome overseas territories, especially in Africa and Egypt. These pressures were exacerbated by internal tensions, too, as the Whig and Radical factions each jockeyed to shift the balance of power in their favour.[1] The animosities which forced a political realignment at Westminster in the wake of the Home Rule crisis had their own reverberations out in the constituencies, particularly those with large Irish populations. In the long term Cowen's departure from the political scene in 1886 served to weaken rather than strengthen the Liberals' powerbase on Tyneside. A new radical demagogue with his own paper pulpit, Charles Diamond, emerged to preach the doctrine of independence not alliance, and harnessed Irish energies to the nationalist cause. With labour representation still in its infancy in the closing decades of the nineteenth century, it was the Conservatives who gained most from the fault lines in the Liberal ranks.[2]

In the mid-1870s Cowen had seemed eager to forge friendships with his fellow radicals on the Liberal benches. He had been only too pleased to introduce Joseph Chamberlain to the House in 1876 but they soon fell out over the Eastern Crisis and the caucus.[3] His relationship with John Morley fared no better. While their relationship was not close, for a time it was certainly amicable and cooperative. Cowen had so much regard for Morley's talents in 1877 that he saw fit to recommend him to the Newcastle Liberals as a possible second candidate. By 1883, however, they were barely on speaking terms. To a certain extent, conflict between these two highly ambitious men was bound to arise given that Cowen had been a thorn in Gladstone's side ever since their clash over the Royal Titles Bill. Morley was, if nothing else, in awe of Gladstone and repeatedly courted his patronage. Nevertheless, it is almost certain that some of this rancour stemmed from a series of highly critical articles which Morley published in early January 1883 in the *Pall Mall Gazette*. A full page article entitled 'A Wasted Force in Politics' described Cowen as 'impotent…a source of lamentable division inside his own constituency without influence or following'. It proceeded to argue that

Cowen had 'contributed nothing beyond one or two set pieces of sterile decla-
mation' and took him to task for quarrelling with Gladstone's foreign policy on
Egypt while having no workable strategy of his own:

> Neither individual, nor group will be of any service or command any re-
> spect in the country, so long as they reserve all of their sarcasms for their
> friends, and all of their compliments for their enemies, so long as their just
> censure of what is wrong is never varied by just praise for what is good and
> right, and so long as they show themselves unable to impress their mark
> on a single piece of policy, or any one of their strangest views on the mind
> of the nation.[4]

The timing of the piece suggests that it was deliberately calculated to undermine
Cowen's position in the critical weeks leading up to Morley's selection. The fol-
lowing day's edition carried extracts from other newspapers which lambasted
Cowen's 'evil communications'[5] on Egypt and sarcastically portrayed him as a
'politician of caprices...a Tory in Scotland and England, an irreconcilable in
Ireland, a non-interventionist abroad.... Mr C, in short, is nothing, if not anti-
Liberal.'[6]

At a meeting of the Liberal Five Hundred in Northumberland Hall in February
1883 Morley politely expressed his admiration and respect for Cowen's many
talents before proceeding to highlight the 'fundamental difference' between
them: *he* was a supporter of the government whereas Cowen was not.[7] Having
spent the weekend with Chamberlain at Highbury, Morley was well-briefed in
how to endear himself to his prospective new constituency.[8] His commitment
to support the Liberal Party, even if its policies fell short of his own agenda for
reform, was exactly what Robert Spence Watson and his friends wanted to hear.
With Morley in place they would finally be able to connect themselves to the
Gladstonian inner circle. The Cowen camp judged this to be a pledge to uphold
the caucus at any price and made great capital of it. They attempted to field
their own candidate, Isaac Lowthian Bell, but he pleaded ill health and old age
and would not stand. A working-class candidate, Elijah Copland, was chosen
instead but the Newcastle Liberal Association took great exception to Cowen's
interference in the selection process. Spence Watson claimed that Copland
'would be a traitor in the Liberal camp' and insisted that Morley would defeat
the Tory and 'the sham working man's candidate'.[9] Cowen's decision to support
Copland aroused considerable ill-feeling and it is nothing less than extraordinary that, on this occasion, Thomas Burt did not object to Spence Watson's
bad tempered outburst. Burt was already held in poor odour in some quarters
because of his support for Irish coercion and some of his constituents were

concerned that he was far too deferential to the Liberal hierarchy, especially Gladstone.[10] Contrasting Burt's 'sheeplike' behaviour with Cowen's energetic support, Copland's backers concluded that he was 'one of the best Radicals in England'.[11]

It has been claimed that Cowen's actions were part of a careful strategy to dismantle the caucus and that Copland was pressed forward 'in quite a sectarian spirit', the suggestion being that this was a shameful act.[12] Dismantling the caucus was, indeed, precisely what Cowen set out to achieve but he was not remotely apologetic or embarrassed about it. In his opinion, the caucus was not just anti-democratic but unpatriotic. Many of his campaign speeches were couched in the old 'oppositional vocabulary of patriotism',[13] and the Newcastle caucus were repeatedly accused of corruption – of 'representing their own interests'.[14] Men who paid taxes, defended their country and created the wealth, Cowen later reasoned, 'ought to be more than mere spectators in the legislative drama'.[15] Ultimately, Cowen's willingness to back Copland in opposition to the official Liberal candidate exposed the deep fragility of the Radical/Liberal alliance on Tyneside. Morley's candidature was formally approved by Thomas Burt, Samuel Storey, J. C. Laird and J. W Pease at a mass meeting in the Circus and a contest soon followed.[16] When Copland's defeat seemed inevitable, despite the vigorous backing of the Cowen press, the Irish made good their threat to support the Tory candidate, Gainsford Bruce, who also picked up the Catholic and the Jewish vote.[17]

The deep divisions between the two Newcastle Liberal members overshadowed the final years of Cowen's parliamentary career. At Westminster, Morley sought the company of old friends like Chamberlain and Mundella, to whom he complained of the 'constant struggle' of dealing with Cowen and his friends.[18] As for Cowen and Morley, their public courtesies fooled no-one; their friendly overtures lacked sincerity and Morley confided to Spence Watson that he would 'smash, pulverise and destroy him when the time comes'.[19] Cowen's supporters, who had previously accused Ashton Dilke of being Spence Watson's 'puppet' were no more enamoured of Morley, whose attitude to Irish reform had been a source of contention in 1881 and who they deeply distrusted.[20]

Not even for a second did Cowen contemplate working with Morley to secure Irish reform, though they would have made a formidable team. Together they could have courted parliamentary power and the Irish vote to considerable effect. Typically, Cowen blamed others rather than himself for his diminished status. As Cowen's vision of establishing a militant democracy failed to materialise, he began to distance himself from those organisations which, he believed, had betrayed the radical principles he had fought so hard to inculcate. As early as 1879, he conceded that his enthusiasm for politics had begun to dissipate:

I have lost, it is true, much of my old political fervour…A good deal of the poetic enthusiasm that once characterized the aspirations of the English workman has been dampened. There is now not a single Utopia which inspires his confidence or enlists his sympathies…The English workman is pre-eminently practical, somewhat materialistic, and I fear I must add a little conservative…he is to a large extent indifferent to anything that is not obvious and immediate, that is not pressing and present.[21]

Local trade unionism, he believed, had let him down by succumbing to the blandishments of the Liberal Association executive. When the Northumberland and Durham miners supported Morley and the Liberals he found himself in direct confrontation with the very group who had had been his most loyal followers.[22] In 1883, too, he declared that he was 'completely out of the temperance agitation' and that he had 'never had a good opinion of the teetotal people'; although he supported their aspirations, he 'distrusted many of their methods'.[23]

The failings of the north-east Co-operative movement were singled out for particularly harsh criticism. Conflict amongst the Blaydon members in 1868, which had resulted in the formation of a rival store (Blaydon Working Men's Co-operative Society), had proved galling to Cowen who regarded his local store as the flagship of north-east co-operation. The management had been accused of laxity when fixed stock had to be depreciated at 5 per cent; in the ensuing row several members withdrew. With a mere 194 members in 1872, it never seriously undermined the original store which had a membership of 1,874 and assets of £16,221, but it remained a source of singular embarrassment to Cowen.[24] In the 1870s the *Newcastle Weekly Chronicle* had been highly critical of the poor working conditions of co-operative employees, whose 'hands and feet have been almost worn to the bone – and this at a time when stores were reputedly enjoying a 'roaring and profitable trade'. The dividend, it was suggested, should be extended to those who had secured the profits and wages brought in line with those of other trade unionists.[25] These attempts to pressurize aberrant co-operative societies to keep faith with the Rochdale ideal had only limited success. In a speech to the North of England Travellers Association in 1884, Cowen deplored the failings of many co-operators who knew nothing of their founder and were 'as ignorant of its system of rational society as they are of Buddhism'.[26] Despite Cowen's efforts to educate the movement into a more progressive view of what co-operation should be, the deep-rooted insularity of some societies prevailed and it was the vexed question of inequitable working practices which finally led him to sever his connection with the Movement in 1891:

of all the meannesses in God's creation…the modern co-operator is the worst living embodiment. 'I know of things', continued Mr C, 'done and being done in the North here, of dishonest dealings, of underpaying, of sweating the life's blood out of the unemployed, of a wanting of the littlest of the doctrines of honest commercialism, that makes one despair of the success of great schemes over the baseness of human schemes.[27]

In 1870 Cowen had given firm support to Bright's Bill to extend the franchise to women and he had been invited to join the committee of the National Society for Women's Suffrage.[28] When the issue was revived during the Third Reform Act campaign in 1884, Cowen willingly spoke in favour of Woodall's amendment,[29] despite the prevailing opposition which scared off scores of other radicals such as John Morley.[30] For Cowen, the issue was perfectly simple:

Justice and logic, precedence and experience, are in favour of her inclusion in the roll of citizenship. What is against it? Two potent forces – prejudice and pride. The prejudice engendered by organised selfishness of human nature, and the pride induced by ages of predominance. Nothing more. Woman, it is said, is inferior intellectually to man. What then? Do not the humblest and the feeblest, as well as the most gifted, enjoy the same civil rights?. If women wish to be politicians, let us remove all legal impediments.[31]

At his selection, Morley had promised Spence Watson that he would support women's suffrage but, once elected, he soon calculated that it would not win him any plaudits from those who mattered. He was later obliged to admit to Spence Watson that he would no longer lend his support.[32]

The singular consistency of Cowen's radical beliefs, which led him to pursue his own agenda at the expense of a successful political career, was the defining feature of his life. His commitment to the cause of Irish nationalism earned him an almost unrivalled reputation as the champion of liberty and yet this is uniquely at odds with his later pronouncements on British superiority, especially the right to defend the Empire at any cost and by force if necessary.[33] Cowen's imperialism was extremely complex: even though he became a fierce defender of the Empire, he remained deeply opposed to 'aimless extension or factious meddling in the affairs of other nations'.[34] In any case, his turn to imperialism was by no means rare in Liberal circles in the last quarter of the nineteenth century.[35] He was fundamentally at odds with Gladstonian 'Little Englanders' such as Morley and H. J. Wilson but, interestingly enough, not Chamberlain. Like so many of his contemporaries, Chamberlain's views of Empire changed markedly in the later decades of the nineteenth century.[36] Whereas in 1878 he had portrayed himself as a 'red-hot Little England Radical',[37] when association with the peace lobby was judged to be politically advantageous, he welcomed the purchase of the Suez shares shortly afterwards as 'a clever thing'.[38] The Liberal Party became deeply divided over the issue and the radical movement as a whole failed to develop a convincing anti-imperialist critique.[39] As the editor of the *Tyneside Echo* noted in 1885, the Peace party had been 'noisy enough when in opposition but since the Liberals followed the same course they have piped as softly as any bullfinch'.[40] Cowen was one of the few 'freelancers' prepared to join a vote of censure against the Liberal's Egyptian policy in 1884.[41] Essentially, Cowen's imperialism has to be viewed against a backdrop of confused attitudes and responses. For example, prominent socialists, including Henry Hyndman and Robert Blatchford, opposed expansion earnestly enough and yet were still committed to the defence of existing territory.[42]

Cowen's imperialist views did not endear him to the Newcastle Liberals and even his Irish friends were disturbed by the aggressive tone of his later speeches.[43] There are several pathways through this apparent confusion in his later politics. In the first instance, Cowen's conversion to imperialism can be located in the prevailing climate of rising nationalism. Cowen was an avid reader who had always been deeply influenced by the currency of nineteenth century ideas and philosophies. His later speeches and writings reflect a belief in the civilizing effects of British rule. Equally, the commercial advantages of an imperialist foreign policy must be regarded as a compelling factor. Cowen was an extremely shrewd businessman who never allowed sentiment to colour his financial judgement, as this statement to the electorate in 1885 reveals:

> Our imperial supremacy has secured us mercantile supremacy. If one leaves us the other will follow; and if our trade is destroyed the whole fabric of our prosperity will go by the run...We have the Empire, we must hold it, and to do so we must be prepared to defend its interests in Council and fight for them in the field or in the ocean.[44]

The Bulgarian Atrocities agitation is commonly regarded as the 'baptism of fire of Liberal imperialism' and inevitably Cowen attracted the hostility of his opponents who disliked the 'imperialist' tone of his speeches.[45] Addressing the Commons in February 1878, Cowen reminded members of a time 'When none was for party, and all were for State', insisting that, 'patriotism and good sense' required them to put aside party considerations at times of national crisis and 'remember only that we are Englishmen, and present a united front to the world'.[46] While Cowen had no qualms about supporting the foreign policy of the opposition, and was more than prepared to risk damaging his political career in the process, his opinion of Conservatism remained fundamentally unchanged: 'A Tory', he said, 'was the embodiment of all that was objectionable in a citizen'.[47] Holyoake once suggested that if Cowen transferred his allegiance to the Conservatives he might thereby achieve high office:

> Disraeli is dead. Do you not see that you may take his place if you will? It is open. His party has no successor among them. He had race, religion and want of fortune against him. You have neither of these against you. You are rich, and you can speak as Disraeli never could – He had neither the tone nor the fire of conscience. You have the ear of the House and the personal confidence of the country, as he never had. In his place you would fill the ear of the world.[48]

His proposal was not as fanciful as it appears. When the Conservatives circulated Cowen's speech on foreign policy during the 1880 election it was hardly surprising that his enemies assumed that a switch of allegiance was a mere formality.[49] Cowen, however, was quick to disabuse them. As he told Holyoake, 'There is one difficulty, I am not a Tory.'[50]

The row over Egypt and the Sudan, the threatened crisis over the Budget, and the ongoing saga of Irish rebellion bedevilled Gladstone's Second Ministry. It is only remarkable that unity was preserved for a full term of office and some have credited Gladstone with holding the party together during such a testing period.[51] Yet even those who would cast the 'Grand Old Man' in this role admit that Liberal unity was extremely 'precarious'.[52] Jenkins sees things rather differently, viewing the perennial uncertainty over Gladstone's retirement as profoundly 'destabilising'.[53] His return to politics in 1880 had been mooted as only a temporary expedient and, on some level, Gladstone's sudden volte-face in 1886 on the question of Home Rule was a strategy designed to justify his decision to stay in office as leader.[54] In the circumstances, he was bound to discover yet 'another speciality which only he had the political expertise to deal with'.[55] Viewed as a leadership issue, the adoption of Home Rule makes a good deal of sense and this need not preclude arguments by D. G. Boyce and others which stress the sea change in Gladstone's thinking, or the pressing need to unify Whig and Radical factions.[56] What it does offer is a more plausible pecking order of the motivating factors.

The greatest obstacle to reconciling Cowen's subsequent imperialism is thought to be his high profile commitment to the cause of Home Rule. His unflagging efforts on behalf of the Irish nationalists do seem strangely contradictory when juxtaposed with his later determination to retain the Empire at all costs. A number of explanations suggest themselves here. Firstly, at the time when he was most actively pressing for Irish constitutional reform, in the early 1880s, he was also an outspoken opponent of the Liberals' foreign policy and consistently voted against the annexations in Egypt and the Sudan.[57] He considered the accretion of more territory to be extremely unwise and greatly regretted that there were not enough independent Liberals to deter the majority 'who follow the government blindly and without question'.[58] Even in 1885 when his views had hardened considerably, he still denounced the 'scramble for material prosperity', arguing that 'the most dexterous special pleader, or the most belated panegyrist cannot reconcile this catalogue of annexations, occupations and protectorates with the ascetic programme promulgated by the Government four years ago'.[59]

It is important, too, to understand exactly what Cowen was advocating when he championed Irish demands for Home Rule. He never, at any time, supported Irish independence. Even in 1874, when Irish votes were crucial to his election and he might have been tempted to prevaricate, his opposition to it is explicitly stated. While the principle of Home Rule had his wholehearted approval, he stated that he 'was not in favour of dismemberment' of the British Empire and questioned whether even the supporters of Home Rule would go so far.[60] The introduction of Irish Home Rule, he repeatedly maintained, would deliver 'improved union, not separation'.[61] When the Home Rule Bill was finally debated in the Commons in 1886, Cowen still reiterated his conviction that the unity of the Empire was not at issue. The Bill, he claimed, was a 'decentralising not a disuniting' measure.[62] In this light, the seeming contradiction between conceding Home Rule to the Irish and advocating an imperialist policy is not nearly as incongruous as it might first appear.

With Home Rule as a campaigning cause for the 1885 election, Cowen's political future should have been secure and, in a sense, it was, in so far as the available Irish votes were pledged to him on Parnell's directive. His position in Newcastle was, however, rapidly becoming untenable. Cowen had relinquished his place in the Liberal fold without even attempting to retain a modicum of influence. While he still had many friends within Liberal circles, they were not powerful enough to counter the formidable opposition that was being mounted against him. Cowen's determination to help working men into political office had not diminished. As he had previously explained to the electors in December 1883, he looked to working men to 'lift politics out of the idealess level of hucksters and drill sergeants'.[63] Once again he aligned himself with the labour representation lobby, this time backing Lloyd Jones against a local coal owner, James Joycey, for the Chester-le-Street seat.

As it transpired, the Durham Miners' Association had already brokered an electoral pact with the Liberals and they refused to back down, even though they were well aware that Joycey's reputation as a ruthless capitalist would make him an unlikely candidate for the working-class vote. Cowen's unwelcome intervention caused a serious rift with the miners. Once again, Cowen's motives are perceived to be somewhat mixed. Aside from his desire to thwart the Newcastle Liberals, Cowen is thought to have been prompted to exert some revenge for Joycey's financial support of a rival 'Liberal' newspaper, the *Newcastle Leader*.[64] Cowen readily acknowledged that the 'Liberal Association people' would plump for Morley and yet he stubbornly refused to canvass for support. Dogged with ill-health, and obviously weary, he told the listening crowds that if he lost he would not complain, arguing that 'he either fears his fate too much, or his desert too small, who dares not put it to the test, to win or lose it all'.[65] The campaign for labour representation made some gains and, aside from Burt, Charles Fenwick, William Crawford and John Wilson were all elected. While this was cause for great celebration at the time, in the longer term the success of labour candidates in 1885 served to strengthen the Lib-Lab pact and, ultimately, this acted as a brake on the challenge to Liberalism.[66]

Britain's dependent territories focused heavily in the speeches Cowen delivered during the 1885 election campaign. 'Nationality', he maintained, 'is the soul which animates and exalts the whole brotherhood of associated men... and is the link of life between England and her colonies'.[67] He shared Thomas Brassey's dream of a federation which hinged upon the expectation that, at times of national crisis, the imperial colonies would provide Britain with an insuperable fighting force. This same speech reveals, beyond all doubt, the extent to which he had absorbed Darwinian ideas:

> No inferior race ever displaced a superior one, except when the superior
> one had first become demoralised. Inferior races have swept over the lands
> as scavengers – clearing the way for better tenants. They have never held
> what they won. The ultimate victory has always been for the fittest and it
> will be so with England.[68]

Even though he had been a fierce opponent of the Liberal's policy on Egypt in 1884, he contended that 'semi-civilized' people would always be defeated in a conflict with a superior power:

> The marvel is that men versed in affairs should have ever dreamed, when
> once we went there, overthrew the government and destroyed its defences
> that we could leave as easily as a crowd leaves a public meeting...From the

character of the two races, retention and advance on our part are inevitable. It is our destiny and theirs. We can no more escape from it than a man can escape from his shadow. Civilization marches at the rear of conquest. This experience is as universal and unvarying as cause and effect.[69]

He believed that Britain had a duty and a responsibility to 'turn its freedom to noble uses' by civilizing 'unoffending savages'.[70] This belief in a civilizing mission was widely shared, especially among religious groups such as Quakers who linked the question to their long-standing campaign against slavery.[71] Robert Spence Watson, for instance, appears to have had little difficulty in reconciling his commitment to the cause of peace with a belief in an 'imperial ideal'.[72] In a letter to his daughter, he claimed that a mission to Africa would confer mutual benefits on both countries: 'What is right is best, and what is good and pleasant for ourselves is good and pleasant for others…the missionaries are going first to prepare the way and then our merchants will soon follow…this will put down the slave trade.'[73] W. E. Adams was among those who had consistently spoken out against the expansion of British territory and yet he later came to view African imperialism in a less negative light. The anti-slavery argument persuaded him that in British hands the Empire could be a force for good in the world and, in 1896, was utilized as an equally powerful justification for his strident opposition to the Boers who were 'born slave-holders'.[74]

Biagini has dismissed Cowen's 1885 election campaign as 'the futile last battle of a romantic supporter of the old, 'direct' style of popular politics', and contends that he was out of step with 'the real needs of the working classes'.[75] Yet, it was a successful last battle: Cowen still topped the poll (10,489: 10,129), albeit with Tory votes and the narrowest of margins. At the start of the campaign Morley had exuded a certain confidence and bragged of his success in cultivating the support of the men at Armstrong's engineering works by helping to avert a strike. There were, of course, other sectional interests to consider and, unhappily for Morley, he conspicuously failed to win over Irish voters on Tyneside, who mostly judged him to be insincere.[76] In late November, the Liberals were beginning to feel the pressure and Elizabeth Spence Watson confided to her daughter Mabel that she feared the election would go badly.[77] Cowen was one of only a handful of candidates excluded from Parnell's plan to use Irish votes against the Liberals and so exert pressure for Irish reforms.[78] Bernard McAnulty's eve-of-contest endorsement for Cowen effectively ensured that the Irish would give him all of their plumpers.[79] Morley was ill-prepared for what followed. He did not enjoy being hustled by the boisterous 15,000-strong crowd or the threat of losing his seat. In the immediate aftermath he vowed 'never again to contest an election'.[80] As for Cowen, who had refused to canvass and had managed his own campaign through the pages of the *Chronicle*, he sought to present his victory as a powerful testimonial against the caucus. He was, nonetheless, forced to confront the unpalatable fact that Tory votes had helped to secure his victory; he made up his mind to retire from political life. Thanking his supporters for their 'unsolicited approval', he asserted that he had not been

> stung into political life by penury and I don't remain in it for gain…the meanness, the implacability, the vindictiveness and the personal rancour of our local politicians have become unbearable and I have therefore resolved, notwithstanding the result of this election, not again to contest the city.[81]

The breach with the miners, officially marked by his resignation as a Trustee of the DMA,[82] coupled with his dependence upon Tory votes to win the 1885 election, convinced Cowen that his political career was over. The radicalism he had espoused for so long and which 'once was a voice', was 'now only an echo'.[83] Cowen's supporters urged him to reconsider, claiming with some justification that Morley had taken unfair advantage of his decision not to canvass. His agents were accused of having 'urged voters to plump for him as you would be receiving part Conservative and the whole of the Irish vote, and your election would be safe'.[84] Slater's Private Detection Agency wrote to Cowen, offering to investigate known cases of corruption but he refused to pursue it.[85]

Nationally, the election result was a great disappointment to the Liberals, who failed to take a large number of English boroughs and were returned with a considerably diminished majority. The Irish nationalists were the real victors, securing eighty-six seats, which left them holding the balance of power and Gladstone with the problem of how to respond.[86] According to Peter Marsh what happened next was a 'tale of rival captains and bemused followers fighting in a fog'.[87] Gladstone's careful 'soundings' of Dublin opinion had been ongoing for some time as he struggled to find a solution to the growing unrest in Ireland.[88] During the 1885 Christmas holidays he had commissioned Mundella to travel 'privately' to Dublin on his behalf before reporting back to Hawarden.[89] In the event, Gladstone's abandonment of local government reform in favour of a Home Rule Bill took many in his party by surprise, and Chamberlain's defection to form the Liberal Unionist Party spearheaded a complete realignment of Liberal politics.[90] It was not just the parliamentarians who struggled to accept this new agenda; at constituency level the party faithful were forced to reconsider their position. After testing deliberations, in April 1886 the Newcastle Liberal Association voted overwhelmingly in favour of Home Rule[91] – a policy which Cowen had long advocated, and they had so persistently opposed. Timing, which had been so much in his favour at the start of his career, deserted Cowen at the end:

> He has, in fact, in a large degree, educated the people of Newcastle on the question. And now, after he had prepared the ground and sowed the seed, Mr. John Morley (Irish Secretary) steps in and reaps the harvest. This is lucky, to say the least of it, for Mr. Morley. Had Mr. Cowen felt inclined, had he flattered Ministers, had he generally voted with his party, had he exercised less independence and shown less acrimony, he might have been Chief Secretary for Ireland, with a seat in the Cabinet.[92]

Cowen's retirement from political life not only marked the end of his political career but also the breakdown of the old alliance between Irish nationalists and Tyneside radicals. In seeking to explain the political conservatism of the interregnum between the 'militant democracy' of the Cowen era and the precocious socialism of the turn of the century, historians have mostly cited generational factors and the strength of the Lib-Lab pact.[93] The suggestion here is that the newfound independence of the Irish vote on Tyneside after 1886 should be a key element in that explanation. Following Cowen's retirement, the Irish sought leadership and political direction from the ardent nationalist and press entrepreneur Charles Diamond who had, even then, already staked his claim upon the loyalties of the Tyneside Irish.

Charles Diamond was born into a large Irish Catholic family in Maghera, Co Derry, in 1858.[94] His father was one of thousands of rack-rented farmers who were evicted in the 1870s and eventually driven out of Ireland by the hostility and abuse of the Orange Order. The family were devout Catholics and sufficiently wealthy to provide a good education for their six children 'alongside some of the finest intellects of the day'.[95] When Diamond arrived in Newcastle upon Tyne in 1878 he initially found work as a spirit traveller and paper merchant[96] and, by 1880, he was owner of a highly lucrative paper manufactory and stationers. He produced paper bags for grocers and drapers, confectioners and fruiterers – even hat-boxes for Newcastle's milliners. Printing and publishing was a natural extension to this paper empire, and by 1884 he was publishing almanacs and printing a range of quality stationery.[97]

Diamond was an extremely ambitious man. Publishing a newspaper was the obvious next step, after all he had the paper and the printing expertise, but making his fortune was not the primary motivation. By 1884, Diamond had established his political credentials, not least in his role as Secretary to the Newcastle branch of the Irish National Land League (INLL) and later as branch President. When the National Land League of Great Britain decided to hold their first convention in Newcastle at the end of August 1881 Diamond wrote to Cowen's parliamentary office, and invited him to attend a major public demonstration in Newcastle Town Hall which was to be hosted by the Newcastle branch.[98] Cowen was only too happy to oblige. The INLL meeting in Newcastle proved auspicious and Cowen was subsequently elected to serve on the INLL executive. This was a singular honour given that the League was then dominated by a 'Dublin and London clique'.[99] The occasion also marked the beginning of a strong friendship between Diamond and Cowen. It is hardly surprising that when Diamond considered setting up a new Irish weekly journal he should turn to Cowen first of all for approval and then, when that was secured, for support and encouragement.[100]

A close scrutiny of the first edition of the *Irish Tribune* reveals a great deal about the negotiations between the two newspaper entrepreneurs. Launched on 13 December 1884 with an ornate masthead of entwined shamrock and Irish harp, the oversized gothic typeface proclaimed the arrival of the *Irish Tribune: An Irish Journal for England and Scotland*. This was a clever move because its claim upon a national rather than a provincial readership precluded any fears, real or imagined, that it might threaten the *Chronicle*'s circulation. The *Tribune*'s eight pages were cheap enough for even the poorest of Irish readers to afford and offered a lively mixture of commercial advertising, Irish home news, INLL branch news, 'Catholic intelligence', a survey of British parliamentary and American news, and stirring political editorial. Diamond's debut editorial was notably combative and upbeat. 'The times', he declared, 'are changed. . . the Irish race is a force, which in the future will influence largely the destiny of this land'.[101] Exuding confidence, Diamond's editorial dispatched any suggestion that the *Tribune* was to be a vehicle for alliance politics. The *Tribune* aimed to 'bind Irishmen, if possible, more closely together. . . Against Whig, Tory, Liberal, or Radical, we shall not fail to warn them always.' A long single column outlined the *Tribune*'s mission statement:

> [It was]...to become the organ of Irish national thought in this country,
> to represent and possess the confidence of all Irishmen – priest and lay-
> men, labourers and merchants, rich and poor – who on the broad national
> platform can meet and work together.

The Irish were directed to forget English politics and consider only 'what is best for Ireland?... Tory and Liberal are, so far as Ireland is concerned, synonymous titles for the factions who alternately rule England, and against one and another we shall always warn our people.' From the outset, the *Tribune* made it plain to its readers that Morley was not to be trusted; that he was the sort of man who would 'keep a promise to the ear, but break it to the hope'. [102]

In the second issue, too, Diamond distanced himself from the Democratic Federation, rejecting outright the notion that the Irish needed the support or advice of English democrats. Diamond was not at all impressed by Hyndman's sudden adoption of the Irish cause and he was probably concerned that a new socialist initiative would peel off the articulate, politically active Irish and undermine the Nationalists' plans. Diamond reminded his readers that America and Canada would still be dependent territories if they had not rebelled and, more pointedly, that the British government 'hold India with a selfish iron grasp, and without the least compunction wring the last rupee from the starving population'. In typically pugnacious style, Diamond asserted that only the 'combined irresistible force of a determined Irish peasantry' would deliver national independence. As for Hyndman and the newfound democrats, Diamond asserted, 'What they will not do for themselves, they are less likely to do for others.' [103]

The *Tribune*'s circulation rates went from strength to strength: at the end of the first quarter, the paper bragged of 20,000 weekly sales; at the end of the first year of trading Diamond was publishing a number of separate editions aimed at particular provincial readerships, including Newcastle, Glasgow, Liverpool, Manchester and London. [104] And, in keeping with its demonstrably Catholic Irish loyalties, a special edition was published for all four towns in the Nottingham diocese (Derby, Lincoln, and Leicester). By 1886, too, the paper had twelve pages of newsprint and sixty columns to fill. Diamond ensured that his readers were kept informed about the everyday activities of local Foresters' branches, Irish Literary Institutes, the meetings of the INL as well as educated in Catholic dogma and Irish history. The provision of Irish history is particularly significant. At a time when the teaching of history in Catholic schools was judged to be 'too controversial' for the Commissioners to agree upon an approved textbook, [105] a regular column dedicated to an heroic account of Irish history in the *Tribune* adds weight to the claim made here that, under Diamond's control, the *Tribune* became a primary vehicle for cultivating the independence of Irish nationalist politics.

Diamond was well on the way to creating a press empire by the time that Cowen abandoned political life. In April 1885, his reputation was such that he was asked to travel north to Glasgow and revive the struggling fortunes of the *Glasgow Observer*. [106] He used the *Observer* to secure Catholic representation on School Boards and three candidates were successfully elected at the end of April 1885. [107] Other newspaper ventures followed, including the *Catholic Household, A Weekly Journal for every Catholic Home* (1887), and he could claim with some confidence that an advertisement in the *Tribune* 'could reach four million Irish and Catholic people in England and Scotland'.[108]

Much of Diamond's new journalism, it should be stressed, was modelled on Cowen's *Newcastle Weekly Chronicle* and like Adams, who launched his 'Children's Corner' in 1876 to further his environmentalist and good citizenship agenda,[109] Diamond was keen to recruit the 'rising generation' to the Irish cause. He introduced his own 'Boys and Girls' column presided over by a 'Guardian' and as it became required reading in all Catholic schools the membership of 'young friends' rapidly expanded.[110] Recruitment of the young: as readers, as Catholics and as Irish patriots was intended to ensure the newspapers' commercial viability and serve the cause of Ireland in the longer term. In this, Diamond could depend upon the powerful backing of the Catholic hierarchy who ensured that his newspapers were available in Catholic churches and schools.

Meanwhile, the hard political line continued to be as strong as ever, and if anything, the editorials grew more aggressive and confident. Diamond unequivocally denounced the subversive activities of the Irish loyalists, and questioned why the British authorities ignored their activities. Home Rule, he proclaimed, was 'inevitable, and these stupid, unteachable wretches are howling and vapouring, as powerless to stop its march as a rat to stop an elephant'.[111] In 1886, Diamond was blatantly using his newspaper as a campaigning vehicle for Parnell's parliamentary fund, raising money not just from British branches of the National League but in America too. The paper reported that a collection in Syracuse, New York State had raised $153,550 for the fund, and Diamond urged his readers on to greater fund raising efforts, suggesting that the forthcoming St Patrick's Day celebrations should be given over entirely to fund raising activities.[112] Unlike Morley, Cowen could depend upon Diamond's support and if he *had* chosen to fight another election, the pages of the Diamond press would have been an invaluable source of political propaganda.[113]

Cowen's departure left a political hiatus that threw the Irish back on their own resources and created a vacancy that the Liberals found difficult to fill. For more than a century, Newcastle upon Tyne had been the cornerstone of those industrial energies which had delivered so much that was progressive and new. As the old staple industries based on carboniferous capital came under threat from rising international competition, the uncertainty and doubt which characterised the final decade of the nineteenth century began to eat away at entrepreneurial confidence.[114] Arguably, Northern industrial towns felt the transition both earlier and more keenly than other urban areas; they registered the financial and social hegemony of London and mourned the slippage in their own prestige.[115] Jose Harris has observed that in the late Victorian period the 'fulcrum of economic life' no longer resided in the North, and the apparent political slough served to accentuate the general concern that all that was distinctive and progressive had been lost. As a new Tyneside journal, *The Citizen,* declared, Irish affairs dominated the political landscape: Newcastle was 'as apathetic and as mute as if its political soul were dead'.[116]

In 1887 Adams responded by launching a new journal, the *Monthly Chronicle of North Country Lore and Legend,* in a bid to 'to preserve the great wealth of history and tradition' and to reaffirm Northern provincial identity. It was lavishly illustrated and gathered together a 'rich legacy of legend and history, poetry and song, dialect and folklore'- some of which had appeared before in earlier editions of the *Newcastle Weekly Chronicle* but which Adams feared would not survive in newspaper form.[117] A radical to the last, Adams opened the second volume with a report of Jean Paul Marat's visit to Newcastle in the early 1770s. He hoped that the *Monthly* would help to recapture the great events of the past and memorialise the achievements of those who, like Cowen, had been 'Men of Mark'. By the time that the last issue was published Adams was satisfied that it had been available for the 'bookshelf of the cottager' or his richer neighbours.[118]

In his retirement Cowen continued to give generously to good causes and was much in demand as a public speaker. The punishing regime that he had set for himself throughout his life gave way, for a brief period, to the tranquillity of Stella Hall and its impressive estate.[119] Ill-health, including failing eyesight, forced him to decline most invitations, while even his own correspondence proved too much for him to manage without the assistance of William Longstaffe.[120] He relied heavily upon his two children, especially Jane, an author in her own right who had frequently acted as his amanuensis.[121] One of the last letters he wrote was to W. E. Adams and it is a token of the esteem in which he held his radical compatriot that it was written in his own hand.[122] 'Great work', said Cowen in his last speech on the Empire in 1897, 'requires great effort, and great effort is the essence of life'.[123] The Irish, it seems were prepared to make that effort and, for a time, what was left of radicalism passed into their hands. Diamond's political message was firmly anchored to the new cultural nationalism[124] and this bred not only confidence but power too. As for the Liberals, whose domination of Tyneside politics during the Cowen era had been little more than a chimera, they were a spent force.[125]

Cowen's death on 18 February 1900 did not pass by unremarked and even those who had quarrelled most with him in his lifetime were moved to acknowledge his contribution to political life.[126] His career had traversed some of the most turbulent decades of the nineteenth century and he had been involved at the highest level in all of the popular campaigns for democratic and social reform, not merely in his own country but in Europe and overseas. One of his biographers, E.R. Jones, suggested that his troublesome relationship with the

Liberal party had actually been instrumental in honing his acclaimed oratorical powers, that it forced him to spend hours writing and redrafting his speeches in a bid to ensure that his views were clearly articulated.[127] This is, perhaps, to put a positive spin on his querulous response to challenge from any quarter – he simply dug his heels in and sought to overcome opposition by a war of words, determined that his views would prevail. Many of the difficulties he encountered were of his own making: his vaulting self belief would admit of no wrong; his ambitious programme of reform made him impatient, irascible and, at times, arrogant in his dealings with others. From one vantage point his was a career marked by the echoes of what might have been, but his failure to achieve high office ought not to detract from what was accomplished by him and by those democrats who followed in his footsteps.

Notes

Introduction

1   Patrick O'Brien, 'Is political biography a good thing?', *Contemporary British History*, 10:4, 1996, p. 66.
2   Ibid. The same volume offers three responses by way of a counter argument. See, for example, John Derry, 'Political Biography: A Defence (2)', pp. 75-80.
3   E. R. Jones, *The Life and Speeches of Joseph Cowen*, London, 1885.
4   William Duncan, *The Life of Joseph Cowen*, London, 1904; Nigel Todd, *The Militant Democracy: Joseph Cowen and Victorian Radicalism*, Newcastle, 1990.
5   Antony Taylor, 'Post-Chartism: Metropolitan Perspectives on the Chartist Movement in Decline 1848-80', in Matthew Cragoe and Antony Taylor (eds.), *London politics 1760-1914*, Basingstoke 2005, pp. 75-97; Rohan McWilliams, 'Liberalism Lite?', *Victorian Studies*, 48:1, 2005, pp. 103-11.
6   Owen R. Ashton and Paul Pickering, *Friends of the People. Uneasy radicals in the age of the Chartists*, London, 2002, p. 2. A discussion of 'gentlemen leaders' is also ventilated in Dorothy Thompson, 'Who were the 'the People' in 1842?', in M. Chase and I. Dyck (eds.), *Living and Learning: essays in honour of J. F. C. Harrison*, Aldershot, 1996, pp. 118-132.
7   At his death, Cowen had assets of over £501,000. See probate, 29 May 1900, CGPLA Eng. & Wales (1900).
8   TWAS, Cowen Papers.
9   While the Cowen papers contain a good deal of press material, copies of the *Chronicle* newspapers are best accessed in Newcastle City Library, Local Studies Department which has one of the best newspaper libraries in England.
10   SUSC.
11   Greater London Record Office.
12   I am very grateful to Professor David Saunders for locating a microfilm copy of this collection at the International Institute of Social History in Amsterdam.
13   For example, see John Belchem, *Popular Radicalism in Nineteenth-Century Britain*, Basingstoke, 1996; Margot C. Finn, *Class and Nation in English Radical Politics, 1848-1874*, Cambridge, 1996; Miles Taylor, *The Decline of British Radicalism, 1847-60*, Oxford, 1995; E. F. Biagini and A. J. Reid (eds.), *Currents of Radicalism. Popular radicalism, organised labour and party politics in Britain, 1850-1914*, Cambridge, 1991.
14   For instance, see T. J. Nossiter, *Influence, Opinion and Political Idioms in Reformed*

England. *Case studies from the North East 1832-1874*, Brighton, 1975, p. 2 ; F. W. Hirst, *Early Life and Letters of John Morley*, 2 vols., London, 1927, II, p. 144.

15   Owen R. Ashton, *W. E. Adams, Chartist, Radical and Journalist, 1832-1906*, Whitley Bay, 1991 p. 108.

16   T. A. Jenkins, *Gladstone, Whiggery and the Liberal Party*, Basingstoke, 1994, p. 12; John Vincent, *The Formation of the British Liberal Party, 1857-1868*, Harmondsworth, 1976, pp. 17-18.

17   There are numerous instances where local issues and conditions determined the reactions of the electorate, for example the pro-Disraeli response to the Eastern Question at Greenwich; see also A. R. Ball, *British Political Parties: The emergence of a modern party system*, London, 1981, p. 27 who states that politics was community-based until the end of the nineteenth century.

18   M. A. Busteed, *Geography and Voting Behaviour*, London, 1975; Vincent, *Formation of the British Liberal Party*, p. 24ff.

19   Eugenio F. Biagini, *Liberty Retrenchment and Reform*, Cambridge, 1992, p. 4, and ch. 4 which deals at length with Gladstone's crucial contribution to the success of the Liberal party. See also Michael Bentley, *Politics Without Democracy 1815-1914*, London, 1996; Martin Pugh, *The Making of Modern British Politics 1867-1931*, London, 1982.

20   Eugenio F. Biagini, 'Popular Liberals, Gladstonian finance and the debate on taxation, 1860-1874', in Biagini and Reid (eds.), *Currents of Radicalism*. p. 157.

21   Joseph Cowen, *Speeches on Public Questions and Political Policy*, Newcastle upon Tyne, 1874, speech on 'Trade. Taxation. Republicanism', p. 86.

22   David Eastwood, *Government and Community in the English Provinces 1700-1870*, Basingstoke, 1997, p. 60.

23   Dawson was a founder member of the Society for the Friends of Italy and a close friend of Taylor and the radical engraver W. J. Linton. For details see F. B. Smith, *Radical Artisan: W. J. Linton, 1812-97*, Manchester, 1973, pp. 108-9; Ashton, *Adams*, pp. 32, 54; Asa Briggs, *Victorian Cities*, Middlesex, 1963, pp. 195-201.

24   Smith, *Radical Artisan*, p. 107. Sketchley is said to have been greatly impressed by Linton and seriously disillusioned by the internal wrangling among the Chartist leadership. On Taylor and Leicester politics, see Bill Lancaster, *Radicalism, Cooperation and Socialism: Leicester Working Class Politics, 1860-1906*, Leicester, 1987, pp. 76-9, 83.

25   TWAS, CP/A633, Subscription List, 1 January 1859. The list of possible subscribers included P. A. Taylor. Lancaster, *Radicalism, Cooperation and Socialism*, pp. 76-7 suggests that he was more interested in domestic reform, but it is quite possible that Biggs' financial support was kept quiet.

26   R. Jay, *Joseph Chamberlain. A Political Study*, Oxford, 1981, p. 20.

27   J. Allen and O. R. Ashton (eds.), *Papers for the People. A Study of the Chartist Press*, London, 2005; Mark Hampton, 'Liberalism, the press and the construction of the public sphere: theories of the press in Britain, 1830-1914', *Victorian Periodicals Review*, 37:1, 2004, pp. 72-92.

28   Hampton, 'Liberalism, the press and the construction of the public sphere', p. 78.

29   Ibid., p. 72. See also Hannah Barker, *Newspapers, Politics and English Society, 1695-1855*, Harlow, 2000, pp. 1-2.

30   Eastwood, *Government and Community in the English Provinces*, pp. 73-5.

31   Alan Lee, *The Origins of the Popular Press, 1855-1914*, London, 1976, p. 138. See also Vincent, *Formation of the British Liberal Party*, p. 65.

32   W. S. Fowler, *A Study in Radicalism and Dissent: The Life and Times of Henry Joseph Wilson 1833-1914*, Slough, 1961.

33   Ibid., p. 34.

34   SUSC, MP/LC, Mundella to Robert Leader, 18 January 1874. See also SUSC, MP, Goldwin-Smith to Mundella, November 1870 advocating closer links with the Sheffield radicals.

35   SUSC, WP, Mundella to Wilson, 6 October 1875; 8 October 1875.

36   Lee, *Origins of the Popular Press*, p. 141.

37   Jay, *Joseph Chamberlain*, p. 40.

38   Vincent, *Formation of the British Liberal Party*, p. 64; Lee, *Origins of the Popular Press*, p. 142.

39   Lancaster, *Radicalism, Cooperation and Socialism*, ch. 6.

40   Lowell Satre, *Thomas Burt, Miners' MP, 1837-1922*, Leicester, 1999.

41   Lancaster, *Radicalism, Cooperation and Socialism*, p. 81 notes that Leicester trade union leaders became 'part of the fixtures of local Liberalism'.

42   K. D. Brown, 'Nonconformity and trade unionism: the Sheffield outrages of 1866', in Biagini and Reid (eds.), *Currents of Radicalism*, p. 105.

43   Jonathan Spain, 'The Labour Law reforms in 1875', in Biagini and Reid (eds.), *Currents of Radicalism*, p. 126.

44   Ibid., p. 127.

45   See Alan O'Day, 'The Political Organisation of the Irish in Britain, 1867-1890', in Roger Swift and Sheridan Gilley (eds.), *The Irish in Britain, 1815-1939*, London, 1989, p. 190.

46   SUSC, MP/LC, Mundella to Leader, 26. February 1881. Mundella disputed T. P. O'Connor's claim that Irish votes had helped him to win the election in 1880.

47   O' Day, 'Political organisation of the Irish in Britain', p. 186.

48   SUSC, MP, Jesse Collings to Mundella, November 1869.

49   SUSC, WP, Mundella to Wilson, 14 January 1881.

50   SUSC, MP/LC, Mundella to Leader, 1 February 1881.

51   Roger Swift, 'Crime and the Irish in Nineteenth Century Britain', in Swift and Gilley (eds.), *The Irish in Britain 1815-1939*, pp. 171, 178.

52   Jay, *Joseph Chamberlain*, p. 22.

53   Graham D. Goodlad, 'Gladstone and his rivals: popular Liberal perceptions of the party leadership in the political crisis of 1885-1886', in Biagini and Reid (eds.), *Currents of Radicalism*, pp. 163-5.

54   Roland Quinault, 'Joseph Chamberlain: A reassessment', in T. R. Gourvish and A. O'Day (eds.), *Later Victorian Britain, 1867-1900*, Basingstoke, 1988, p. 81.

55 Goodlad, 'Gladstone and his rivals', p. 164.

56 Biagini and Reid (eds.), *Currents of Radicalism*.

57 Taylor, 'Post-Chartism', p. 75.

58 W. Purdue, 'The ILP in the North East of England', in David James, Tony Jowitt and Keith Laybourn (eds.), *The Centennial History of the Independent Labour Party*, Halifax, 1992, p. 17.

59 Joan Allen, "Keeping the Faith': The Catholic press and the preservation of Celtic identity in Britain in the late nineteenth century', in Pamela O'Neill (ed.), *Exile and Homecoming*, Sydney, 2004, pp. 78-91.

60 Todd, *Militant Democracy*, p. 162 notes that when the ILP launched the first issue of the *Northern Democrat* they acknowledged their indebtedness to Joseph Cowen.

Chapter 1

1 H. T. Dickinson, *Radical Politics in the North-East of England in the Later Eighteenth Century*, Durham, 1979; See also H. T. Dickinson, *Liberty and Property. Political Ideology in Eighteenth Century Britain*, London, 1977, especially Part 3; John Belchem, *Popular Radicalism in Nineteenth Century Britain*, Basingstoke, 1996, pp. 9-15.

2 John Vincent, *The Formation of the British Liberal Party, 1857-1868*, Harmondsworth, 1976, Introduction to the 1st edn., p. *xxix*.

3 Eugenio F. Biagini, 'Liberalism and direct democracy: John Stuart Mill and the model of ancient Athens', in Eugenio F. Biagini (ed.), *Citizenship and Community. Liberals, radicals and collective identities in the British Isles, 1865-1931*, Cambridge, 1996, p. 29.

4 Biagini, 'Liberalism and direct democracy', pp. 40-1 draws upon John Stuart Mill's 'On Civilization' to make the case that 'reciprocal censorship' was most perfectly realised in small villages and towns.

5 John Sykes, *Local Records; or Historical Register of Remarkable Events...*, 2 vols. Newcastle, 1866, Vol. II, p. 123 records the involvement of the Winlaton reform societies in a protest meeting in October 1819; *Newcastle Courant*, 16 October 1919; 'Early Reform Demonstrations', *Newcastle Daily Chronicle*, 20 January 1867. See also M. W. Flinn, *Men of Iron: The Crowleys in the early iron industry*, Edinburgh, 1962; Peter Cadogan, *Early Radical Newcastle*, Consett, 1975, pp. 30-3.

6 Joyce Ellis, 'The 'Black Indies'. The economic development of Newcastle, *c*. 1700-1840', in Robert Colls and Bill Lancaster (eds.), *Newcastle upon Tyne. A Modern History*, West Sussex, 2001, p. 24. See also, Keith Wrightson and David Levine, *The Making of an Industrial Society, Whickham 1560-1765*, Oxford, 1991.

7 John K. Walton, 'North', in D. M. Palliser, Peter Clark and Martin Daunton (eds.), *The Cambridge Urban History of Britain*, 3 vols. Cambridge, 2000-1, vol. II: Peter Clark (ed.), *1540-1840*, p. 122 ; Ellis, 'Black Indies', p. 2. D. J. Rowe's analysis tends to emphasise the limitations rather than the strengths of the north-east economy, and he notes that much of Newcastle's prosperity was gained at the expense of ad-

jacent towns such as Gateshead and Sunderland. See D. J. Rowe, 'The North East', in F. M. L. Thompson (ed.), *The Cambridge Social History of Britain 1750-1950*, 3 vols. pbk edn. Cambridge, 1990, vol. I: *Regions and Communities*, p. 417.

8   Most notably T. S. Ashton, *The Industrial Revolution, 1760-1830*, Oxford, 1996. See also John E. Archer, *Social Unrest and Popular Protest in England 1780-1840*, Cambridge, 2000, especially ch. 4; E. J. Hobsbawm, *Labouring Men*, London, 1968; E. P. Thompson, *The Making of the English Working Class*, new edn. London, 1980.

9   John Stevenson, *Popular Disturbances in England 1700-1832*, 2nd edn. Harlow, 1992, p. 153.

10   Stevenson, *Popular Disturbances in England*, pp. 157-8; Robert Colls, *The Pitmen of the Northern Coalfield: work, culture, and protest, 1790-1850*, Manchester, 1987.

11   David Ridley, 'Shoot the Damn Dogs: The 1734 Dispute at Newbottle Colliery, County Durham', *North East History*, vol. 37, 2006, pp. 88-105.

12   G. D. H. Cole and R. Postgate, *The Common People, 1746-1946*, London, 1938, pp. 21, 172 note that in 1746 Newcastle had a number of Friendly Societies, 'some of them embryonic forms of Trade Union', and that the Newcastle Shoemakers Society was established as early as 1719. See also P. M. Ashraf, *The Life and Times of Thomas Spence*, Gateshead, 1983, p. 34 which notes the 'awakening political consciousness' of Newcastle in 1774.

13   Matthew Cragoe and Anthony Taylor (eds.), *London Politics, 1760-1914*, Basingstoke 2005, pp. 2-4. Also, in the same volume, see Matthew McCormack, 'Metropolitan 'Radicalism' and electoral independence, 1760-1820', pp. 18-36.

14   Stevenson, *Popular Disturbances in England*, p. 86. See also, Richard Fynes, *The Miners of Northumberland and Durham*, Sunderland, 1873, pp. 10-11; Dickinson, *Radical Politics in the North-East of England*, p. 13.

15   Dickinson, *Radical Politics in the North-East of England*, p. 16

16   Ibid., pp. 4-5. For a discussion of print culture in the north east see Joan Hugman, 'Print and preach. The entrepreneurial spirit of Tyneside politics', in Colls and Lancaster (eds.), *Newcastle*, pp. 116-20.

17   Dickinson, *Radical Politics in the North-East of England*, p. 6.

18   C. J. Hunt, *The Book Trade in Northumberland and Durham to 1860*, Newcastle upon Tyne, 1975; J. C. Day and W. M. Watson, 'History of the Book Trade in the North', in Peter Isaac (ed.), *Six Centuries of the Book Trade in Britain*, Winchester, 1991; C. Clair, *A History of Printing in Britain*, London, 1965.

19   Jeff Smith, 'The making of a diocese 1851-1882', in Colls and Lancaster (eds.), *Newcastle*, pp. 96-9.

20   The Glassite community in Forster Street was an independent branch of a former Scottish Presbyterian church and they established their meeting house in Forster Street in 1766-7. See Ashraf, *Life and Times of Thomas Spence*, p. 11.

21   Cole and Postgate, *Common People*, p. 184. See also Trygve Tholfsen, *Working Class Radicalism in Mid-Victorian England*, London, 1976, p. 32ff; Dorothy Thompson, *The Chartists*, London, 1984, pp. 166, 243.

22 Ashraf's *Life and Times of Thomas Spence* provides helpful details on Spence's writings, but Malcolm Chase's study '*The People's Farm*': *English Radical Agrarianism, 1775-1840,* Oxford, 1988 has done most to raise Spence's profile. For Spence's later career, see David Worrall, *Radical Culture, Discourse, Resistance and Surveillance,* Detroit, 1992.

23 Chase, '*People's Farm*'.

24 Edward Royle, 'Chartism', in A. Digby and C. Feinstein (eds.), *New Directions in Economic and Social History,* London, 1989, p. 162ff; Thompson, *The Chartists,* London, 1984, p. 302.

25 Ashraf, *Life and Times of Thomas Spence,* p. 34.

26 Jeffrey Smith, 'James Murray (1732-1782): Radical and Dissenter', *North East History,* vol. 32, 1998, p. 56.

27 Among other matters, the Society debated the American question at the time of the war in 1775. See Dickinson, *Radical Politics in the North-East of England,* p. 9.

28 For a biographical sketch of Spence see T. M. Parsinnen, 'Thomas Spence', in J. O. Baylen and N. J. Gossman (eds.), *Biographical Dictionary of Modern British Radicals,* 5 vols. Brighton, 1984-8, II: *1830-1870,* 1984, p. 455.

29 Ashraf, *Life and Times of Thomas Spence,* p. 29.

30 Rachel Hammersley, 'Jean-Paul Marat's *The Chains of Slavery* in Britain and France, 1774-1833', *Historical Journal,* 48.3, 2005, p. 651. On Corresponding Societies, see Mark Philp, *The French Revolution and British Popular Politics,* Cambridge, 1991.

31 Ibid., p. 38.

32 Ashraf, *Life and Times of Thomas Spence,* p. 146.

33 Belchem, *Popular Radicalism in Nineteenth Century,* pp. 22-3.

34 Malcolm Chase, 'Paine, Spence and the Rights of Man', *Bulletin of the Society for the Study of Labour History,* vol. 52.3, p. 35.

35 Dickinson, *Radical Politics in the North-East of England,* p. 15.

36 TWAS, CP/ B248, Speech in Newcastle, 28 January 1882; TWAS, CP/B349, Speech, 1885; TWAS, CP/B415, Undated letter from Joseph Cowen to H. B. Thompson; *Northern Liberator,* 24 March 1838.

37 Ashraf, *Life and Times of Thomas Spence,* p. 127.

38 Flinn, *Men of Iron*; Norman McCord, *Northeast England. The region's development 1760-1960,* Bristol, 1979, pp. 47-8; Winlaton and District Local History Society [WDLHS], *A History of Blaydon,* Gateshead, 1975, pp. 28-49; Chris Evans, 'The Hawks Family of Gateshead and the Tyneside mode of metal production', *Bulletin of the North East Labour History Society,* 30, 1996, p. 22; T. J. Nossiter, *Influence, Opinion and Political idioms in Reformed England. Case studies from the North East 1832-1874,* Brighton, 1975, p. 13.

39 Flinn, *Men of Iron,* p. 250; WDLHS, *History of Blaydon,* p. 44.

40 Evan Rowland Jones, *The Life and Speeches of Joseph Cowen, MP,* London, 1885, pp. 8-9.

41 Flinn *Men of Iron,* pp. 227-9.

42 Ibid., pp. 222, 229.

156 JOSEPH COWEN AND POPULAR RADICALISM ON TYNESIDE

43 *Northern Tribune* was a republican journal published by Cowen in the mid-1850s. Volume I, 1854, p. 63 carried a lengthy account of the history and politics of Winlaton: 'class feeling is bitter and rife and there is little mutual confidence or respect between employer and employed'.

44 For a discussion of the politics of deference in the workplace see Patrick Joyce, *Work, Society and Politics: The culture of the factory in later Victorian England*, Brighton, 1980, especially ch. 4. See also John K. Walton, *Lancashire. A Social History, 1558-1939*, Manchester, 1987, pp. 132-3.

45 Jane Cowen's unpublished biography [hereafter JCM] of her father, Joseph Cowen Jnr. provides a history of the family and is held in TWAS, in the Cowen Papers [CP], E436. John Cowen and his wife, Mary Newbigin, had six children. Joseph Cowen Snr. was the eldest.

46 I am greatly indebted to the late Keith Harris for much of the family history and social background contained in this section and to Mrs M. Harris who generously provided access to his papers. Keith Harris unpublished Ms., ch. 1. See also WDLHS, *History of Blaydon*, p. 24.

47 Jones, *Life and Speeches of Joseph Cowen*, p. 13. To avoid confusion Joseph Cowen's father will be referred to hereafter as Sir Joseph even though his Knighthood was not actually conferred until 1871.

48 Harris Ms., p. 2; TWAS, CP/E436, JCM, p. 16.

49 Harris Ms., p. 4 notes that Sir Joseph Cowen left over £100,000, as well as extensive business interests and property when he died in 1873; see 'Obituary', *Sunderland Daily Echo*, 22 December 1873.

50 S. Middlebrook, *Newcastle upon Tyne. Its Growth and Achievement*, Newcastle, 1950, p. 180; Sykes, *Local Records*, Vol. II, p. 123.

51 TWAS, CP/E436, JCM, p. 14. See also Colls, *Pitmen of the Northern Coalfield*, p. 270.

52 *Newcastle Journal*, 15 May 1832; *Northern Tribune*, Vol. I, 1854, p. 376.

53 *Northern Liberator*, 29 December 1838. Report of a Chartist meeting at Sandhill, Newcastle. See also W. Hamish Fraser, *Dr John Taylor, Chartist Ayrshire Revolutionary*, Ayr, 2006.

54 *Northern Liberator*, 15 September 1838; 15 June 1839. See also Thomas Ainge Devyr, *The Odd Book of the Nineteenth Century*, New York, 1982, p. 180.

55 *Northern Tribune*, Vol. I, 1854, p. 63.

56 *Northern Liberator*, 15 June 1839.

57 *Northern Liberator*, 3 November 1838. See also Colls, *Pitmen of the Northern Coalfield*, p. 282, who notes that the Chartist, Robert Lowery, was presented with a Winlaton pike, 'a formidable weapon'.

58 Nigel Todd, *The Militant Democracy. Joseph Cowen and Victorian Radicalism*, Whitley Bay, 1991, p. 25.

59 TWAS, CP/E436, JCM, p. 3.

60 Ibid.

61 Harris Ms., ch.1, p. 6.

62   Colls, *Pitmen of the Northern Coalfield*, p. 70. For a more detailed account of the 1844 strike see Raymond Challinor and Brian Ripley, *The Miners' Association. A Trade Union in the Age of the Chartists,* London, 1968, new edn., Whitley Bay, 1990, pp. 126-55.

63   Anon, *Radical Monday. A letter from Bob in Gotham town to his cousin Bob in the country, containing an account. . .,* Newcastle upon Tyne, 1821; TWAS, CP/E436, JCM, p. 4; Jones, *Life and Speeches of Joseph Cowen,* p. 4. See also D. Read, *Peterloo: the 'Massacre' and its Background,* Manchester, 1973.

64   TWAS, CP/E436, JCM, p. 20.

65   David Ridley, 'The Spital Fields Demonstration and the Parliamentary Reform Crisis in Newcastle upon Tyne, May 1832', *Bulletin of the North East Labour History Society,* 26, 1992, pp. 4-35 noting the national importance of the activities of the NPU. See also Nancy D. Lopatin, *Political Unions, Popular Politics and the Great Reform Act of 1832,* Basingstoke, 1999, pp. 19, 145.

66   TWAS, CP, various, especially CP/A246; TWAS, CP/A270 for an account of the Foreign Affairs Committee, and references to the involvement of Charles Attwood; TWAS, CP/C6, Northern Reform Union minutes.

67   Todd, *Militant Democracy,* p. 24.

68   Harris Ms., p. 6, 72n.

69   TWAS, T371/1/3, Gateshead Board of Guardians [GBG], Minutes, 2 February 1847.

70   Editorial, *Gateshead Observer,* 29 July 1848.

71   TWAS, T371/1/3, GBG, Letter from Somerset House, 18 July 1850.

72   Speech at Newcastle, 30 December 1873, and provided in Cowen, *Speeches on Public Questions and Political Policy,* Newcastle, 1874, p. 3.

73   TWAS, CP/E436, JCM, p. 33.

74   *Newcastle Guardian,* 12 January 1850; *Gateshead Observer,* 12 January 1850.

75   TWAS, CP/ B118, *Liverpool Journal,* 27 January 1872; Jones, *Life and Speeches of Joseph Cowen,* p. 10.

76   'Joseph Cowen Obituary', *Newcastle Daily Chronicle,* 19 February 1900.

77   TWAS, CP/E447, Speech by Joseph Reed in 1929 referring to Cowen's management of his newspaper business.

78   Flinn, *Men of Iron,* p. 228.

79   TWAS, CP/E436, JCM, ch. II, p. 7.

80   Harris Ms., p. 8.

81   Jones, *Life and Speeches of Joseph Cowen,* p. 11.

82   Alex Tyrrell, *Joseph Sturge and the Moral Radical Party in Early Victorian Britain,* London, 1987, p. 125; NCLLS, Local Tracts, T. W. P. Taylder, *History of the Rise and Progress of Teetotalism in Newcastle,* Newcastle upon Tyne, 1885, p.14 notes that Ritchie lectured in Newcastle in 1841; TWAS, CP/B148, Speech by Joseph Cowen, 13 May 1873.

83   Todd, *Militant Democracy,* p. 26.

84   Jones, *Life and Speeches of Joseph Cowen,* p. 11.

85   TWAS, CP/E436, JCM, ch. II, p. 9.

86   TWAS, CP/F12, Joseph Cowen, Ms., 'Notes, Hints and Observations on Daily Life', July 1846.

87   For a detailed account of the life of W. E. Adams, who was Cowen's editor at the *Weekly Chronicle*, see Ashton, *W. E Adams*. For details of his involvement in the abolition movement see pp. 105-8.

88   TWAS, CP/D217, Letter from William Lloyd Garrison to Joseph Cowen, 8 January 1868.

89   Jones, *Life and Speeches of Joseph Cowen*, pp. 15-16; TWAS, CC/E436, JCM, ch. II, p. 27.

90   Denis V. Reid, 'Panizzi, Gladstone, Garibaldi and the Neapolitan Prisoners', *Electronic British Library Journal*, 2005, pp. 1-15, explores the furore surrounding the affair. See also Roland Sarti, 'Giuseppe Mazzini and his opponents', in John A. Davis (ed.), *Italy in the Nineteenth Century: 1796-1900*, Oxford, 2000, p. 91.

91   TWAS, CP/E8, Joseph Cowen to Major Jones, 2 June 1885. See also Jones, *Life and Speeches of Joseph Cowen*, pp 15-16; TWAS, CP/E433, Albert Harrison, 'Joseph Cowen: Orator, Patriot and Englishman', 1900. The Cowen Papers have an extensive collection of documents relating to Cowen's friendship with Mazzini, including their correspondence between 1860 and 1872.

92   TWAS, CP/E8, Letter from Joseph Cowen to Major E. R. Jones, 2 June 1885.

93   TWAS, CP/F12, p. 4

94   Ibid.

95   Ibid., p. 23.

96   TWAS, CP/E436, JCM, ch. 2.

97   Harris Mss., p. 10, n. 98 states that Cowen was not expelled from University for his political activities.

98   TWAS, CP/E436, JCM, ch. 3.

99   TWAS, CP/A8; A9; A16, Address of the People's International League and related correspondence.

100   Thomas Cooper, *The Life of Thomas Cooper*, London, 1872, new edn. Leicester, 1971; F. B. Smith, *Radical Artisan: W. J. Linton, 1812-97*, Manchester, 1973; D. Vincent (ed.), *Testaments of Radicalism: Memoirs of Working Class Politicians 1790-1885*, London, 1977.

101   F. G. and R. M. Black (eds.), *The Harney Papers*, Assen, 1969; TWAS, CP, various, especially A241, A247. See also A. R. Schoyen, *The Chartist Challenge*, London, 1958.

102   TWAS, CP/F9, Joseph Cowen, 'The Tyranny of the Higher Classes', May 1846.

103   TWAS, CP/E436, JCM, ch. 3; TWAS, CP/B15, *Almanack for the Times*, British Anti-State Church Association, 1851. The Association (later the Liberation Society) was formed in 1842 and the first meeting was held in London on 30 April 1844. See Ian Machin, 'Disestablishment and Democracy, c.1840-1930', in Eugenio F. Biagini (ed.), *Citizenship and Community. Liberals, Radicals and Collective Identities in the British Isles, 1865-1931*, Cambridge, 1996, pp. 120-48; David M. Thompson,

'The Liberation Society, 1844-1868', in Patricia Hollis (ed.), *Pressure from Without in early Victorian England,* London, 1974, pp. 210-38. Vincent, *Formation of the British Liberal Party,* pp. 68-76 for an account of its later history as the Liberation Society.

104 GLRO, A/LIB/275, Proceedings of the first Anti-State Church Conference, 30 April 1844.

105 TWAS, CP/B5, B8.

106 GLRO, A/LIB/89, Anti-State Church Association Cashbook, 1844 -1853, entry dated 5 May 1848.

107 TWAS, CC/E436, JCM, ch. 3 states that Cowen's handwritten minutes 'came to an abrupt termination'.

108 GLRO, A/LIB/89, various entries including 3 April 1845, 13 March 1846, 29 November 1847, 28 March 1850, 1 January 1851, 27 November 1852 show the extent of Newcastle support. Although David Thompson's study does not include Newcastle in his list of active committees the Cashbooks have regular entries until 1852. Thompson, 'Liberation Society', pp. 229, 237-8. See also *Newcastle Guardian,* 13 April 1850 which carried a report of the second triennial conference in London.

109 Thompson, 'Liberation Society', p. 210.

110 For an appraisal of the insanitary condition of north east colliery villages see Colls, *Pitmen of the Northern Coalfield,* pp. 263-4. See also Neville Kirk, *The Growth of Working Class Reformism in England,* London, 1985, p. 108, *passim* for a review of public health initiatives in Manchester and Salford during the mid-century ; Anthony S. Wohl, *Endangered Lives. Public Health in Victorian Britain,* London, 1983, especially ch. 6.

111 Tholfsen, *Working Class Radicalism in Mid-Victorian England,* pp. 143, 149 note that articles in the *Peoples Journal* in 1849 stressed the importance of mutual effort for the happiness of the community as a whole. It seems likely that Cowen drew heavily upon this material when preparing his speech.

112 TWAS, CP/D20, Report of the Winlaton and Blaydon Sanitary Association; TWAS, CP/D23, Inaugural meeting, 26 January 1848; TWAS, CP/E436, JCM, ch. 3.

113 *Newcastle Guardian,* 27 April 1850.

114 TWAS, CP/D57, Speech by Joseph Cowen 5 May 1852.

115 J. F. C. Harrison, *Learning and Living, 1790-1960,* London, 1961; Kirk, *Growth of Working Class Reformism in England,* p. 190.

116 TWAS, CP/D5, 2 February 1847.

117 TWAS, CP/ D16, August 1847.

118 TWAS, CP/E436, JCM, ch. 4.

119 *Northern Tribune,* I, 1854, p.1.

Chapter 2

1 For example, Norman McCord, *North East England: The Region's Development, 1760-1960,* London, 1979, p. 79 found 'little evidence for the existence of a con-

tinuous very widespread popular support for radical political agitations'. See also D. J. Rowe, 'Some Aspects of Chartism on Tyneside', *International Review of Social History*, 16, 1971, pp. 17-39.

2   Kate Tiller, 'Late Chartism: Halifax 1847-58', in James Epstein and Dorothy Thompson (eds.), *The Chartist Experience. Studies in Working-Class Radicalism and Culture, 1830-1860*, London, 1982, pp. 311-44; Bill Lancaster, *Radicalism, Cooperation and Socialism: Leicester Working Class Politics, 1860-1906*, Leicester, 1987; E. F. Biagini and A. J. Reid (eds.), *Currents of Radicalism. Popular radicalism, organised labour and party politics in Britain, 1850-1914*, Cambridge, 1991.

3   See Appendices. Lists were compiled using the Cowen Papers, newspaper reports of meetings and demonstrations and the bibliographical data in D. J. Rowe, 'Tyneside Chartism', in Norman McCord (ed.), *Essays in Tyneside Labour History*, Newcastle, 1977, pp. 62-87.

4   For example, see Gareth Stedman Jones, 'The Language of Class', in James Epstein and Dorothy Thompson (eds.), *The Chartist Experience. Studies in Working–Class Radicalism and Culture, 1830-1860*, London, 1982, p. 52 who claims that the 'changing character and policies of the state' rendered the language of radicalism bankrupt.

5   Joan Hugman, 'Print and Preach': The entrepreneurial spirit of Tyneside politics', in Robert Colls and Bill Lancaster (eds.), *Newcastle A Modern History*, Chichester, 2001, pp. 116-19. For a discussion of the links between an oral and literary culture see Owen R. Ashton, 'The Western Vindicator and Early Chartism', in Joan Allen and Owen R. Ashton (eds.), *Papers for the People. A Study of the Chartist Press*, London, 2005, pp. 66-7.

6   Joan Hugman, 'A small drop of ink': Tyneside Chartism and the *Northern Liberator*', in Owen Ashton, Robert Fyson and Stephen Roberts (eds.), *The Chartist Legacy*, Woodbridge, 1999, pp. 24-47.

7   Margot Finn, *After Chartism. Class and Nation in English Radical Politics, 1848-1874*, Cambridge, 1993.

8   Margot Finn, "A vent which has conveyed our principles': English radical patriotism in the aftermath of 1848', *Journal of Modern History*, 64: 4, 1992, p. 639. On the international dimension of early radical Tyneside, see J. H. Gleason, *The Genesis of Russophobia in Britain*, Harvard, 1950, p. 261 who observes that David Urquhart's Russophobic campaign in 1840 was most successful in Newcastle and Glasgow. See also R. G. Gammage, *The History of the Chartist Movement, 1837-1854*, London, 1894, repr. New York, 1969, p. 189.

9   *Newcastle Courant*, 24 July 1819, 7 August 1819; NCLLS 324. 2, *Address of the Reformers of Fawdon to their brothers the Pitmen, Keelmen and other labourers on the Tyne and Wear*, 1819; *Northern Reformers Monthly Magazine and Political Register*, I, January 1823. For Political Unions, see Nancy D. LoPatin, *Political Unions, Popular Politics and the Great Reform Act of 1832*, Basingstoke, 1999; David Ridley, 'The Spital Field Demonstration and the Parliamentary Reform Crisis in Newcastle upon Tyne', *Bulletin of the North East Labour History Society*, 26, 1992,

pp. 4-35 analyses the pivotal role of the NPU in securing the successful passage of the 1832 Reform Act.

10   *Democratic Review*, 1849-1850, p. 349 ff.

11   Tiller, 'Late Chartism: Halifax' states that 'the ideas and policies of Chartism continued to be independently articulated after 1858, later putting considerable pressure on established Liberalism'. See also Antony Taylor, 'Post-Chartism: Metropolitan Perspectives on the Chartist movement in Decline, 1848-80', in Matthew Cragoe and Antony Taylor (eds.), *London Politics, 1760-1914*, Basingstoke, 2005, p. 75 who argues for a 'fault line in the relationship between Liberalism and the radical constituency'.

12   Joan Allen, "Resurrecting Jerusalem': The late Chartist press in the north- east of England', in Allen and Ashton (eds.), *Papers for the People*, pp. 176-83.

13   TWAS, CP/various, especially C152, Letter from J. A. Langford to Joseph Cowen, 20 August 1858; C267, Letter from J. P. Cobbett to Joseph Cowen, 9 November 1858.

14   Trygve Tholfsen, *Working Class Radicalism in Mid-Victorian England*, London, 1976, p. 325 emphasises the force of radicalism expressed through Chartism compared with the 'softer form' of mid-Victorian radicalism.

15   On middle class values and mechanics' institutes as instruments of social control, see Harold Perkin, *The Origins of Modern English Society, 1780-1880*, London, 1969; John K. Walton: *Lancashire. A Social History, 1558-1939*, Manchester, 1987; J. F. C. Harrison, *Learning and Living, 1790-1960*, London, 1961.

16   Ray Boston, *British Chartists in America,1839-1900*, Manchester, 1971. On Tyneside, Robert Blakey, who had masterminded Chartist activity via the pages of the *Northern Liberator*, abandoned politics in 1840 for an academic career. See Hugman, 'A small drop of ink', p. 33.

17   Aled G. Jones, *Powers of the Press. Newspapers, Power and the Public in Nineteenth Century England*, Aldershot, 1996, p. 73.

18   Jones, 'Language of Class', p. 13.

19   Malcolm Chase, 'Wholesome Object Lessons: The Chartist Land Plan in Retrospect', *English Historical Review*, CXVIII: 475, 2003, pp. 61-85; David Martin, 'Land reform', in Patricia Hollis (ed.), *Pressure from Without in Early Victorian England*, London, 1974, p. 155; Royden Harrison, *Before the Socialists. Studies in Labour and Politics 1861-1881*, London, 1965, p. 214ff; Denis Judd, *Radical Joe. A Life of Joseph Chamberlain*, Cardiff, 1993, pp. 56-61.

20   Brian Harrison and Patricia Hollis (ed.), *Robert Lowery: Radical and Chartist*, London, 1979.

21   *Northern Liberator*, 15 September 1838.

22   This theme has been explored by Paul Pickering, 'Class without Words: Symbolic communication in the Chartist Movement', *Past and Present*, 112 (1986), pp. 144-62. See also J. A. Epstein, 'The constitutional idiom, radical reasoning, rhetoric and action in early nineteenth-century England', *Journal of Social History*, 23, Spring

1990, pp. 553-74; Robert Poole, 'The march to Peterloo: politics and festivity in late Georgian England', *Past and Present*, 192, August 2006, pp. 109-155.

23 *Northern Tribune*, 2, 1854, p. 376; *Newcastle Journal*, 15 May 1832.

24 TWAS, 1074/111, Handbill: 'Speech by Charles Larkin at a dinner for Charles Attwood and Thomas Doubleday', 2 December 1833. See also TWAS, 1074/115, Poster advertising Daniel O'Connell's visit to Newcastle, 14 September 1835, wherein the aristocracy were denounced as 'those who had fed and fattened upon public soil'.

25 *Northern Liberator*, 1 June 1838.

26 Ibid., 25 May 1839; P. M. Ashraf, *Life and Times of Thomas Spence*, Gateshead, 1983, p. 48.

27 *Northern Liberator*, 29 December 1838.

28 T. J. Nossiter, *Influence, Opinion and Political Idioms in Reformed England. Case Studies from the North East, 1832-1874*, Brighton, 1975, p. 153ff; *Newcastle Weekly Chronicle*, correspondence, 27 September 1884. For counter arguments see W. H. Maehl, 'The dynamics of violence in Chartism: A case study in north-east England, 1839', *Albion*, 7, 1975, p. 107; W. H. Maehl, 'Augustus Hardin Beaumont: Anglo-American Radical (1798-1838)', *International Review of Social History*, XIV, 1969, pp. 237-51. On revolutionary Chartism more generally, see Edward Royle, *Revolutionary Britannia? Reflections on the threat of revolution in Britain, 1789-1848*, Manchester, 2000.

29 Thomas Ainge Devyr, *The Odd Book of the Nineteenth Century or Chivalry in Modern Days*, New York, 1882, pp. 159-204.

30 Dorothy Thompson, *The Chartists: Popular Politics in the Industrial Revolution*, London and New York, 1984, p. 54 describes the *Liberator* as one of the 'longest-lived and liveliest' of the Chartist papers.

31 Hugman, 'A small drop of ink', pp. 39-41; *Northern Liberator*, 5 January 1839.

32 *Northern Liberator*, 12 January 1839.

33 *Northern Star*, 29 December, 1839.

34 This accords with the view that the years between 1838 and 1840 were the 'high point' of Chartism. See Dorothy Thompson, 'The Chartists in 1848', in Terry Brotherstone, Anna Clark and Kevin Whelan (eds.), *These Fissured Isles: Ireland, Scotland and British History, 1798-1848*, Edinburgh, 2005, p. 172.

35 On the Anti-Corn Law League see Paul Pickering and Alex Tyrrell, *The People's Bread. A History of the Anti-Corn Law League*, Leicester, 2000.

36 TWAS, 1074/126, Poster, 'Sketches of A System by a Tyne Chartist', 1840, including the 'Address of the Working Men of Newcastle to the Manufacturing, Trading and Middle Classes of the United Kingdom'.

37 TWAS, 1074/127, Poster, 'Defeat of the O'Connellite Anti-Corn Law Conspirators', 1840.

38 TWAS, 1074/126, 'Sketches of A System'; TWAS, 1074/128, Poster, 'The Radicals Remembrancer', nd, stated that the Corn Laws would 'famish yourselves and your families, that the landlord might have £200,000 instead of £100,000 per year'.

39 Jones, 'Language of Class', pp. 3-58 offered a sustained argument that Chartism was not a class-based movement. For counter arguments see Dorothy Thompson, 'The Languages of Class', *Bulletin of the Society for the Study of Labour History*, 52: 1, 1987, pp. 54-7; Neville Kirk, 'In Defence of Class', *International Review of Social History*, 1, 1987, pp. 3-46.

40 Norman McCord, *The Anti-Corn Law League*, London, 1958, p. 45ff.

41 There was no Association in Newcastle until February 1842. See Pickering and Tyrrell, *People's Bread*, Appendix 1, p. 256.

42 TWAS, 1666/7/8, Poster, Chartist Meeting in the Joiners' Hall, Newcastle, December 1839.

43 *Northern Tribune*, vol. 1, p. 406; *Newcastle Courant*, 30 October 1819; TWAS, Thomas Wilson Collection, vol. IV/1832-5, Handbill, 'Why has Fife left the Northern Political Union', 28 June 1832.

44 *Newcastle Journal*, 23 March 1832; TWAS, CP/A270, Letter from Charles Attwood to Joseph Cowen objecting to John Fife's membership of the Newcastle Foreign Affairs Committee and referring to the events of 1832, 12 December 1854.

45 McCord, *Anti-Corn Law League*, p. 50.

46 Ibid., p. 150; Martin, 'Land reform', p. 144.

47 Malcolm Chase, "We wish only to work for ourselves': The Chartist Land Plan', in M. Chase and I. Dyck (eds.), *Living and Learning: Essays in honour of J. F. C. Harrison*, Aldershot, 1996, pp. 133-48; Chase, 'Wholesome Object Lessons'.

48 John Saville, *Ernest Jones, Chartist*, London, 1952, p. 212; Gammage, *History of the Chartist Movement*, Introduction by John Saville, pp. 48-62.

49 Rowe, 'Tyneside Chartism', p. 81.

50 Roy Church, 'Chartism and the Miners: A Reinterpretation', *Labour History Review*, 56:3, 1991, pp. 23-36 singles out Northumberland and Staffordshire as exceptions. On mining and radical politics, see R. Colls, *Pitmen of the Northern Coalfield*; Keith Wilson, 'Political Radicalism in the North East of England 1830-60', unpublished University of Durham Ph.D thesis, 1987.

51 *Northern Liberator*, 25 May 1839.

52 Ibid.

53 Ibid., various dates throughout 1839-1840 for references to 'missions' to Seghill, Sheriff Hill, Walker, Elswick and Benwell.

54 TWAS, 1102/2, Inquiry into Children's employment in mines in Northumberland and Durham Collieries, 1842, p. 673.

55 Church, 'Chartism and the Miners', p. 33.

56 Patrick Joyce, *Visions of the People. Industrial England and the Question of Class*, Cambridge, 1991, p. 39 but also see chapter 2 generally.

57 R. Challinor and B. Ripley, *The Miners' Association: A Trade Union in the Age of the Chartists*, Whitley Bay, repr. 1990, p. 224; Raymond Challinor, *A Radical Lawyer in Victorian England: W. P. Roberts and the Struggle for Worker's Rights*, Whitley Bay, 1990; Keith Laybourn, *A History Of British Trade Unionism c. 1770-1990*, Stroud, 1992, p. 34

58 Challinor and Ripley, *Miners' Association*, p. 217. Thomas Slingsby Duncome was MP for Hertford 1826-32 and Finsbury 1834-61. He presented the Charter to the House of Commons in 1842, was President of the United Trades for the Protection of Labour, a campaigner for mining reforms and a member of the People's International League.

59 *Miners Advocate,* various dates, especially 18 May 1844, 27 July 1844. The *Illustrated London News,* 3 August 1844 noted that it was the 'longest strike ever recorded' in the mining industry.

60 *Newcastle Chronicle,* 4 May 1849 stated that the majority attending the meeting were 'working class'. See also Malcolm Chase, 'Out of Radicalism: The mid-Victorian Freehold Land Movement', *English Historical Review,* 106, April 1991, pp. 319-45.

61 *Newcastle Chronicle,* 4 May 1849. The inaugural meeting was addressed by 'Charlton, Wilkie and Dodds'.

62 Ibid., 2 November 1849 claimed that the skilled working class were sustaining the radical movement.

63 Chase, 'Land and the Working Classes', p. 250 states that the Metropolitan Parliamentary and Financial Reform Association comprised many former Anti-Corn Law Leaguers such as Richard Cobden and John Morley.

64 *Democratic Review,* 'The Charter and Something More', February 1850, p. 350. See also Schoyen, *Chartist Challenge,* p. 148.

65 F. B. Smith, *Radical Artisan, William James Linton 1812-97,* Manchester, 1973, p. 108.

66 *Democratic Review,* June 1849. 'Terrigeneous' also contributed to the *Red Republican.* In an article dated 9 November 1850, Harney refers to 'Terrigeneous' as 'a working man'.

67 Ibid., February 1850, p. 352.

68 *Red Republican,* 1, 22 June 1850.

69 Martin, 'Land reform', p. 150ff suggests that Cobden's involvement in land reform was important; by keeping agrarianism at the top of the agenda he was able to ensure that the Liberals obtained and retained radical support.

70 TWAS, CP/A247, Newcastle FAC meeting, 29 November 1854.

71 *Northern Liberator,* 15 September 1838.

72 TWAS, CP/E436, JCM, ch. 7.

73 See Michael Rush, *The Role of the Member of Parliament since 1868. From Gentlemen to Players,* Oxford, 2001, pp. 183-7.

74 *Northern Liberator,* 15 September 1838; Augustus Beaumont, *Adventures of Two Americans in Brussels by One of Them,* Cornhill, 1830, p. 4. See also Iorwerth Prothero, 'Chartists and Political Refugees', in Sabine Freitag (ed.), *Exiles from European Revolutions. Refugees in Mid-Victorian England,* New York and Oxford, 2003, pp. 211-12, 215.

75 Nossiter, *Influence, Opinion and Political Idioms in Reformed England,* p. 152; *Northern Liberator,* 17 February 1838.

76 *Northern Liberator,* 17 February 1838, Valedictory Address, Newcastle WMA.

77 O.R. Ashton and P.A. Pickering, *Friends of the People, Uneasy Radicals in the Age of the Chartists,* London, 2002, p. 2.

78 Miles Taylor, 'The old radicalism and the new: David Urquhart and the politics of opposition, 1832-1867', in Biagini and Reid (eds.), *Currents of Radicalism,* pp. 23-43.

79 See J.O. Baylen and N.J. Gossman (eds.), *Biographical Dictionary of Modern British Radicals,* 5 vols, Brighton, 1984-8, pp. 25-26.

80 LoPatin, *Political Unions, Popular Politics and the Great Reform Act*; Carlos Flick, *The Birmingham Political Union and the Movements for Reform in Britain, 1830-39,* Hampden, CT, 1979. Flick's account barely mentions Charles, even though the two Unions were closely linked.

81 TWAS, CP/D87, *Northern Tribune,* II, 1855, p. 321.

82 Devyr, *The Odd Book of the Nineteenth Century,* p. 164.

83 Gleason, *Genesis of Russophobia,* p. 284. See also Richard Shannon, 'David Urquhart and the Foreign Affairs Committees', in Hollis (ed.), *Pressure from Without,* p. 247; Patricia Hollis and Brian Harrison, 'Chartism, Liberalism and the Life of Robert Lowery', *English Historical Review,* 82 (1967), pp. 503-35.

84 Gleason, *Genesis of Russophobia,* p. 284.

85 Alexander Wilson, *The Chartist Movement in Scotland,* Manchester, 1970, p. 113.

86 Gammage, *History of the Chartist Movement,* p. 189; Schoyen, *Chartist Challenge,* p. 241 notes that Urquhart split the Chartists in 1840.

87 TWAS, CP/A197, Speech in Newcastle, 12 December 1853.

88 TWAS, CP/A42, 19 May 1851; John Belchem, 'Britishness, Asylum Seekers and the Northern Working Class: 1851', *Northern History,* XXXIX:1, March 2002, pp. 70-2.

89 A number of historians have identified internationalism as a unifying factor. For example, Finn, *After Chartism.* F. M. Leventhal, *Respectable Radical: George Howell and Victorian Working Class Politics,* London, 1971, p. 45; James Hinton, *Labour and Socialism,* Brighton, 1983, p. 10; John Vincent, *The Formation of the British Liberal Party, 1857-1868,* Harmondsworth, 1976.

90 Asa Briggs, *Victorian People: Some reassessments of people, institutions, ideas and events, 1851-67,* London, 1954.

91 *Newcastle Chronicle,* 31 August 1849. Other delegates included Victor Hugo, Richard Cobden, Henry Vincent and Joseph Sturge.

92 Smith, *Radical Artisan,* p. 91.

93 TWAS, CP/A8. Address of the People's International League. The members included P. A. Taylor, James Stansfield, W. J. Linton, J. H. Parry, Thomas Slingsby Duncome and William Shaen. It was founded by William Ashurst Jnr in 1847, and was later absorbed into the Society of the Friends of Italy. Cowen was active in both organisations.

94 Quoted in Smith, *Radical Artisan,* p. 91.

95 *Democratic Review,* October 1849.

96   F. G. and R. M. Black (eds.), *The Harney Papers*, Amsterdam, 1969, Letter from Harney to Friedrich Engels, 30 June 1846.

97   Ibid. Harney founded the Fraternal Democrats in 1845.

98   Ibid. Letter from Mazzini to Harney, 1845; *Northern Star,* various editions throughout March 1849.

99   John Saville (ed.), *Red Republican*, 1850, vol. I. Introduction, p. x.

100 Schoyen, *Chartist Challenge*, p. 240ff; TWAS, CP/A247, NFAC minutes; TWAS, CP/E436, JCM, ch. 9 states that the Committee was 'Cowenite'.

101 TWAS, CP/B41.The Blaydon Store first opened in March 1859.

102 *Newcastle Guardian,* 29 April 1848.

103 *Gateshead Observer,* 15 April 1848. The Association included George Crawshay, Thomas Wilke, George Charlton, John Blakey, J. T. Gilmour, Robert Bainbridge and John Mawson.

104 TWAS, CP/F12, 1846.

105 *Newcastle Chronicle,* 2 November 1849. For speeches in similar vein see TWAS, CP, various including D19, Speech at Scotswood, Newcastle.

106 TWAS, CP/A153, Letter from Joseph Cowen to J. Passmore Edwards, 22 March 1852 asking for a donation to the Subscription for European Freedom. Edwards wanted the money to be spent on peace tracts not guns.

107 TWAS, CP/A152, Letter from Joseph Cowen to Samuel Beale, 24 March 1852, re his criticism of the 'warlike attitude' of the members of the Subscription.

108 Prothero, 'Chartists and Political Refugees', p. 227.

109 TWAS, CP/A16, Circular letter of the People's International League.

110 TWAS, CP/A17, Address of the People's International League.

111 Ibid.

112 Smith, *Radical Artisan*, p. 60. Linton described the Address as 'one of the most momentous harbingers of the present world'.

113 Ibid., p. 102. The *English Republic* was published in monthly editions from January 1851 to April 1855 and financed by Cowen. See Allen, 'Resurrecting Jerusalem' in Allen and Ashton (eds.), *Papers for the People,* pp. 171-3.

114 Adams was a Cheltenham Chartist and ardent republican who later edited the *Newcastle Weekly Chronicle* as well as publishing in his own right. See Ashton, *W. E Adams*, pp. 49-50, 65; W. E. Adams, *Memoirs of a Social Atom*, New York, 1903; rept. New York, 1967; Introduction by John Saville; W. E. Adams, *Our American Cousins*, 1883; rept. New York, 1992; Introduction by Owen R. Ashton and Alan Munslow.

115 TWAS, CP/C480, Letter from Cowen to J. Baxter Langley, 6 February 1859; TWAS, CP/C481, Reply from Baxter Langley, same date.

116 TWAS, CP/A42, 19 May 1851; TWAS, CP/A60, Concert by the Band of Hope to raise funds for the refugees. See also Belchem, 'Britishness, Asylum Seekers and the Northern Working Class', pp. 70-3.

117 TWAS, CP/E436, JCM, ch. 5, meeting dated 19 May 1851.

118 TWAS, CP/A152, 24 March 1852.

119 Krzysztof Marchiewicz, 'Continuities and Innovations: Polish Emigration after 1849', in Freitag (ed.), *Exiles from European Revolutions,* pp. 111-14.

120 TWAS, CP/E436, JCM, ch. 5; TWAS, CP/A189. This correspondence, which was originally written in invisible ink, details the strategies adopted to conceal Bulewski's plans. Other correspondence relating to Cowen's seditious activities were destroyed by his daughter after his death.

121 TWAS, CP/E436, JCM, ch. 9, p. 26 gives an account of Orsini's visit. See also Finn, *After Chartism,* pp. 181-186; Maurizio Isabella, 'Italian Exiles and British Politics before and after 1848', in Freitag (ed.), *Exiles from European Revolutions,* pp. 77-8.

122 TWAS, CP/A104, 28 October 1851.

123 TWAS, CP/A152, Letter dated 1 March 1852.

124 TWAS, CP/A150, Circular letter, 3 March 1852.

125 TWAS, CP/E436, JCM, ch. 9, p. 3.

126 TWAS, CP/A159, nsp. cutting, 10 March 1852.

127 *Memoirs of a Social Atom,* pp. 280-2; AIISH, AP222/1/2, diary entries 20 November 1854-27 March 1855; AP222/1/48, fragment of a letter (nd); AP/222/1/49, Adams letter dated 7 March 1856.

128 TWAS, CP/D87, *Northern Tribune,* I, January 1854. It began circulation as a monthly journal and later became a weekly.

129 TWAS, CP/D187, Letter from Cowen to George Tweddell, 12 January 1854.

130 Allen, 'Resurrecting Jerusalem', p. 174.

131 *Northern Tribune,* II, p. 64; TWAS, CP/A241, Petition for a public meeting with 180 signatures, August 1854.

132 Miles Taylor, 'The old radicalism and the new: David Urquhart and the politics of opposition, 1832-1867', in Biagini and Reid (eds.), *Currents of Radicalism,* pp. 23-43.

133 TWAS, CP/A270, Letter from Charles Attwood to Joseph Cowen, 8 December 1854.

134 TWAS, CP/A246, NFAC Account book, shows that Cowen was the largest contributor. Although officially he was the Secretary, he also controlled all of the group's activities, including its finances.

135 Schoyen, *Chartist Challenge,* p. 89ff.

136 Taylor, 'The old radicalism and the new', p. 36 notes the independence of the Newcastle Committee.

137 Joan Allen, 'George Crawshay', *New Dictionary of National Biography,* Oxford, 2004.

138 *Northern Tribune,* II, 12 March 1855.

139 TWAS, CP/E436, JCM, ch. 10, speech by Joseph Cowen at Nelson Street Lecture Rooms, 12 December 1853.

140 TWAS, CP/A270, Letter from Cowen to Charles Attwood, 22 January 1855.

141 *Northern Tribune,* II, p. 105; *Republican Record,* January 1855.

142 *Republican Record,* January 1855.

143 The slogan was used in both the *English Republic* and the *Democratic Review*.
144 On Italian unification, see John A. Davis (eds.), *Italy in the Nineteenth Century*, *1796-1900*, Oxford, 2000, especially chapters 3 and 5.
145 TWAS, CP/various including D87, E8, E443, A648. The sword was manufactured at Birmingham and the testimonial cost £10.13s.3d; the deficit of £1.16s.10d was paid by Cowen.
146 TWAS, CP/E436, JCM, ch. 7, Letter from Garibaldi to Joseph Cowen, 27 July 1860.
147 Allen, 'Resurrecting Jerusalem', p. 172. For an interesting insight into late Chartist activity in Cheltenham, see AIISH, AP222/1/2, various diary entries, including 5 April 1850, 12 April 1850, 6 June 1850, 28 July 1850 and 23 May 1851.
148 *Reasoner and London Tribune*, 16 May 1855; TWAS, CP/A241.
149 Finn, *After Chartism*, p. 188.
150 *Northern Daily Express*, 13 May 1857, Speech by Joseph Cowen.
151 George Jacob Holyoake, *Sixty Years of An Agitator's Life*, 2 vols, II, London, 1906, pp. 19-30.
152 TWAS, CP/C6, NRU Minutes.
153 Ibid., NRU, Quarterly Minutes, 5 April 1858.
154 On the *Northern Reform Record*, see Allen, 'Resurrecting Jerusalem', pp. 176-82
155 For a biographical study of Reed, see Owen. R. Ashton and Paul A. Pickering, *Friends of the People. Uneasy Radicals in the Age of the Chartists*, London, 2002, ch. 6.
156 TWAS, CP/C6, 5 April 1858.
157 Ibid., Circular, 21 September 1858.
158 Ibid., October 1858.
159 Ibid., Quarterly Meeting, 19 September 1859.
160 Ibid., Circular of the NRU, 11 October 1859.
161 TWAS, CP/E386, Obituary, *Cheltenham Examiner*, 28 February 1900.
162 *Daily Chronicle and Northern Counties Advertiser*, 11 January 1859.
163 Eric J. Evans, *Parliamentary Reform, c. 1770-1918*, Harlow, 2000, p. 41; TWAS, CP/C230, Letter from Edward Miall to Cowen, 22 October 1858; C233, Letter from Herbert Ingram to Cowen, same date.
164 TWAS, CP/ C139, Letter from Caroline Ashurst Briggs to Reed, 4 August 1858; 12 August 1858; C316, Letter from G. E. Harris to Reed re paupers; C707, Letter from Lord Teynham to Reed, 27 August 1859
165 *Newcastle Daily Chronicle*, 8 December 1859. Holyoake used a pseudonym, '*Disque*'.
166 TWAS, CP/C21, 11 January 1858.
167 TWAS, CP/C377, 2 January 1859.
168 TWAS, CP/C800, 19 October 1859.
169 *Northern Reform Record*, September 1858.
170 TWAS, CP/C1009, 27 December 1859.

171 Nossiter, *Influence, Opinion and Political Idioms in Reformed England*, p. 159. See also C. Muris, 'The Northern Reform Union 1858-1862', unpublished University of Durham MA thesis, 1959.

172 Finn, *After Chartism*, p. 197.

173 Ashton and Pickering, *Friends of the People*, especially pp. 132-7.

174 TWAS, CP, various including C181, C152, C279, C190.

175 TWAS, CP/C380, Letter from Thomas Bott to Reed, 5 January 1859; C431, Letter from Henry Cooper to Reed, 25 January 1859

176 TWAS, CP/C196, Letter from Thomas Doubleday to Joseph Cowen, 4 October 1858.

177 TWAS, CP/C464, Letter dated 4 January 1859 gives details of the attempt by Felice Orsini to assassinate Louis Napoleon. See also G.J. Holyoake, *Sixty Years of an Agitator's Life*, 2 vols. London, 1906; Todd, *Militant Democracy:* pp. 8-9.

178 TWAS, CP/C355, Letter from Frank Grant to R.B. Reed, 23 December 1858.

179 TWAS, CP/C387, Letter from Thomas Thompson to R. B. Reed, 10 January 1859.

180 TWAS, CP/C391, Letter from John Tennant to R. B. Reed, 10 January 1859.

181 TWAS, CP/C547, 28 February 1859.

182 TWAS, CP/C1029, Letter from H. J. Slack to R. B. Reed, 31 December 1859; C956, Letter from Cowen to Bright, 14 December 1859.

183 TWAS, CP/C512, copy of a letter to the *Daily Chronicle* by 'A Democrat', 14 December 1859.

184 TWAS, CP/C750, 20 September 1859.

185 TWAS, CP/E436, JCM, ch. 11, p. 26; Ashton and Pickering, *Friends of the People*, p. 136.

186 Janet Fyfe (ed.), *Autobiography of John McAdam, 1806-1883*, Edinburgh, 1980, Letter from J. McAdam to R. B. Reed, 10 September 1860, p. 133.

187 TWAS, CP/C1022, 25 December 1859; see also *Reasoner*, 27 May 1860.

188 *Northern Reform Record*, July 1858, p. 9.

189 TWAS, CP/C6, 20 May 1858; 19 September 1859. T. E. Headlam polled 2,687; George Ridley 2,680; Taylor 463.

190 TWAS, CP/C696, Letter from E.S. Pryce to Cowen, 11 August 1859.

Chapter 3

1 *Newcastle Daily Chronicle*, 22 February 1900.

2 Joseph Cowen, speech delivered at The Circus, Newcastle, 22 December 1883. See Jane Cowen (ed.), *Joseph Cowen's Speeches on the Near Eastern Question: Foreign and Imperial Affairs: And on the British Empire*, Newcastle upon Tyne and London, 1909, p. 171.

3 Vincent, *Formation of the British Liberal Party*, p. 245.

4 H.C.G. Matthew, 'Gladstone, Rhetoric and Politics', in Peter Jagger (ed.), *Gladstone*, London, 1998, p. 214; Stuart Hall, 'Variants of Liberalism', in J. Donald and S. Hall (ed.), *Politics and Ideology*, London, 1986, ch. 3.

5   For example, see R. J. Morris, *Class, Sect and Party. The Making of the British Middle Class, Leeds 1820-1850*, Manchester and New York, 1990, p. 15.

6   John Walton, *Lancashire. A Social History, 1558-1939*, Manchester, 1987, p. 247 cites the 'cumulative impact' of paternalistic control, and notes that the teaching of political economy may have helped to 'win the assent of an educated working class to the existing social system'.

7   Harold Perkin, *Origins of Modern British Society*, repr. London, 1994, ch. 8.

8   Vincent, *Formation of the British Liberal Party*, p. 115

9   For instance, see Perkin, *Origins of Modern British Society*, p. 380ff.

10   Rohan McWilliam, 'Radicalism and popular culture: The Tichborne case and the politics of 'fair play', in E.F. Biagini and A.J. Reid (eds.), *Currents of Radicalism*, p. 45, argues that 'Tichbornism provides evidence for the survival of such radicalism beyond Chartism'.

11   Robert Gray, 'The platform and the pulpit: cultural networks and civic identities in industrial towns, c. 1850-70', in Alan Kidd and David Nicholls (eds.), *The Making of the British Middle Class. Studies of regional and cultural diversity since the eighteenth century*, Stroud, 1998, pp. 121-47.

12   J. F. C. Harrison, *Learning and Living, 1790-1960: A Study in the History of the English Adult Education Movement*, London, 1969, p. 126.

13   Jones, *Life and Speeches of Joseph Cowen*, p. 96

14   *Newcastle Guardian*, 15 April 1848.

15   Harrison, *Learning and Living*, p. 82. See also Morris, *Class, Sect and Party*, ch. 11.

16   Harrison, *Learning and Living*, p. 79ff. See also Morris, *Class, Sect and Party*, pp. 93-4

17   TWAS, CP/D1, Rules, January 1847. The Newcastle Mechanics' Institute opened on 26 February 1824. See TWAS, 1074/230.

18   TWAS, CP/D5, Address, 2 February 1847.

19   Ibid.

20   TWAS, CP/E436, JCM, ch. 3.

21   TWAS, CP/D14, August 1847.

22   TWAS, CP/D16, Address, August 1847.

23   TWAS, CP/D25, Half Yearly Report, 10 July 1848 notes that placards advertising the programme had been torn down.

24   Jones, *Life and Speeches of Joseph Cowen*, p. 99.

25   H. H. Gerth and C. Wright Mills (eds.), *From Max Weber. Essays in Sociology*, London, 1948, p. 247.

26   TWAS, CP/D87, *Northern Tribune*, II, January 1854-March 1855, p. 211; *Newcastle Guardian*, 4 May 1850.

27   See W. E. Adams. *Memoirs of a Social Atom*, London, 1903, pp. 114, 155.

28   TWAS, CP/D220, 4 August 1858. Joseph Cowen Speech at the 12th Annual Festival; TWAS, CP/A648, Meeting in Blaydon Mechanics' Institute, 14 September 1859.

29   *Newcastle Guardian*, 26 January 1850.

30   Ibid., 5 January 1850.

31 Ibid., 27 May 1848.

32 Ibid., 18 March 1848.

33 TWAS, CP/D55, 5 May 1852.

34 TWAS, CP/E436, JCM, ch. 4, p. 9.

35 Ibid., p. 19.

36 Ibid., p. 27.

37 TWAS, CP/D36, 28 October 1869.

38 *Northern Daily Express,* 19 August 1856.

39 Todd, *Militant Democracy,* pp. 27-30, gives a good account of Cowen's educational ventures and the opposition he encountered as a result.

40 Harrison, *Learning and Living,* pp. 149-51 highlights an abortive attempt by the Halifax middle class radicals to rescind the rule excluding politics and religion.

41 TWAS, CP.E436, JCM, ch. 4, p. 28.

42 TWAS, CP/D220, 4 August 1858.

43 TWAS, CP/D88, 1 January 1854. The new title reflected its regional circulation.

44 TWAS, CP/D87, *Northern Tribune,* January 1854-March 1855, p. 349.

45 *Newcastle Daily Chronicle,* 24 January 1883, report of a meeting in Walker Mechanics' Institute to raise subscriptions to alleviate distress in Ireland. See also *Newcastle Daily Chronicle,* 13 July 1871, which has an account of the 18th Anniversary of Marley Hill Mechanics' Institute; *North of England Farmer,* 18 September 1876, report of the Jubilee of Morpeth Mechanics' Institute.

46 *Newcastle Daily Chronicle,* 3 October 1867, Editorial commenting upon the counter attractions to betting shops.

47 NCLLS, *Minute Book of the Northern Union of Mechanics' Institutes, 1872-1887,* 4 October 1879, report of the annual essay competition. Thomas Burt was one of the appointed judges and the winning entries were published in the *Newcastle Weekly Chronicle.*

48 TWAS, CP/D87, *Northern Tribune,* II, p. 349. On the establishment of Newcastle Public Library, see Owen R. Ashton and Joan Hugman, 'Letters from America: George Julian Harney, Boston, USA and Newcastle upon Tyne, England, 1863-1888', *Proceeding of the Massachusetts Historical Society,* 107, 1995, pp. 186-7.

49 *Northern Tribune,* II, p. 93.

50 G. J. Holyoake, *Self Help by the People: History of Co-operation in Rochdale,* London, 1858.

51 TWAS, CP/D318, Joseph Cowen speech to the Annual Meeting of the Northern Union of Mechanics' Institutes, 17 September 1884; *Newcastle Daily Chronicle,* 12 April 1873.

52 Joan Hugman, 'Joseph Cowen and the Blaydon Cooperative Store: a north east model', in Bill Lancaster and Paddy Maguire (eds.), *Towards a Cooperative Commonwealth,* Loughborough, 1996, pp. 63-74.

53 TWAS, CP/B135, B137; R. Challinor, *A New Harmony?,* Newcastle, 1990, p. 4.

54 TWAS, CP/B137, Joseph Cowen speech to the Newcastle Cooperative Congress, 12 April 1873.

172   JOSEPH COWEN AND POPULAR RADICALISM ON TYNESIDE

55 Ibid.
56 On the rise of co-operation, see Sidney Pollard, 'Cooperation: from Community Building to Shopkeeping', in Asa Briggs and John Saville (eds.), *Essays in Labour History*, vol. 1, 1969, pp. 99-100; G. D. H. Cole, *A Century of Co-operation*, Manchester, 1944, p. 89. More generally, see Lancaster and Maguire, (eds.) *Towards a Cooperative Commonwealth*; Peter Gurney, *Co-operative Culture and the Politics of Consumption in England, c.1870-1930*, Manchester, 1996; Paul Johnson, *Saving and Spending. The Working Class Economy in Britain, 1870-1939*, Oxford, 1985.
57 Gurney, *Co-operative Culture and the Politics of Consumption*, p. 10.
58 Edward Morton, *An Adventure in Co-operation among the Working Classes in North Shields*, Pelaw-on-Tyne, 1925, p. 72; D. Gledson, *Jubilee Souvenir. A Short History of the New Delaval Equitable Industrial Co-operative Society Limited, 1862-1912*, Pelaw-on-Tyne, 1913, p. 149.
59 TWAS, CP/B137.
60 Ibid.
61 TWAS, CP/E436, JCM, ch. 14, p. 7.
62 TWAS, CP/B122, *North of England Co-operative Almanack*, 1873.
63 TWAS, CP/B41, Northern Co-operative Union Minute Book, 11 March 1862-17 May 1864. It is notable that the meetings were held in the Northern Reform Union Office.
64 Cole, *Century of Co-operation*, p. 154; Todd, *Militant Democracy*, p. 107.
65 TWAS, CP/E436, JCM, ch. 14.
66 W. Simpson, *Jubilee Souvenir. A Short History of the Cramlington District Co-operative Society Ltd., 1861-1911*, Manchester, 1912, p. 27.
67 *Handbook of the Twenty Sixth Annual Co-operative Congress*, Sunderland, 1894, p. 78.
68 TWAS, CP/E436, JCM, ch. 14, p. 43. The deputation told Cowen that they were unwilling to move nearer to their place of work because they would no longer qualify for a vote and they would not be near the Co-op store. Cowen successfully negotiated with the railway authorities on their behalf.
69 E. Allen, J. F. Clarke, N. McCord and D. J. Rowe, *The North-East Engineers' Strikes of 1871: The Nine Hours' League*, Newcastle, 1971 provides the most detailed account of the background and progress of the strike.
70 Ibid., p. 123. Debate about the merits of producer co-operatives were ongoing throughout the 1860s.
71 Todd, *Militant Democracy*, pp. 108-9. By 1871 there was a Cabinetmakers' Society (1867), a Corn Mill (1868) and a Tailoring Co-operative (1871).
72 Dr John Hunter Rutherford was a local educationalist with an active involvement in the Newcastle Mechanics' Institute. He collaborated with Cowen on various reform projects but he is particularly renowned as a prominent co-operator who sponsored the Ouseburn venture. See Cole, *Century of Co-operation*, pp. 163-4 which gives a short account of his co-operative activities A brief biography of

Rutherford's life and career can also be found in Richard Welford, *Men of Mark 'Twixt Tyne and Tweed*, Newcastle, 1892, 3 vols., III, pp. 338-41. For Rutherford's educational activities, see Joan Allen and Richard Buswell, *Rutherford's Ladder: The Making of the University of Northumbria*, Newcastle, 2005.

73 *Newcastle Daily Chronicle*, 1 July 1871.
74 Ibid.
75 The mining co-operative Briggs & Co. was established in Yorkshire in 1865. Cole, *Century of Co-operation*, p. 160 was dismissive, stating that it was 'no more than a profit-sharing arrangement of a singularly unfortunate kind' but its importance lies in that other producer co-operatives, including the Ouseburn Engine Works, adopted the same 10 per cent fixed reserve on capital before any dividend was payable. In 1874 the shareholding arrangements were abandoned following a protracted strike.
76 *Newcastle Daily Chronicle*, Editorial, 4 July 1871.
77 Ibid., 1 July 1871.
78 Ibid., 6 July 1871.
79 Ibid., 7 August 1871.
80 TWAS, CP/B120, Returns of Co-operative Societies to the House of Commons, 1872, record that the Blaydon Society had assets worth £16,221 and 1,774 members.
81 *Newcastle Daily Chronicle*, 28 August 1871.
82 Ibid., 7 October 1871.
83 Ibid., 8 November 1871.
84 Ibid., 31 October 1871. Rutherford contested and won the Elswick seat.
85 TWAS, CP/B122, Alex Scorer, 'The Ouseburn Engine Works', *North of England Co-operative Almanack*, 1873.
86 R. Oakeshott, *The Case for Workers' Co-ops*, London, 1978, p. 57 gives a brief summary of the history of worker's co-operatives and states that Ouseburn was 'another false start'. See also Cole, *Century of Co-operation*, pp. 163-7; Benjamin Jones, *Co-operative Production*, Oxford, 1894.
87 H. D. Lloyd, *Labour Co-partnership*, London, 1899, pp. 103-7; B. Lancaster, *Radicalism, Cooperation and Socialism: Leicester Working Class Politics 1860-1906*, Leicester, 1987, ch. 10, especially pp. 137-8; L. Magnanie, 'National Cooperative Festivals', in S. Yeo (ed.), *New Views of Cooperation*, London, 1988, pp. 181-3, who notes that dissent over share holding and partnership created a rift and led to the creation of an 'alternative' festival based in the North.
88 Lloyd, *Labour Co-partnership*, p. 183 noting that the Hebdon Bridge Fustian Works encountered such problems. See also Lancaster, *Radicalism, Cooperation and Socialism*, p. 138.
89 Oakeshott, *Case for Workers' Co-ops*, p. 58.
90 Todd, *Militant Democracy*, p. 122.
91 TWAS, CP/B122, *North of England Co-operative Almanack*, 1873; Nigel Todd, 'The Red Herring War of 1872: Women's rights, Butchers and Co-ops in the

Northern Coalfield', in Lancaster and Maguire, (eds.) *Towards the Cooperative Commonwealth*, pp. 55-62. See also M. I. Thomis and J. Grimmet, *Women in Protest 1800-1850*, New York, 1982, ch. 2 which gives a detailed appraisal of early-nineteenth century food riots,

92 *Newcastle Guardian*, 1 April 1848 refers to the 'unwearied exertions' of the women which kept many mechanics' institutes solvent.

93 *North of England Farmer*, 15 June 1872.

94 Ibid., 22 June 1872.

95 Ibid.

96 Ibid., 6 July 1872.

97 Ibid., 22 July 1872.

98 Ibid., 31 August 1872. The editor asserted that high food prices were a direct result of the shorter working hours that the working classes had agitated for in 1871.

99 TWAS, CP/B137, Speech to Newcastle Cooperative Congress, 13 April 1873.

100 Perkin, *Origins of Modern British Society*, pp. 384-90 states that by the 1860s the Co-operative movement was 'an instrument of working class amelioration rather than social revolution'. See also Johnson, *Saving and Spending*, p. 126 who asserts that most members were 'more interested in money than in social development'. Walton, *Lancashire*, pp. 245-7 states that the Co-operative movement in Lancashire diverted the working classes away from radical reform, although elsewhere in the volume he also points out that co-operatives gave the working classes access to libraries and educational facilities, and overall this produced significant improvements in standards of living. Ibid., p.301.

101 TWAS, CP/B137.

102 Ibid.

103 *Wallsend Industrial Co-operative Society Jubilee History, 1862-1912*, Manchester, 1913.

104 Ibid.

105 Simpson, *Jubilee Souvenir, Cramlington*. See also *Blaydon and District Industrial and Provident Society Centenary History, 1858-1958*, Newcastle, 1958; *Newcastle Daily Chronicle*, 3 March 1873 notes the establishment of the Newcastle Industrial Land and Building Society 'on co-operative principles'.

106 Simpson, *Jubilee Souvenir, Cramlington*, p. 174.

107 TWAS, CP/B122, *North of England Co-operative Almanack, 1873*.

108 TWAS, CP/D320. Speech on the Blue Ribbon Movement, 19 January 1884.

109 NCLLS, Local Tracts, *North of England Temperance League Centenary Handbook, 1858-1958*, 1958, states that the first Newcastle Temperance Society was formed on 1 January 1830 and the Northern Union was established by 1836.

110 Brian Harrison, *Drink and the Victorians: The temperance question in England, 1815-1872*, London, 1971, ch. 5.

111 Ibid., p. 113 states that Whittaker was a 'poor factory lad'; T. W. P. Taylder, *The History of the Rise and Progress of Teetotallism in Newcastle*, Newcastle, 1885, pp. 9-10.

112 *British and Foreign Temperance Intelligencer*, 1 January 1840.

113 Extract from the United Kingdom Alliance 4th Report, 1856, and cited in Taylder, *History of the Rise and Progress of Teetotalism*, p. 77.

114 *Newcastle Guardian*, 27 April 1850.

115 TWAS, CP/B148, Speech by Joseph Cowen at the opening of a Temperance Church Bazaar, North Shields, 13 March 1873.

116 TWAS, CP/D87, *Northern Tribune*, I, March 1854.

117 Joseph Cowen, *Speeches on Public Questions and Political Policy*, Speech in the Glassmakers' Arms, Newcastle upon Tyne, 2 January 1874, p. 59.

118 *Durham Chronicle*, 24 May 1870; *North of England Farmer*, 28 October 1871. On Bruce's Licensing Act, see Richard Shannon, *Gladstone. Heroic Minster 1865-1898*, London, 2000, p. 96; John Ramsden, *An Appetite for Power. A History of the Conservative Party since 1830*, London, 1999, pp. 111-12; T. A. Jenkins, *The Liberal Ascendancy, 1830-1886*, Basingstoke, 1994, pp. 133-4.

119 *North of England Farmer*, 31 August 1872.

120 R. Colls, *Pitmen of the Northern Coalfield: Work, Culture and Protest, 1790-1850*, Manchester, 1987, p. 131.

121 Anon., *Testimony for the Millions*, Newcastle, January 1847.

122 An analysis of the debate is provided in Robert Moore, *Pitmen, Preachers and Politics*, Cambridge, 1974, p. 225. See also Lowell J. Satre, *Thomas Burt, Miner's MP, 1837-1922. The Great Conciliator*, Leicester, 1999, pp. 8-9.

123 NCLLS, *Local Tracts*, 'A Defence of Working Men', 1850.

124 Ibid.

125 *Newcastle Daily Chronicle*, 1 June 1859.

126 Ibid., 10 July 1860.

127 Ibid., 26 July 1860. The 'Garibaldi March' was written by a Tyneside man, T. S. Watson.

128 *Northern Tribune*, I, 1854, p. 211, has a report of a speech by Joseph Cowen at Newburn, as well as a review of the Middlesbrough Temperance movement which noted that 'the leaders of the Temperance movement are the leading men in the Mechanics'.

129 NCLLS, 'Newcastle As It Is', An Address by the Newcastle Temperance Society, Newcastle, 1854.

130 Taylder, *History of the Rise and Progress of Teetotallism in Newcastle*. pp. 10-11.

131 The *North of England Temperance League Register* lists the annual income of the Newcastle Temperance Providence Insurance as £114,000 and the Newcastle Permanent Land and Building Society as £77,000.

132 *Newcastle Daily Chronicle*, 22 January 1872 stated that members of the Good Templars were the 'better class of temperance reformers'.

133 Cole, *Century of Co-operation*, p. 77.

134 Harrison, *Drink and the Victorians*, p. 174.

135 Based on information from the *North of England Temperance League Register*, and the *North of England Co-operative Almanac*, Newcastle, 1873.

136 The *Co-operator* was circulated as *The Anti-Vaccinator* from January 1871 until December 1871. Thomas Burt was prosecuted for failing to have his children vaccinated against smallpox. There are numerous newspaper reports of the local campaign in which Temperance activists played a prominent part. For example, see the *North of England Farmer,* 21 October 1871.

137 J. M. Baernreither, *English Associations of Working Men,* London, 1889. The statistics quoted are extracted from the *Fourth Report of the Royal Commission,* 1874, p. 163. See also Perkin, *Origins of Modern British Society,* p. 381 who states that friendly societies had four times more members than trade unions and twelve times as many members as the co-operative societies. On Friendly societies more generally, see Johnson, *Saving and Spending,* pp. 13-65.

138 For many years P. H. J. H. Gosden, *The Friendly Societies in England, 1815-75,* Manchester, 1961 was the most comprehensive available study, but see also Simon Cordery, *British Friendly Societies 1750-1914,* Basingstoke, 2003; Eric Hopkins, *Working Class Self- Help in Nineteenth-Century England,* London, 1995. On Freemasonry, see John Halstead and Andrew Prescott, 'Breaking the Barriers: Masonry, Fraternity and Labour', *Labour History Review* (Special Issue), 71: 1, 2006, pp. 3-9 and, more generally, other contributions in the same volume.

139 Elaine Knox, 'The Body Politic, Bodysnatching, the Anatomy Act and the Poor on Tyneside', *Bulletin of the North East Labour History Society,* 24, 1990, p. 131 states that in 1850 there were more than 300 Burial Societies in Newcastle. See also Ruth Richardson, *Death, Dissection and the Destitute,* London, 1987.

140 Baernreither, *English Associations of Working Men,* p. 217ff.

141 NCLLS, *Rulebook of the Friend Societies of Matrons* (Newburn), established 15 October 1821.

142 NCLLS, *Rulebook of the Friendly Society of Women* (North Shields), established 1819.

143 Peter Bailey, *Leisure and Class in Victorian England,* London, 1978; Hugh Cunningham, *Leisure in the Industrial Revolution,* London, 1980, p. 122.

144 Winlaton and District Local History Society, *History of Blaydon,* Gateshead, 1975, p. 62.

145 *Newcastle Daily Chronicle,* 29 August 1865.

146 Baernreither, *English Associations of Working Men,* p. 225.

147 *Newcastle Daily Chronicle,* 26 July 1850.

148 NCLLS, *The Loyal Order of Ancient Shepherds (Ashton Unity) Guide & Directory 1887/8.* The Order was founded in 1826 and had a recorded membership in 1888 of 64,525.

149 TWAS, CP/D320, Cowen Speech on the Blue Ribbon Movement, 19 January 1884; *Newcastle Daily Chronicle,* 9 June 1870, with a report of Cowen's speech at a celebratory dinner for the Ancient Order of Druids.

150 Perkin, *Origins of Modern British Society,* p. 381ff; Johnson, *Saving and Spending,* p. 65.

151 *Newcastle Daily Chronicle,* 9 January 1867, 28 January 1867.

152 R. Whitfield, *History of the Lodge of Industry*, Newcastle, 1934, p. 50ff gives a full account of Reed's executive role in the Lodge and a brief biographical sketch of his political activities. Whitfield was Master of the Lodge in 1879. See also Ashton and Pickering, (eds.) *Friends of the People*, p. 142.

153 Robert Burt, 'The British Non-Ferrous Mining Industry', *Labour History Review*, 71: 1, 2006, pp. 69, 72.

154 Baernreither, *English Associations of Working Men*, p. 162; G.D.H. Cole and R. Postgate, *Common People, 1746-1946*, London, 1938, p. 235.

155 R. Challinor and B. Ripley, *The Miners' Association. A Trade Union in the Age of the Chartists*, London, 1990.

156 *Newcastle Weekly Chronicle*, 8 February 1873 publicised the 1873 campaign to extend the franchise to those mining districts anomalously excluded under the provisions of the 1868 Reform Act.

157 Ibid., 6 January 1872.

158 *Newcastle Daily Chronicle*, 16 August 1871.

159 *Northern Tribune*, I, 1854, p. 102. Samuel Kydd was a prominent Chartist. For Kydd, see Stephen Roberts, *Radical politicians and poets in early Victorian Britain: the voices of six Chartist leaders*, Lampeter, 1993.

160 Ibid.

161 *Newcastle Guardian*, 13 August 1859. See also K. D. Brown, 'Nonconformity and trade unionism: the Sheffield outrages of 1866', in Biagini and Reid, (eds.) *Currents of Radicalism*, p. 96 in which he argues that nonconformists employed the radical language of equity and fair play in their discussion of trade unionism.

162 SUSC, MP/LC, 10 September 1860; W. H. G. Armytage: *A. J. Mundella, 1825-1897*, London, 1951; R. Harrison, *Before the Socialists, Studies in Labour and Politics 1861-1881*, London, 1965, p. 37ff;. Ashton, *W. E. Adams*, p. 97.

163 *Newcastle Daily Chronicle*, 15 September 1871.

164 Ibid., 21 September 1871.

165 SUSC/MP, 6P/4/12/1, Thomas Cooper to A. J. Mundella, 19 September 1871, 20 September 1871.

166 Ibid.

167 SUSC/MP, 6P/4/12/6, Mundella to R. Leader, 1 October 1871.

168 Allen, Clarke, McCord and Rowe, *North East Engineers Strike of 1871*, p. 173ff; Todd *Militant Democracy*, p. 88.

169 *Newcastle Daily Chronicle*, 16 October 1871 notes similar demands being made in Manchester and Leeds; Ibid., 29 January 1872 notes that membership of the Amalgamated Society of Engineers increased from 34,805 to 37,840 because of the strike's success.

170 *Newcastle Weekly Chronicle*, 6 January 1872.

171 J. P. D. Dunbabin, *Rural Discontent in Nineteenth-Century Britain*, London, 1974, ch. VII, especially p. 161; Alun Howkins, *Reshaping Rural England: A Social History 1850-1925*, London, 1991.

72 Nigel Scotland, 'The National Agricultural Labourer's Union and the demand for

a stake in the soil, 1872-1896', in E.F. Biagini, (ed.) *Citizenship and Community, Liberals, radicals and collective identities in the British Isles, 1865-1931*, Cambridge, 1996, pp. 151-67.

173 *North of England Farmer*, 2 March 1872.
174 Ibid., 26 February 1872: Editorial.
175 *Newcastle Daily Chronicle*, 5 March 1872.
176 Ibid., 15 March 1872; 18 March 1872 ; 27 March 1872; 28 March 1872.
177 Ibid., 28 March 1872.
178 *Newcastle Daily Chronicle*, 19 February 1883.
179 *Newcastle Weekly Chronicle*, 17 February 1883, 24 February 1883, 31 January 1884. See also, Todd, *Militant Democracy*, pp. 150-1, 158.
180 *Newcastle Daily Chronicle*, 3 January 1872, 7 February 1872.
181 For a discussion of charismatic leadership see Eugenio. F. Biagini, *Liberty Retrenchment and Reform. Popular Liberalism in the Age of Gladstone, 1860-1880*, Cambridge, 1992, ch. 7.
182 H.H. Gerth and C.W. Mills, (eds.) *From Max Weber. Essays in Sociology*, London, 1948, p. 249.

Chapter 4

1   The Irish-born population was 31,167 in 1851, some 4.4 per cent of the total population. See Frank Neal, 'Irish settlement in the north-west and the north-east of England', in Roger Swift and Sheridan Gilley (eds.), *The Irish in Victorian Britain. The Local Dimension*, Dublin, 1999, p. 76. See also Roger Swift, 'The Irish in Britain', in Patrick O'Sullivan (ed.), *The Irish World Wide, History Heritage, Identity*, 6 vols, London, 1992-2000, II: *The Irish in the New Communities*, 1992, p. 57, who notes that 5.4 per cent of the population of Durham was Irish.
2   Roger Cooter, *When Paddy Met Geordie. The Irish in County Durham and Newcastle, 1840-1880*, Sunderland, 2005. See also Caroline L. Scott, 'A comparative re-examination of Anglo-Irish relations in Nineteenth Century Manchester, Liverpool and Newcastle upon Tyne', unpublished University of Durham PhD thesis, 1998.
3   Frank Neal, *Sectarian Violence. The Liverpool Experience 1819-1914*, Manchester, 1988; J. Walton, *Lancashire. A Social History, 1558-1939*, Manchester, 1987, pp. 252-4; Joan Smith, 'Labour Tradition in Glasgow and Liverpool', *History Workshop Journal*, 17, Spring 1984, pp. 32-56; M. A. G. Ó Tuathaigh, 'The Irish in Nineteenth Century Britain: Problems of Integration', in Roger Swift and Sheridan Gilley (eds.), *The Irish in the Victorian City*, London, 1985, pp. 149-73.
4   There is a vast and still growing literature on anti-Irish hostility in Britain after 1847. For example, Donald M. MacRaild, *Irish Migrants in Modern Britain 1750-1922*, London, 1999, ch. 6 and his *Culture, Conflict and Migration. The Irish in Victorian Cumbria*, Liverpool, 1998; Steve Fielding, *Class and Ethnicity. Irish Catholics in England, 1880-1939*, Manchester, 1993; Paul O'Leary (ed.), *Irish Migrants in Modern Wales*, Liverpool, 2004; Graham Davis, *The Irish in Britai*

1815-1914, Dublin, 1991; Tom Gallagher, *Glasgow. The Uneasy Peace, Religious Tension in Modern Scotland*, Manchester, 1987.

5   Donald M. MacRaild, *Faith, Fraternity and Fighting. The Orange Order and Irish Migrants in Northern England, 1850-1920*, Liverpool, 2005 has provided the first substantive study of Orangeism in the North of England while Frank Neal in his 'English-Irish conflict in the north-east of England', in Patrick Buckland and John Belchem (eds.), *The Irish in British Labour History* (Conference Proceedings in Irish Studies, 1), Liverpool, 1993, pp. 59-85 has identified some instances of inter-communal conflict, particularly in the west of the region.

6   Neal, 'English-Irish conflict', p. 79.

7   Terence McBride, 'Irishness in Glasgow', *Immigrants and Minorities*, 24.1, 2006, p. 3. See also, David Fitzpatrick, 'A Curious Middle Place: The Irish in Britain , 1871-1921', pp. 36-40, in Roger Swift and Sheridan Gilley (eds.), *The Irish in Britain 1815-1939*, London, 1989.

8   Sir Joseph Cowen, Cowen jnr and his son, also called Joseph. The latter helped to establish the Tyneside Irish Brigade at the time of the Boer War (1898-1902). See Felix Lavery (ed.), *Irish Heroes in the War*, London, 1917.

9   T. P. O'Connor, 'The Irish in Great Britain', in Lavery, (ed.) *Irish Heroes in the War*, p. 27 notes that Cowen was 'one of only seven Englishmen who stood up in the Commons to protest' about the Coercion Act in 1881.

10   Some local security measures were implemented, as directed by the government, but they were always regarded as precautionary. Attempts to arm the police were rigorously resisted. Even the 'conservative' *Newcastle Journal* conceded that 'while Fenian partisans are not wanting in Newcastle and the vicinity. . . there was no fear of any unrest', 25 November 1867.

11   Malcolm Chase, 'The Teesside Irish in the nineteenth century', in Buckland and Belchem (eds.), *Irish in British Labour History*, pp. 47-58.

12   C. G. Pooley, 'Segregation or Integration? The residential experience of the Irish in mid Victorian Britain', in Swift and Gilley (eds.), *The Irish in Britain,* p. 61 exposes the flaws in the censuses, not least the absence of data on age, gender and counties of origin, See also Roger Swift, 'The Irish in nineteenth-century Britain: towards a definitive history', in Buckland and Belchem (eds.), *Irish in British Labour History*, pp. 11-18.

13   Pooley,'Segregation or Integration?', p. 66 provides a list of the 'top twenty' Irish towns in Britain in 1851. Also see Neal, 'Irish settlement in the north-west and the north-east of England', pp. 76-7.

14   J. G. Lynch, 'The Irish Population in Darlington 1841-1851', *Durham Local History Society Bulletin*, 43, December 1989, p. 45 states that immigrants frequently left Scotland and travelled on to Tyneside.

15   Cooter, *When Paddy met Geordie*, p. 22.

6   Lavery, (ed.) *Irish Heroes in the War*, p. 328 claims that Monsignor McCartan 'sent to Newcastle a constant stream of lads from his native county'.

17 Graham Davis, 'Little Irelands', in Swift and Gilley, (eds.) *Irish in Britain*, pp. 103-33; Ó Tuathaigh, 'Irish in Nineteenth Century Britain', pp. 13-36; Fielding, *Class and Ethnicity*, pp. 27-31.

18 Pooley, 'Segregation or Integration?', p. 80 argues that a 'substantial minority' of skilled Irish workers were also widely dispersed in the residential suburbs. See also T. P. MacDermott, 'The Irish Workers on Tyneside in the 19th century', in Norman McCord (ed.), *Essays in Tyneside Labour History*, Newcastle, 1977, p. 163 who claims that there is no evidence that the Irish were coerced or pressured into residential 'ghettos'.

19 Cooter, *When Paddy met Geordie*, p. 20.

20 'Our Colliery Villages', *Newcastle Daily Chronicle*, 25 January 1873.

21 Tom Gallagher, 'A Tale of Two Cities: Communal Strife in Glasgow and Liverpool Before 1914', in Swift and Gilley (eds.), *Irish in the Victorian City*, p. 108.

22 Ó Tuathaigh, 'Irish in Nineteenth Century Britain', p. 20.

23 Gallagher, 'A Tale of Two Cities', p. 109. See also Smith, 'Labour Tradition in Glasgow and Liverpool', p. 46.

24 Cooter, *When Paddy met Geordie*, pp. 39-40; Davis, 'Little Irelands', pp. 64-5; Neal, 'English-Irish conflict in the north-east of England', p. 79.

25 Davis, 'Little Irelands', pp. 64-5, 115 contrasts the experience of the Irish on Tyneside with the hostile response in Cardiff.

26 *Gateshead Observer*, Editorial, 29 July 1848: 'In no part of the kingdom can the Poor Law be more faithfully administered. . . the resident and the casual poor alike enjoy the relief'.

27 *Newcastle Daily Chronicle*, Editorial, 'Irishmen in England', 24 December 1867 also noted that there had been no municipal enactments against Irish immigrants and expressed concern that 'honest' Irish workers in London might be sacked in reprisal for the recent Fenian outrages.

28 Smith, 'Labour Tradition in Glasgow and Liverpool', p. 48ff notes that the Liverpool job market was mainly transport and commerce and that there was greater competition in this sector. See also Neal, 'Irish settlement in the north-west and the north-east', pp. 92-6.

29 Gallagher, 'A Tale of Two Cities', p. 110; Walton, *Lancashire*, p. 252.

30 Cooter, *When Paddy met Geordie*, pp. 128-34. On the 1844 strike, see Richard Fynes, *The Miners of Northumberland and Durham*, Sunderland, 1873, pp. 49-103.

31 Dorothy Thompson, 'Ireland and the Irish in English Radicalism before 1850', in James Epstein and Dorothy Thompson (eds.), *The Chartist Experience. Studies in Working-Class Radicalism and Culture, 1830-1860*, London, 1982, p. 130.

32 MacRaild, *Irish Migrants in Modern Britain*, pp. 128-31; Swift, 'Irish in Britain', pp. 62-3.

33 Examples are numerous, for instance, 'The Address of the London Friendly Society of Operative Carpenters of Great Britain and Ireland', published in the *Northern Liberator*, 24 March 1838.

34 *Poor Man's Guardian* 1831-35, 12 February 1832, Rptd. London, 1969, p. 274.
35 *Newcastle Daily Chronicle*, 29 January 1867 carries a detailed account of previous Tyneside radical demonstrations, including the 1819 meeting. See also see John Belchem, '1848: Feargus O' Connor and the collapse of the Mass Platform', in J. Epstein and D. Thompson (eds.), *The Chartist Experience. Studies in Working Class Radicalism and Culture, 1830-1860,* London, 1982, p. 88 noting that the Spenceans' plan to build up a General Union of the Non- Represented of the United Kingdom of Great Britain and Ireland was promoted through their 'aptly named journal'.
36 *Newcastle Daily Chronicle*, 29 January 1867 states that the official Reform League banner was 'blue for Scotland, red for England and green for Ireland'.
37 *Northern Liberator*, 29 December 1838. Political speeches were interspersed with appropriate songs – in this instance 'Sprig of Shillelagh' ('With his sprig of shille-lagh, and shamrock so green/His heart is good-humoured, 'tis honest and sound/ no malice or hatred is there to be found'). Harney's reference to Robert Emmett, the renowned United Irishman executed in 1803 for his seditious activities would have been considered inflammatory by the authorities.
38 Ibid.
39 Ibid., 1 July 1838.
40 See Peter Doyle's Chartist Letters printed in the *Newcastle Weekly Chronicle*, 21 July 1883 and 27 September 1884. Doyle claimed to have thrown a piece of broken granite at the Mayor, Sir John Fife, during the 'Battle of the Spital'. He also claims that 'seditious schemes were concocted . . . and a diabolical project planned to burn the town' in the offices of the *Northern Liberator*.
41 *Newcastle Weekly Chronicle*, 27 September 1884, McKinney described himself as the son of a farmer from Londonderry, dispossessed by the laws of primogeniture and subsequently sacked by a Scottish clergyman for his political views. He had met with similar treatment in other parts of England. Other speakers, including James Ayr (mason), Richard Ayre (publican and treasurer of the NPU), Mr Parker ('delegate of four factories on the Tyne') actively promoted Irish interests.
42 *Northern Liberator*, 1 September 1838, 'Address of the WMA of North Shields to the Democrats of Great Britain and Ireland', 24 August 1838. The signatories were James Waugh and James McKean Henderson.
43 Ibid., 13 April 1839, John Rucastle (druggist) addressing a public meeting in the Guild Hall.
44 Ibid., Speech by William Thomason of the NPU.
45 Ibid., NPU Council meeting at Howdon Pans. The sub-committee comprised Richard Ayre, James Ayr and John Mason (shoemaker).
46 Ibid., 29 December 1838. Parker remarked upon the 'beautiful sight. . . of his fair Radical country women'.
47 *Newcastle Journal*, 1 April 1848 complained of the 'disorderly spirit' of the crowd and the way that 'a Mr Kidd raved about Ireland'.
48 John Saville, *1848. The British State and the Chartist Movement*, Cambridge, 1987, pp. 73-4. Saville agrees with Dorothy Thompson's claim for strong links between

English and Irish Radicals, particularly in the Northern industrial towns, but re-
gards 1848 as the moment when closer working relationships were forged.

49   *Newcastle Journal*, 7 October 1848; *Gateshead Observer*, 15 April 1848.

50   Cooter, *When Paddy Met Geordie*, p. 61; *Northern Liberator*, 25 May 1839. See
also 3 March 1838, 'Deputation of the WMA to a meeting of pitmen at Wylam,
with men from three collieries in the district and to the miners of the St Lawrence
Colliery'. The St Lawrence colliery was located in the All Saints area and the shaft
was sunk between 1832 and 1833.

51   T.A. Devyr, *The Odd Book of the Nineteenth Century, or Chivalry in Modern Days*,
New York, 1882, p. 162.

52   TWAS, CP/C547, 28 February 1859.

53   *Newcastle Daily Chronicle*, 3 January 1872, Speech by Thomas Connolly to the
Tyneside Engineers.

54   John Newsinger, *Fenianism in Mid-Victorian Britain*, London, 1994, pp. 50-3.

55   Norman McCord, 'The Fenians and public opinion in Great Britain', in Maurice
Harmon (ed.), *Fenians and Fenianism*, Dublin, 1968, p. 38.

56   Belchem, '1848: Feargus O'Connor', p. 278; *Newcastle Journal*, 29 October 1867
claimed that wealthy middle class supporters would be discouraged if the Reform
League did not publicly denounce Fenianism.

57   P. Quinliven and P. Rose, *The Fenians In England: A Sense of Insecurity*, London,
1982, pp. 65-72

58   Statistics quoted by Fitzpatrick, 'A Curious Middle Place', p. 33. See also *Newcastle
Weekly Chronicle* which published a series of articles on secret societies in 1878,
especially 2 February 1878 stating that Newcastle, London, Liverpool, Manchester
and Glasgow were all major centres of the IRB in 1864. L. W. Brady, *T. P. O'Connor
and the Liverpool Irish*, London, 1983, p. 32 estimates that there were 5,000 Fenians
in Lancashire in the 1860s.

59   O'Connor, 'Irish in Great Britain', p. 47.

60   *Newcastle Daily Chronicle*, 13 December 1865, Editorial, criticising the harsh sen-
tences imposed on the Fenians and denouncing the tendency to 'brand Irish people as low, ignorant and indolent'.

61   Ibid., 2 October 1867. Editorial, 'Fenianism: Its Cause and Its Cure'.

62   Ibid., 6 July 1866; Todd, *Militant Democracy*, p. 69; D. J. Jackson, ' 'Garibaldi or the
Pope!'. Newcastle's Irish Riot of 1866', *North East History*, 34, 2001, pp. 49-82.

63   'Garibaldi Riots' occurred in other towns too. See S. Gilley, 'The Garibaldi riots of
1862', *Historical Journal*, 16:4, 1973, pp. 697-732.

64   Ashton, *W. E. Adams*, p. 109, notes that the Testimonial committee set up to ar-
range a civic reception 'maintained its existence indefinitely. . . it became essentially the parent. . . of the Northern Reform League'.

65   Michael Morris and Leo Gooch, *Down Your Aisles. The Diocese of Hexham and
Newcastle*, Hartlepool, 2000, p. 12 estimates that there were 26,000 Catholics in
Northumberland and Durham in 1851, rising to 190,000 by 1914.

66   *Newcastle Daily Chronicle*, 6 July 1866.

67 *Newcastle Courant*, 20 July 1866.

68 *Newcastle Daily Chronicle*, 19 July 1866.

69 Walton, *Lancashire*, p. 261. See also MacRaild, *Irish Migrants in Modern Britain*, pp. 176-8; Quinliven and Rose, *Fenians in England*, ch. 4 gives a detailed account of the Murphy Riots.

70 Roger Swift, 'Crime and the Irish', in Swift and Gilley (eds.), *Irish in Britain*, p. 170 surveys anti-Catholic and anti-Irish disorder after 1850 and links this to the resurgence of popular Protestantism. p. 172.

71 Quinliven and Rose, *Fenians in England*, pp. 33-4. See also Walton, *Lancashire*, p. 261.

72 *Newcastle Daily Chronicle*, 26 August 1867.

73 T. P. MacDermott, 'Charles Larkin, Radical Reformer 1800-1879', *Northern Catholic History*, 28 August 1988, pp. 13-17.

74 *Newcastle Weekly Chronicle*, 'Larkin's Letters', 1 February 1868. Larkin was careful to insist upon justice for the Irish as a cure for Fenianism, not punitive action.

75 MacRaild, *Culture, Conflict and Migration*, p. 179.

76 MacRaild, *Faith Fraternity and Fighting*, pp. x, 55.

77 Ibid., p. 10; Tony Gray, *The Orange Order*, London and Toronto, 1972, p. 89; MacDermott, 'Irish Workers on Tyneside', p. 160 states that disturbances tended to be located south of the Tyne. For reported clashes between Fenians and Orangemen see *North of England Farmer*, 18 February 1871 (Consett), and 15 July 1871 (West Hartlepool); 4 February 1871 (Hartlepool); 11 February 1871 (Bishop Auckland).

78 *Newcastle Guardian*, 28 January 1871.

79 Robert Kee, *The Green Flag. A History of Irish Nationalism*, London 1972, ch. 18; Newsinger, *Fenianism in Mid-Victorian Britain*, pp. 53-4, 60-5.

80 *Newcastle Daily Chronicle*, 26 September 1867; 28 September 1867. The police were said to be 'on the alert' and steamers leaving Hartlepool were rigorously searched.

81 Editorial in the *Newcastle Daily Chronicle*, 11 October 1867.

82 Neal, 'English-Irish conflict in the north-east of England', pp. 72-3; *Birmingham Journal*, May 1867; *Sheffield Independent*, 7 May 1867.

83 *Newcastle Daily Chronicle*, 10 October 1867, 16 October 1867, 8 November 1867.

84 Ibid., 2 September 1867.

85 Quinliven and Rose, *Fenians in England*, p. 72; *Newcastle Daily Chronicle*, 9 October 1867, Editorial: 'We have every confidence in the loyalty of the Irish element in our towns.'

86 Ibid., 23 November 1867; *Newcastle Weekly Chronicle*, 6 December 1867.

87 *Newcastle Daily Chronicle*, 25 November 1867.

88 *Newcastle Journal*, 16 December 1867.

89 *Newcastle Daily Chronicle*, 16 December 1867.

90 *Newcastle Journal*, 16 December 1867. See also Quinliven and Rose, *Fenians in England*, p. 97.

91   See *Newcastle Daily Chronicle* throughout December 1867, especially 24 December, Editorial: 'Irishmen in England'.

92   Ibid. Sir Joseph Cowen claimed that he had been to Ireland and witnessed the injustice they suffered at first hand.

93   *Newcastle Journal*, 25 November 1867, 6 December 1867.

94   *Newcastle Daily Chronicle*, 11 December 1866. There is a large cache of papers on the Reform League in the Cowen papers. See TWAS, CP/1740-1852.

95   *Newcastle Daily Chronicle*, 11 March 1867.

96   Ibid., 29 January 1867.

97   F. M. Leventhal, *Respectable Radical: George Howell and Victorian working class politics*, London, 1971, p. 98.

98   *Newcastle Journal*, 25 October 1867.

99   *Newcastle Daily Chronicle*, 29 January 1867. Irish Trade delegates included Ralph Anderson, DMA; John Charlton NMA; George Hill, Newcastle Society of Boilermakers; John Cummings, Brassfounders and Brass-finishers; and James Campbell, Boilermakers and Iron Shipbuilders (Jarrow).

100   Michael Bentley, *The Climax of Liberal Politics: British Liberalism in theory and practice, 1868-1918*, London, 1987, p. 60; Walton, *Lancashire*, p. 262 who notes the importance of the sectarian issue during the 1868 election.

101   Cooter, *When Paddy Met Geordie*, p. 239 n.80.

102   J. P. Dunbabin, 'Electoral Reforms and their Outcome in the U.K. 1865-1900', in T. R. Gourvish and A. O'Day (eds.), *Later Victorian Britain, 1867-1900*, Basingstoke, 1988, pp. 118-21.

103   Walton, *Lancashire*, p. 262 states that 'religious affiliation was remarkably effective as a touchstone for political alignment'.

104   Ibid., p. 260 who highlights the divisions caused by the Liberals' education reform in the Lancashire area. On Cowen's education strategy, see Joan Allen and Richard Buswell, *Rutherford's Ladder: The Making of the University of Northumbria 1871-1996*, Newcastle, 2005, pp. 27-8.

105   Ashton, *W. E. Adams*, pp. 111-12. See also IISH, AP/222/1/123; AP/222/1/124; AP222/1/125, letters from James Trotter to W.E. Adams.

106   Fynes, *Miners of Northumberland and Durham*, Ch. XLIII. According to Fynes' statistics, Northumberland and Durham had 51,000 members in 1873 compared with 27,000 in Yorkshire.

107   TWAS, CP/C1779.

108   TWAS, CP/various, including C1801, C1804, C1808.

109   TWAS, CP/C1822 Speech, 12 April 1873. See also TWAS, CP/C1779, C1808. For an account of the demonstration see Fynes, *Miners of Northumberland and Durham*, p. 269.

110   *Newcastle Daily Chronicle*, 14 April 1873 (Special edition).

111   Lowell Satre, *Thomas Burt, Miner's MP, 1837-1922*, Leicester, 1999, p. 36.

112   MacDermott, 'Irish Workers on Tyneside', p. 167 notes that McAnulty was the first Irishman to sit on an English Town Council.

113 Alvin Jackson, *Home Rule. An Irish History 1800-2000*, London, 2003, pp. 28-44; Alan O'Day, *Irish Home Rule 1867-1921*, Manchester, 1999, pp. 22-38.

114 T. W. Moody, *Davitt and Irish Revolution, 1846-82*, Oxford, 1981, p. 125. Moody gives a good account of Barry's early life and career as a commercial traveller in Newcastle, and as a member of the Supreme Council of the IRB. See also Joseph Keating, 'The History of the Tyneside Irish Brigade', in Lavery (ed.), *Irish Heroes in the War*, pp. 51-3 who states that Barry organized the 'Irish' vote in Newcastle in the early 1870s.

115 Alan O' Day, 'The political organization of the Irish in Britain, 1867-1890', in Swift and Gilley, (eds.) *Irish in Britain*, pp. 190-5.

116 Ibid., p. 193. O' Day states that 'attempts were made to mould disparate associations into a unified organization'.

117 *Newcastle Weekly Chronicle*, 6 January 1872.

118 Ibid. Key activists at the Town Hall meeting were listed as Bayfield, Barry, M. Curran, John Devine, Charles Flannagan, Joseph Heenan, John Mullen, Patrick Mooney, J. McGill, J. McKay, W. McEvoy, McKintyre, Michael O'Hanlon, Stephen Quin, Matthew Roddy, Edward Savage, Smyth and F. Wallace.

119 O'Day, 'Political organization of the Irish in Britain', pp. 190-1.

120 Leon Ó Broin, *Revolutionary Underground: The story of the Irish Republican Brotherhood, 1858-192*, Dublin, 1976, p. 11. Butt allegedly made a secret agreement with the Fenians, promising to relinquish control to them if, at the end of three years, Home Rule had not been achieved.

121 Letter dated 23 August 1873, and cited in O'Day, 'Political organization of the Irish in Britain', p. 195.

122 *Newcastle Weekly Chronicle*, 18 January 1873, 25 January 1873, 6 February 1875.

123 O'Connor, 'Irish in Great Britain', p. 25. In the same volume, see Keating, 'History of the Tyneside Irish Brigade', p. 27 who describes Cowen's sympathy for the Irish as 'extraordinary'. Cowen, he claimed, was the 'rallying point of British democratic and Irish forces'.

124 TWAS, CP/B399, 8 September 1884.

125 Charles Diamond (1858-1934) was born in Co. Derry in 1858 and moved to Newcastle in the late 1870s. He was President of the Newcastle branch of the the I.N.L. in 1884. In his lifetime Diamond published a large number of other Catholic journals, including the *Glasgow Observer* and the *Weekly Herald* (later the *Catholic Herald*). See Joan Allen, "Keeping the Faith': The Catholic press and the preservation of Celtic identity in Britain in the late nineteenth century', in Pamela O'Neill (ed.), *Exile and Homecoming*, Sydney, 2004, pp. 78-91; O. D. Edwards and P. J. Storey, 'The Irish Press in Victorian Britain', in Swift and Gilley (eds.), *Irish in the Victorian City*, p. 173.

126 TWAS, CP/B244, Cowen to Charles Diamond, 2 February 1886. See also Felix Lavery 'Who's Who of the Tyneside Irish Movement' in Lavery (ed.), *Irish Heroes in the War*, p. 323.

127 The phrase is used by Ó Tuathaigh, 'Irish in Nineteenth Century Britain', p. 23 who states that ethnic social groups and institutions created a 'cultural distance' that was 'very difficult to bridge'.

128 Joan Allen and Richard C. Allen, "Competing identities': Irish and Welsh migration and the North East of England', in Adrian Green and A. J. Pollard (eds.), *Regional Identities in North-East England, 1300-2000*, London, 2007.

129 *Newcastle Weekly Chronicle*, 7 May 1881.

130 M. Milne, *The Newspapers of Northumberland and Durham: A study of their progress during the 'Golden Age' of the Provincial Press*, Newcastle, 1971, p. 29 states that the skilled working class read the *Daily Chronicle*, and the unskilled workers were more likely to read the *Weekly*.

131 *Newcastle Weekly Chronicle*, 3 April 1875, Obituary of John Martin MP who was transported for Fenian activities and later represented Co. Meath as a constitutionalist; ibid., 7 August 1875, Biography of Wolfe Tone, founder of the Society of United Irishmen. Lloyd Jones (1811-86) was born in Ireland of Welsh parentage. He was an active co-operator and trade unionist, member of the SDF and numerous other radical organisations. He wrote for a number of newspapers including the *Glasgow Sentinel* and the *Newcastle Chronicle*.

132 TWAS, CP/E436, JCM, ch. 1l.

133 TWAS, CP/B178, Speech in Newcastle, 18 October 1876.

134 Vincent, *Formation of the Liberal Party*, p. 104ff; Machin, 'Disestablishment and democracy', pp. 120-48.

135 GLRO, A/LIB/297, *The Liberation Society: A Jubilee Retrospect*. For details of Newcastle branch activity, see GLRO, A/LIB/3; A/LIB/381; A/LIB/391.

136 Vincent, *Formation of the Liberal Party*, p. 108 states that 'allegiance was demanded from Liberal candidates. . . in proportion to the strength of dissent in the constituency'. See also Alan Sykes, *The Rise and Fall of British Liberalism, 1776-1988*, London and New York, 1997, pp. 54-7.

137 *Newcastle Daily Chronicle*, 31 October 1867.

138 Ibid., 1 November 1867, 21 April 1871; GLRO, A/LIB/89; A/LIB/1; A/LIB/391.

139 *Newcastle Journal*, 31 December 1867.

140 TWAS, CP/B157, Speech, 30 December 1873; Newcastle Liberal Association minutes: NCLLS, Local Tracts, LO, 42 1878-93.

141 *Newcastle Weekly Chronicle*, 25 September 1875, Demonstration in Elswick Park.

142 TWAS, CP/B178, Speech on Civil and Religious Liberty, 18 October 1876.

143 TWAS, CP/B180, Review of the Political Scene, 27 January 1877.

144 Ibid.

145 TWAS, CP/B181, 27 February 1877, Speech to the Nonconformist Conference.

146 TWAS, CP/D320, 61,000 pledges were made in 1882. For an analysis of Irish Temperance activities see Elizabeth Malcolm, 'Temperance and Irish Nationalism', in F. S. L. Lyons and R. A. J. Hawkins (eds.), *Ireland under the Union: Varieties of Tensions. Essays in honour of T. W. Moody*, Oxford, 1980, pp. 69-114.

147 B. Aspinwall and J. F. McCaffrey, 'A Comparative View of the Irish in Edinburgh in the 19th Century', in Swift and Gilley, (eds.) *Irish in the Victorian City*, p. 137. See also Smith, 'Labour Tradition in Glasgow and Liverpool' p. 47ff, and citing Gramsci who argued that participation in private associations helped to create the individual's 'spontaneous philosophy'. Since those same associations constituted the 'hegemonic apparatus', involvement ensured that, in Glasgow, the shared vision of the world was 'Liberal'; on Tyneside, it was 'Radical'.

148 TWAS, CP/B415, Letter from Cowen to H. B. Thompson, nd: 'I would have the land of the country disposed of as easily and as freely as you would dispose of railway stocks and bank shares.'

149 *Northern Tribune*, I: 2, 1854, p. 63 gives an account of the purchase of 'California' from H. T. Liddell at a cost of £370.

150 TWAS, CP/B122, *North of England Co-operative Almanack*, 1873.

151 TWAS, CP/B349, Cowen's comments on the publication of his election speeches in 1885.

152 J. Belchem, *Popular Radicalism in Nineteenth Century Britain*, Basingstoke, 1996, p. 150; Harrison, *Before the Socialists*, pp. 210-17; Hollis (ed.), *Pressure from Without*, pp. 9-11. Also, in the Hollis volume see D. Martin, 'Land Reform', pp. 131-59; Thomas W. Heyck, *The Dimensions of British Radicalism: The case of Ireland, 1874-95*, Urbana, IL and London, 1974, p. 19ff.

153 J.P. Dunbabin, *Rural Discontent in Nineteenth Century Britain*, London, 1974, pp. 62-84, 155-72, and his 'The 'Revolt of the Field': The agricultural labourers' movement in the 1870s', *Past & Present*, 26, 1963, pp. 68-97; Jeffrey Harvey Porter, 'The 'revolt of the field': The Devon response', *Southern History*, 7, 1985, pp. 163-78.

154 TWAS, CP/B152, Broadsheet of the NALU, May 1873.

155 *Newcastle Weekly Chronicle*, 24 February 1875 report of an NALU rally at Hungerford.

156 TWAS, CP/B288, 27 March 1883. Cowen presided over this meeting of the Liberation Society in Newcastle. See also *Newcastle Weekly Chronicle*, 31 March 1883.

157 TWAS, CP/B125, 3 March 1873. Letter from E. Ashton of Mitford asking Cowen to approach Arch for assistance in setting up a local branch.

158 TWAS, CP/B415, undated but probably 1880-1 when the 1881 Land Act was under consideration.

159 *Newcastle Weekly Chronicle*, 20 March 1875; TWAS, CP/ B210 Meeting in Newcastle Town Hall. Dr Rutherford said Cowen 'linked the Land Question and the Irish Question together'.

160 *Newcastle Weekly Chronicle*, 3 April 1875, London Letter. Arthur Orton was imprisoned in 1872. On the national movement, see R. McWilliams, 'The Tichborne Claimant and the People. Investigations into Popular Culture 1867-1886', unpublished University of Sussex PhD thesis, 1990; and his 'Radicalism and popular culture: the Tichborne case and the politics of 'fair play', 1867-1886', in E.F. Biagini

and A.J. Reid (eds.), *Currents of Radicalism. Popular Radicalism, organised labour and party politics in Britain, 1850-1914*, Cambridge, 1991, pp. 44-64.

161 *Newcastle Weekly Chronicle*, 9 March 1872.

162 Ibid., 16 October 1875. Kenealy, MP for Stoke on Trent, acted as defending counsel for Orton and later presided over the Magna Charta Association.

163 Ibid., various dates, including 27 February 1875, 10 April 1875, 17 April 1875. See also, Adams, *Memoirs*, p. 149.

164 *Newcastle Weekly Chronicle*, 30 May 1875. Cowen had voted against a Royal Commission of Enquiry when the question was debated in the Commons on 1 May 1875.

165 Ibid., Editorial, 24 February 1875.

166 Ibid., 7 June 1884.

167 Heyck, *Dimensions of British Radicalism*, p. 65.

168 *Newcastle Daily Chronicle*, 19 January 1881.

169 Ibid., 31 January 1881, 5 February 1881, 26 February 1881, 17 March 1881, 23 April 1881.

170 TWAS, CP/F43, 3 September 1881.

171 *Newcastle Weekly Chronicle*, 23 February 1881. Ladies Land League had 130 members. For a report of the Gateshead branch recruitment drive see ibid., 5 February 1881, 8 February 1881.

172 Heyck, *Dimensions of British Radicalism*, p. 64, and quoting from *The Times*. Chamberlain reputedly told his constituents that while he hated coercion 'we hate disorder more'.

173 *Newcastle Weekly Chronicle*, 17 March 1881, St Patrick's Day Soirée.

174 TWAS, CP/B245, 29 August 1881; *Newcastle Weekly Chronicle*, 3 September 1881.

175 TWAS, CP/B245. Executives (Tyneside) were Cowen, Bernard McAnulty, John Bryson, John Mullen, Peter Byrne, P. Jennings, M. Conway and E. McHugh.

176 *Newcastle Weekly Chronicle*, 26 November 1881. For a biography of George see E. P. Lawrence, *Henry George in the British Isles*, East Lansing, Mich., 1957; See also Avner Offer, *Property and politics, 1870-1914: Landownership, law, ideology and urban development in England*, Cambridge, 1981, pp. 184-201; Belchem, *Popular Radicalism in Nineteenth Century Britain*, pp. 150-1.

177 Moody, *Davitt and Irish Revolution*, pp. 413-14; Lawrence, *Henry George*, pp. 8, 19.

178 Logie Barrow and Ian Bullock, *Democratic Ideas and the British Labour Movement*, Cambridge, 1996, p. 285; Chushichi Tzuzuki, *H. M. Hyndman and British Socialism*, London, 1961, p. 45; Henry Hyndman, *Record of an Adventurous Life*, London, 1911.

179 Holyoake's letter in the *Newcastle Weekly Chronicle*, 23 April 1881 attributed George's scheme to Devyr. See also *Newcastle Weekly Chronicle*, 'The Gossip's Bowl', 9 February 1884.

180 *Newcastle Weekly Chronicle*, 16 April 1881. The column was signed W. T. (Wm. Trotter)

181 Ibid., 6 January1883, Lloyd Jones, Editorial, 2 February 1884.

182 Ibid., 15 March 1884, Letter from Devyr; also 5 July 1884, report of Devyr's visit.

183 Lawrence, *Henry George*, pp. 32, 52 notes that the Land Reform Union asked George to 'play down' his 'no compensation policy'.

184 *Newcastle Weekly Chronicle*, 5 April 1884, 26 April 1884.

185 Ibid., 5 April 1884, 'Notes from the Farm'; TWAS,CP/D274, List of the executives of the Independent Land and Building Society.

186 *Newcastle Weekly Chronicle*, 19 April 1884, speech by Parnell.

187 Roland Edwin Quinault, 'Joseph Chamberlain: a reassessment', in Gourvish and O'Day, (eds.) *Later Victorian Britain*, pp. 69-92.

188 Ibid., p. 78.

189 TWAS, CP/B378, Speech to the Commons, 7 June 1886.

Chapter 5

1 T.J. Nossiter, *Influence, Opinion and Political Idioms in Reformed England. Case Studies from the North East 1832-1874*, Brighton, 1975, is one of a number of historians who stress the strength of Liberal allegiances in Northumberland and Durham. See also F. W. Hirst, *Early Life and Letters of John Morley*, 2 vols., London, 1927, II, p. 144. On the 1874 election more generally, see Shannon, *Gladstone. Heroic Minister 1865-1898*, p. 138; T. A. Jenkins, *The Liberal Ascendancy, 1830-1886*, Basingstoke, 1994, p. 145.

2 TWAS, CP/B180, Speech dated 21 January 1877.

3 Gladstone judged that victory had been 'swept away. . . by a torrent of gin & beer' along with nonconformist opposition to his educational reforms. Cited in Shannon, *Gladstone. Heroic Minister*, p. 138

4 G. R. Searle, *The Liberal Party, Triumph and Disintegration, 1886-1929*, Basingstoke, 2001, pp. 14-20.

5 Antony Taylor, 'Post-Chartism. Metropolitan perspectives in the Chartist movement', in M. Cragoe and A. Taylor (eds.), *London Politics, 1760-1914*, Basingstoke, 2005, p.76

6 Ibid., p. 93.

7 McCalmont's *Parliamentary Poll Book* was first published in London in 1879. This reprint (1971) is edited by John Vincent and Michael Stenton.

8 Vincent, *Formation of the British Liberal Party*, p. 20.

9 Ibid., p. 33; Searle, *Liberal Party*, p. 19; E.F. Biagini, *Liberty, Retrenchment and Reform. Popular Liberalism in the Age of Gladstone, 1860-1880*, Cambridge, 1992, ch. 7; Simon Peaple and John Vincent, 'Gladstone and the Working Man', in Peter J. Jagger (ed.), *Gladstone*, London and Rio Grande, Ohio, 1998, pp. 71-84.

10 Biagini, *Liberty, Retrenchment and Reform*, p. 379 cites G. J. Holyoake's retrospective review of the visit, published in the *Newcastle Weekly Chronicle*, 18 March 1865, and rehearses similar arguments in his 'Popular Liberals, Gladstonian finance and the debate on taxation', in his edited volume *Currents of Radicalism*, p.

142.

11   *Newcastle Daily Chronicle*, 11 October 1862; *Newcastle Journal*, 9 October 1862; Shannon, *Gladstone: Heroic Minister*, pp. xvi, 14.

12   J. McCabe, *Life and Letters of G. J. Holyoake*, 2 vols., London, 1908, II, p. 14,

13   As Derek Beales has demonstrated in his study 'Gladstone and Garibaldi', in Jagger (ed.), *Gladstone*, pp. 137-56, what mostly linked the two men was their opposition to the Papacy.

14   Ashton, *W. E. Adams*, p. 102, stating that the *Newcastle Daily Chronicle* had a circulation of 40,000 copies per day in 1873, a London office and its own private telegraph system.

15   TWAS, CP/B157, Speech dated 30 December 1873.

16   F.W. Hirst, *Early Life and Letters of John Morley*, London, 1927, II, p. 144.

17   Eric J. Evans, *Parliamentary Reform, c. 1770-1918*, Harlow, 2000, p. 61 notes that the electorate in the boroughs increased by 138 per cent.

18   Vincent, *Formation of the British Liberal Party*, p. 35.

19   R. Harrison, *Before the Socialists. Studies in Labour History and Politics 1861-1881*, London, 1965, p. 133.

20   J. P. Dunbabin, 'Electoral reforms and their outcomes in the UK, 1865-1900', in T.R. Gourvish and A. O'Day (eds.), *Later Victorian Britain, 1867-1900*, Basingstoke, 1988, p. 111 states that 'one cannot point to any fundamental changes in British politics that resulted solely and directly from the electoral reforms'.

21   Ibid., p. 118. Dunbabin notes that politicians became more willing to speak outside of their own constituencies, citing Gladstone's Midlothian campaign as an example.

22   This view has been expressed by many including Vincent, *Formation of the British Liberal Party*, p. 265 and his *Pollbooks: How Victorians Voted*, Cambridge, 1967, p. 47; Martin Pugh, *The Making of Modern British Politics, 1867-1931*, London, 1982, p. 4ff: Trevor Lloyd, *The General Election of 1880*, Oxford, 1968, p. 90.

23   Biagini and Reid, 'Currents of Radicalism', pp. 7-10 in their volume of the same name.

24   James Hinton, *Labour and Socialism: A history of the British labour movement 1867-1974*, Brighton, 1983, p. 13. See also F. B. Smith, *The Making of the Second Reform Bill*, Cambridge, 1966, p. 235.

25   Maurice Cowling, *1867 Disraeli, Gladstone and Revolution: The Passing of the Second Reform Bill*, Cambridge, 1967, represents the 'parliamentary power' school of thought. The case for popular pressure is ventilated by Patricia Hollis (ed.), *Pressure from Without in Early Victorian England*, London, 1974.

26   Jenkins, *Liberal Ascendancy*, pp. 124-8.

27   I. J. Salmon, 'Welsh liberalism, 1865-1896. A study in political structure and ideology', unpublished University of Oxford PhD thesis, 1983, p. 125. See also P. M. Jones, 'Office holding, Politics and Society in Leicester and Peterborough, 1860-1930', unpublished University of Leicester MPhil thesis, 1982, p. 67.

28   TWAS, CP/B200, Speech at North Shields, 3 December 1879.

29 M. Noble, *Short Sketches of Eminent Men in the North of England*, Newcastle upon Tyne, 1885.

30 Michael Bentley, 'Gladstonian Liberals and Provincial Notables: Whitby Politics 1868-1870', *Historical Research*, 65:154, 1991, p. 176ff, notes that W. H. Gladstone refused to pay for coals for the local people even though this was customary.

31 Ibid., p. 185.

32 F.M. Leventhal, *Respectable Radical. George Howell and Victorian Working Class Politics*, London, 1971, p. 123.

33 T. A. Jenkins, *Gladstone, Whiggery and the Liberal Party*, Oxford, 1988, p. 13.

34 TWAS, CP/various; TWAS, T371/1/3, Gateshead Poor Law Board of Guardians, Minutes, 1845-1850.

35 G. R. Searle, *Entrepreneurial Politics in Mid-Victorian Britain*, Oxford, 1993, pp. 13-14 and generally; R. J. Morris, 'A year in the public life of the British bourgeoisie', in Robert Colls and Richard Rodger (eds.), *Cities of Ideas. Civil society and urban governance in Britain, 1800-2000*, Aldershot, 2004, pp. 121-43.

36 Jones, 'Office holding, Politics and Society in Leicester and Peterborough', p. 170.

37 NCLLS, Newcastle Corporation Council Minutes, 9 November 1865-7 October 1868. A large share of the Council's business fell under the jurisdiction of the Town Improvement Committee.

38 For example, see F. K. Prochaska, 'Philanthropy', in F.M.L. Thompson (ed.), *Cambridge Social History of Britain*, III, Cambridge, 1990, pp. 357-93.

39 On Chamberlain, see Peter Marsh, *Joseph Chamberlain, Entrepreneur in Politics*, New Haven, 1994; Denis Judd, *Radical Joe. A Life of Joseph Chamberlain*, Cardiff, 1993. Richard Jay argues that while he rid the city of slum dwellings he failed to re-house the evicted residents and his 'municipal socialism' did not benefit the wider community, see Richard Jay, *Joseph Chamberlain. A Political Study*, Oxford, 1981, p. 26ff.

40 R. E. Quinault, 'Joseph Chamberlain: A reassessment', in T. R. Gourvish and A. O' Day (eds.), *Later Victorian Britain, 1867-1900*, Basingstoke, 1988, p. 91

41 Ibid., p. 76.

42 Ibid. See also R. K. Webb, 'Flying Missionaries: Unitarian Journalists in Victorian England', in J. M. W. Bean (ed.), *The Political Culture of Modern Britain: Studies in memory of Stephen Koss*, London, 1987, p. 13, who states that the influence of Unitarians far exceeded their numerical strength and that 'they weighed more than they measured'.

43 TWAS, CP/B108, Joseph Chamberlain to Cowen, 25 September 1871; TWAS, CP/B109, 29 September 1871.

44 Percy Corder, *The Life of Robert Spence Watson*, London, 1914. See also TWAS/213, Robert Spence Watson Papers [RSWP]; NCLLS, Local Tracts, L042/DY107, Newcastle Liberal Association Minutes 1878-1893; Robert Spence Watson, *The National Liberal Federation from its commencement to the general election of 1906*, London, 1907.

45 Jenkins, *Liberal Ascendancy*, p. 184; Hirst, *Early Life and Letters of John Morley*, II,

p. 183; Corder, *Life of Robert Spence Watson*, p. 204.

46 Hirst, *Early Life and Letters of John Morley*, II, p. 203. On the caucus, see Michael Rush, *The Role of the Member of Parliament since 1868. From gentlemen to players*, Oxford, 2001, pp. 46-51.

47 TWAS, CP/B200, Speech at North Shields, 3 December 1879 (quoting the poet Alexander Pope).

48 For example, Alan R. Ball, *British Political Parties: The emergence of a modern party system*, London, 1981, p. 33 identifies Chamberlain as radicalism's 'most outstanding spokesman before 1886'; George Bernstein, *Liberalism and Liberal Politics in Edwardian England*, London, 1986, p. 9 claims that radicalism was 'largely the creation of Joseph Chamberlain'.

49 Quinault, 'Joseph Chamberlain', p. 71.

50 E. I. Waitt, 'John Morley, Joseph Cowen and Robert Spence Watson: Liberal divisions in Newcastle politics, 1873-1895', unpublished University of Manchester PhD thesis, 1972, p. 10ff.

51 Ibid. Thomas Headlam was an influential Newcastle Whig who had headed the poll in 1859 but was beaten into second place by Sir Joseph Cowen in 1865 and lost his seat in the 1874 poll topped by Cowen jnr. In his autobiography, *Reminiscences of the late Rt. Hon. Robert Spence Watson, 1837-1911*, York, rept.1969, pp. 62, 93 Watson is highly critical of the way the campaign was fought yet he was Cowen's electoral agent at the time. He would have been complicit in any 'sharp practice' and, notably, his comments were made after relations between the two had soured.

52 TWAS, CP/C1210, Holyoake to Cowen, 13 December 1860; CP/B157, Speech dated 30 December 1873.

53 TWAS, CP/B157, Speech dated 30 December 1873.

54 TWAS, CP/B248, Speech at the Circus, Newcastle, 28 January 1882.

55 TWAS, CP/B157, Speech dated 30 December 1873.

56 Ibid.

57 Miles Taylor, 'Republics versus empires: Charles Dilke's republicanism reconsidered', in David Nash and Antony Taylor (eds.), *Republicanism in Victorian Society*, Stroud, 2000, p. 34 argues that Dilke's republicanism went 'far beyond a distaste for the mess of monarchy'. See also, Antony Taylor, *Down with the Crown. British Anti-Monarchism and Debates about Royalty since 1790*, London, 1999.

58 Owen R. Ashton, 'W. E. Adams, Chartist and Republican in Victorian England', in David Howell and Kenneth O. Morgan (eds.), *Crime, Protest and Police in Modern British Society: Essays in memory of David J. V. Jones*, Cardiff, 1999, pp. 135-7; Todd, *Militant Democracy*, p. 94.

59 BLL,CDP/Add. 43909/241 Vol. XXXVI, 1871-1892, Letter from George Dixon to Charles Dilke, 3 January 1872; BLL,CDP/ Add. 43909/243, Letter from Cowen to Dilke, 4 January 1872.

60 E. Royle, *Radicals, Secularists and Republicans. Popular Freethought in Britain, 1866-1915*, Manchester, 1979, p. 201. Royle states that 'respectable republicanism

was dead by 1872'.

61 *Newcastle Daily Chronicle*, Various dates, including 21 May 1872, 13 June 1872, 6 July 1872, 25 June 1872 and 10 March 1873. See also TWAS, CP/B121, Circular of the National Republican Brotherhood, 1872, inviting Cowen to become a member.

62 NCLLS, Local Tracts, L042/DY107, Newcastle Liberal Association, Minutes of the General Meeting, 24 April 1882.

63 Dunbabin, 'Electoral reforms and their outcomes', p. 105. See also L. Satre, *Thomas Burt. Miners' MP 1887-1922*, Leicester, 1999, ch. 3. The other working-class member was Alexander McDonald (Stafford).

64 AIISH, AP222/1/24, Letter William Trotter to Adams, 16 July 1872; AP222/1/25 Trotter to Adams, 18 July 1872; AP222/1/128, Charles Bradlaugh to Adams, 30 June 1873.

65 TWAS, CP/B154, Speech dated 18 October 1873.

66 Keith Robbins, *The Eclipse of a Great Power, 1870-1975*, London, 1983, p. 44.

67 Henry Pelling, *The Origins of the Labour Party, 1880-1900*, Oxford, 1965, p. 4.

68 Bernstein, *Liberalism and Liberal Politics*, p. 14.

69 Lloyd, *General Election of 1880*, p. 117.

70 TWAS, CP/B255, satirical article, 'Caucustown' from *The People* (newspaper cutting), 5 March 1882.

71 TWAS, CP/B178, Speech at Clayton Street, Newcastle, 18 October 1876.

72 TWAS, CP/C1855, Circular of the Gateshead Representation League, undated but archivist annotation suggests 1873.

73 TWAS, CP/various, including B198, Speech in the House of Commons, 2 April 1879; B200, Speech at North Shields, 3 December 1879.

74 TWAS, CP/F43(5) Cowen to George Mitchell, n.d. Annotation by Cowen's secretary states that Mitchell was well known to 'George Potter, Odger, Shipton and Howell' and was 'one from the plough'.

75 *Newcastle Daily Chronicle*, 4 January 1881.

76 TWAS, CP/C1857, Northern Reform Union Conference at Manchester Free Trade Hall, 19 December 1877.

77 TWAS, CP/B137, Speech at the Newcastle Co-operative Congress, 12 April 1873.

78 Adams, *Memoirs*, pp. 496-7.

79 NCLLS, Local Tracts, L042/DY107, Newcastle Liberal Association, Minutes, 24 February 1882.

80 *Pall Mall Gazette*, 'The True True-Blue', 2 February 1880; the same edition quoted from the *Daily Telegraph* which judged his speeches to be 'sagacious and eloquent'.

81 TWAS, CP/B398, *The Times*, 25 December 1883.

82 TWAS, CP/B399, *St James Gazette*, 12 December 1885.

83 TWAS, CP/B397, *Lancashire Evening Press*, 9 February 1893.

84 NCLLS, Local Tracts, L042/DY107, Newcastle Liberal Association, Minutes, Speech by Councillor Thomas Richardson, 24 February 1882.

85 David Eastwood, *Government and Community in the English Provinces, 1700-1870*, Basingstoke, 1997, p. 73. Ashton, *W. E. Adams*, p. 102, notes that Cowen bought the *Daily Chronicle c.*1859/60 and launched the *Weekly* in 1863. Details are provided in M. Milne, *Newspapers of Northumberland and Durham: A Study of their progress during the 'Golden Age' of the Provincial Press*, Newcastle, 1971, p. 31. More generally, see A.G. Jones, *Powers of the Press. Newspapers, Power and the Public in Nineteenth Century England*, Aldershot, 1996, Alan J. Lee, *The Origins of the Popular Press, 1855-1914*, London, 1976, pp. 135-6, 174.

86 Ashton, *W. E. Adams*, p. 104.

87 *Newcastle Weekly Chronicle*, March 1867.

88 Ibid., January 1873.

89 TWAS, CP/F106, newspaper cutting from *The Arrow,* October 1898, vol. II, a monthly journal published in Gateshead.

90 Ashton, *W.E. Adams;* Adams, *Memoirs.*

91 O.R. Ashton and J. Hugman, 'George Julian Harney, Boston USA and Newcastle upon Tyne, England, 1863-1888', in *Proceedings*, Massachusetts Historical Society, 107, 1995.

92 NCLLS, Local Tracts, L042/DY107, Newcastle Liberal Association, Minutes, Speech by Robert Spence Watson, 31 December 1881. See also *Newcastle Daily Chronicle*, 30 January 1882; Lee, *Origins of the Popular Press*, p. 174.

93 Vincent, *Formation of the British Liberal Party*, p. 175.

94 Joseph Cowen speech on entering parliament, quoted in A. Harrison, 'Joseph Cowen: Orator, Patriot and Englishman, Obituary', *Newcastle Daily Chronicle*, 26 February 1900.

95 Vincent, *Formation of the British Liberal Party*, p. 176; Biagini, *Liberty Retrenchment and Reform*, pp. 375-79.

96 TWAS, CP/C512, *Newcastle Daily Chronicle*,14 December 1859; Vincent, *Formation of the British Liberal Party*, p. 233.

97 TWAS, CP/C956, Cowen to John Bright, 14 December 1859; CP/C971, Bright to Cowen, 16 December 1859.

98 TWAS, CP/C657, Thomas Allsopp to R. B. Reed, 8 May 1859.

99 Vincent, *Formation of the British Liberal Party*, p. 216.

100 Ibid., p. 175.

101 Eastwood, *Government and Community in the English Provinces*, p. 60.

102 RLSC, R. W. Martin, *North Country Elections from 1826*, Cowen Cartoons, various.

103 Hugh Cunningham, 'Language of Patriotism', *History Workshop Journal*, 12, 1981, p. 10.

104 Ibid., p. 22.

105 David Beetham, *Max Weber and the Theory of Modern Politics*, Cambridge, 1985, p. 227

106 Ibid., p. 231.

107 Biagini, *Liberty Retrenchment and Reform*, p. 360.

108 Ibid., p. 390.

109 Ibid., p. 394.

110 Clifford Geertz, *Local Knowledge: Further essays in interpretive anthropology*, London, 1993, p. 125.

111 Ibid., p. 144.

112 Ibid., pp. 143-4.

113 TWAS,CP/B135, Cowen's speech to the Co-operative Congress, 12 April 1873.

114 TWAS, CP/B180, Speech at Hood Street, Newcastle, 27 January 1877.

115 Ibid.

116 Anthony Blake, 'The Education Question and Liberal Politics in North East England, 1868-1910', unpublished Newcastle University MLitt thesis, 1984, p. 4.

117 TWAS, CP/D253, Speech at Berwick Street Schoolroom, 23 January 1871.

118 TWAS, CP/B61, 23 October 1869.

119 Ibid.

120 Edward Royle, *Radicals, Secularists and Republicans. Popular free thought in Britain, 1866-1915*, Manchester, 1979, p. 64, notes the remarkable increase in branches of the National Secular Society after 1869.

121 J. W. Chater, *Chater's "Canny Newcassel" Diary and Local Remembrancer, For Bissextile or Leap-Year, 1872*, Newcastle, 1872, p. 11. See also Allen and Buswell, *Rutherford's Ladder*, p. 19. On the development of school boards more generally, see W. B. Stephens, *Education in Britain, 1750-1914*, Basingstoke, 1998, pp. 90-6.

122 TWAS, CP/D253, 23 January 1871.

123 *Newcastle Daily Chronicle*, 25 November 1869.

124 TWAS, CP/various, including B72, B85, B108 and B109.

125 TWAS, CP/B76, S. A. Steinthal to Cowen, 22 January 1870.

126 TWAS, CP/B70, J. Jones to Cowen, 28 December 1869.

127 TWAS, CP/B157, Election speech, 30 December 1873, pp. 11-12.

128 *Newcastle Daily Chronicle*, 25 July 1870.

129 Jenkins, *Gladstone, Whiggery and the Liberal Party*, p. 38.

130 Cowen, *Speeches on Public Questions*, p. 77, speech dated 3 January 1874.

131 TWAS, CP/B255, 'Caucustown', *The People*. See also TWAS, CP/B210, Speech at Newcastle, 4 January 1881; *Newcastle Daily Chronicle*, 23 March 1881.

132 TWAS, CP/B154, Speech, 18 October 1873; TWAS, CP/B157, 30 December 1873.

133 TWAS, CP/B200, Speech at North Shields, 3 December, 1879.

134 Samuel Beer, *Modern British Politics*, London, 1965, p. 38; Rush, *Role of the Member of Parliament since 1868*, p. 48.

135 P. M. Gurowich, 'Party and Independence in the early and mid-Victorian House of Commons: Aspects of political theory and practice, considered with special reference to the period 1832-1868', unpublished University of Cambridge PhD thesis, 1986, p. 181.

136 Rush, *Role of the Member of Parliament since 1868*, pp. 48-9.

137 Jones, 'Office Holding, Politics and Society', p. 70.

138 TWAS, CP/D253, 23 January 1871.

139 TWAS, CP/F46(12), Josephine Butler to Cowen, 1 August 1882.
140 TWAS, CP/F43, D. R. Ruth to Cowen, 14 November 1882.
141 TWAS, CP/B349, c.1885.
142 TWAS, CP/B255, 'Caucustown', *The People*.
143 TWAS, CP/B180, Speech reviewing the political scene, 27 January 1877; Jones, *Life and Speeches of Joseph Cowen*, p. 40.
144 TWAS, CP/B167, Speech at Blaydon, 16 September 1874.
145 Hirst, *Early Life and Letters of John Morley*, II, p. 146.
146 TWAS, CP/C1857, 19 December 1877; Corder, *Life of Robert Spence Watson*, p. 269.
147 TWAS, CP/B340, 27 November 1885.
148 Biagini, *Liberty Retrenchment and Reform*, pp. 328, 333.
149 Ibid., p. 336.
150 Shannon, *Gladstone: Heroic Minister*, p. 162. See also Ian St John, *Disraeli and the Art of Victorian Politics*, London, 2005, pp. 186-7.
151 Justin McCarthy, *A Short History of Our Own Times, from the accession of Queen Victoria to the General Election of 1880*, London, 1897, pp. 409-10.
152 TWAS, CP/B170, Speech, 23 March 1876.
153 McCarthy, *Short History of Our Own Times*, p. 408.
154 *Leeds Mercury*, 26 March 1876.
155 Todd, *Militant Democracy*, p. 124
156 On the Eastern Crisis, see Anne Pottinger Saab, *Reluctant Icon, Gladstone, Bulgaria, and the Working Classes, 1856-1878*, Cambridge, Mass., 1991; A. L. Macfie, *The Eastern Question 1774-1923*, Harlow, 1989; R. T. Shannon, *Gladstone and the Bulgarian Agitation, 1876*, 2nd edn. London, 1975.
157 Shannon, *Gladstone and the Bulgarian Agitation*, p. 72.
158 Ibid., p. 75.
159 Sheffield University Special Collections [SUSC] H. J. Wilson papers [WP], A. J. Mundella to Wilson, 29 April 1877; SUSC, A. J. Mundella Papers [MP], various correspondence, especially 6P/10/14, Gladstone to Mundella, 20 December 1877.
160 Shannon, *Gladstone and the Bulgarian Agitation*, p. 90. See also, Shannon, *Gladstone. Heroic Minister*, pp. 167-8.
161 Shannon, *Gladstone and the Bulgarian Agitation*, p. 92.
162 Jane Cowen (ed.), *Joseph Cowen's Speeches on the Near Eastern Question: Foreign and Imperial Affairs: And on the British Empire*, London, 1909, Speech on the Bulgarian Atrocities, 30 September 1876, p. 1.
163 Ibid.
164 TWAS, CP/B180, 27 January 1877.
165 Cowen, *Joseph Cowen's Speeches on the Near Eastern Question*, Bulgarian Atrocities, 30 September 1876, pp. 1-22.
166 R. T. Shannon, *The Crisis of Imperialism, 1865-1915*, London, 1976, p. 132; Hugh Cunningham, 'Jingoism and the working classes, 1877-78', *Bulletin of the Society for the Study of Labour History*, 19, 1969, p. 6.

167 *Newcastle Daily Chronicle*, 9 February 1878.

168 Ibid., 18 February 1878, advertisement for the 'Great Military Spectacle' at the Tyne Theatre.

169 Royle, *Radicals, Secularists and Republicans*, pp. 209-20.

170 Ibid. p. 198; *Newcastle Weekly Chronicle*, 12 January 1878; *Newcastle Daily Chronicle*, 29 January 1878.

171 *Newcastle Daily Chronicle*, 9 January 1878, 15 January 1878; Satre, *Thomas Burt*, p. 71.

172 *Newcastle Daily Chronicle*, 31 January 1878, Editorial, 15 February 1878. The strike finally ended in mid-February 1878.

173 *Newcastle Weekly Chronicle*, 2 March 1878.

174 Ibid., 12 January 1878. *Newcastle Daily Chronicle*, 31 January 1878.

175 *Newcastle Daily Chronicle*, 17 January 1878; *Newcastle Weekly Chronicle*, 4 May 1878. For a discussion of the anti-war lobby, see Saab, *Reluctant Icon*, pp. 185-91.

176 *Newcastle Weekly Chronicle*, Editorial, 'The Right of Public Meeting', 9 February 1878; Ibid., 'The Gossip's Bowl', 6 April 1878.

177 Ibid., 2 March 1878.

178 *Newcastle Daily Chronicle*, 30 January 1878, 23 January 1878. A letter from 'A Tory' said that Cowen's speech was 'far too good to leave to the mere perusal and fame of even a daily paper'.

179 Corder, *Life of Robert Spence Watson*, p. 220.

180 Ashton, *W. E. Adams*, p. 133.

181 Waitt, 'John Morley, Joseph Cowen and Robert Spence Watson', p. 87; Shannon, *Gladstone and the Bulgarian Agitation*, p. 230ff; Milne, *Newspapers of Northumberland and Durham*, p. 107.

182 Cowen, *Joseph Cowen's Speeches on the Near Eastern Question*, The Eastern Question, 11 February 1878, p. 36.

183 Ibid., Extract from Gladstone's speech in the House of Commons, 11 February 1878, p. 25.

184 Ibid., p. 26.

185 TWAS, CP/E346, JCM, p. 46; Todd, *Militant Democracy*, pp. 131-3.

186 TWAS, CP/B248. Speech at the Haymarket, Newcastle, 28 January 1882.

187 TWAS, CP/F43(2e), Cowen to C. H. A. de. Bille MP, who had supported Cowen's policy on the Near East, June, 1880.

188 Jenkins, *Gladstone, Whiggery and the Liberal Party*, p. 88.

189 Ibid., p. 85.

190 W. E. Gladstone, *The approaching general election: Speeches delivered in Midlothian during the last week of November 1879*, London, 1879, p. 18.

191 Corder, *Robert Spence Watson*, p. 236.

192 Shannon, *Gladstone, Heroic Minister*, p. 244; Todd, *Militant Democracy*, p. 136.

193 NCLLS, Local Tracts, L042/ DY107, Newcastle Liberal Association minutes, 24, February 1882.

194 TWAS, RSWP/213, Elizabeth Spence Watson to her daughter, Mabel, 20 March

1880. Charles Hamond (Cons.) was defeated.

195 Shannon, *Gladstone and the Bulgarian Agitation*, p. 274.

196 Ibid., p. 273; also Bernstein, *Liberalism and Liberal Politics*, p. 10.

197 Michael Bentley, *The Climax of Liberal Politics: British Liberalism in theory and practice, 1868-1918*, London, 1987, p. 67; Jenkins, *Gladstone, Whiggery and the Liberal Party*, p. 277; A. B. Cooke and J. Vincent, *The Governing Passion: Cabinet government and party politics in Britain, 1885-6*, Brighton, 1974, p. 383.

198 Bentley, *Climax of Liberal Politics*, p. 68.

199 Jenkins, *Gladstone, Whiggery and the Liberal Party*, p. 280ff; Shannon, *Gladstone and the Bulgarian Agitation*, p. 277.

200 Shannon, *Gladstone and the Bulgarian Agitation*, p. 276. According to Shannon, Gladstone found the analogy 'distasteful'.

201 Ibid., p. 280.

202 Cowen, *Joseph Cowen's Speeches*, Eastern Question, 11 February 1878, p. 31.

203 TWAS, CP/B176, 2 August 1876. See also TWAS, B181, 2 February 1877.

204 TWAS, CP/B379, Speech by Cowen at Birmingham, 17 June 1886.

205 TWAS, CP/F43, Cowen to William Elliott, June 1880.

206 Alan O'Day, *The English Face of Irish Nationalism: Parnellite involvement in British politics, 1880-86*, Dublin, 1977, p. 83, notes that, apart from the Northern boroughs, English members were largely ignorant of Ireland and its problems.

207 TWAS, CP/B207, Speech to House of Commons, 30 August 1881.

208 *Newcastle Weekly Chronicle*, 12 March 1881; H.M. Hyndman, *The Record of an Adventurous Life*, London, 1911, p. 246; L. Barrow and I. Bullock, *Democratic Ideas and the British Labour Movement*, Cambridge, 1996, ch. 1.

209 *Newcastle Daily Chronicle*, 3 September 1881; TWAS, CP/ F43, Cowen to Thomas Seaton MP, Dublin (n.d.).

210 TWAS, CP/B248, 28 January 1882.

211 Hyndman, *Record of an Adventurous Life*, p. 255ff.

212 TWAS, CP/B349, Cowen, on the publication of his speeches, 1885.

213 O' Day, *English Face of Irish Nationalism*, p. 203.

214 TWAS, CP/B246, 29 August 1881.

215 *Pall Mall Gazette*, 4 January 1881; Hirst, *Life and Letters of John Morley*, II, pp. 90-1.

216 *Pall Mall Gazette*, 7 January 1881, 10 January 1881. See also Shannon, *Gladstone. Heroic Minister*, p. 272

217 *Pall Mall Gazette*, 31 January 1881.

218 TWAS, CP/B220, Speech in the House of Commons, 8 February 1881.

219 TWAS, CP/B224, Cowen to W. T. Martin of the Junior Liberal Club, 10 February 1881.

220 *Pall Mall Gazette*, 10 February 1881.

221 TWAS, CP/B232, Speech to House of Commons, 25 February 1881.

222 Ibid.

223 TWAS, CP/B223, 10 February 1881; B263, 7 July 1882; B248, 28 January 1882.

224 *Pall Mall Gazette*, 24 February 1881.

225 TWAS, CP/B242, 10 May 1881.

226 TWAS, CP/B275, 10 November 1882: 'The Right of Free Speech' (later published as a pamphlet).

227 TWAS, CP/B279, *Midland Free Press*, 18 November 1882.

228 NCLLS, Local Tracts, L042/DY107, Newcastle Liberal Association Minutes, Extraordinary General Meeting, 24 February 1882.

229 TWAS, CP/correspondence, B234-B375. See also NCLLS, Local Tracts, L042/DY107, Newcastle Liberal Association minutes, 31 December 1881.

230 Biagini, *Liberty Retrenchment and Reform*, pp. 360-1; Corder, *Life of Robert Spence Watson*, p. 223ff.

231 Hirst, *Early Life and Letters of John Morley*, p. 153.

Chapter 6

1   Michael Bentley, *Politics Without Democracy 1815-1914*, London, 1984, p. 233 notes that between 1882 and 1885 'every minister threatened or promised to resign at least once'.

2   W. Purdue, 'The ILP in the North East of England', in David James, Tony Jowitt and Keith Laybourn (eds.), *The Centennial History of the Independent Labour Party*, Halifax, 1992, p. 17. For an analysis of Conservative gains elsewhere, see Matthew Roberts, '"Villa Toryism' and Popular Conservatism in Leeds, 1885-1902', *Historical Journal*, 49:1, 2006, pp. 217-46.

3   Denis Judd, *Radical Joe. A Life of Joseph Chamberlain*, Cardiff, 1993, pp. 76-8.

4   *Pall Mall Gazette*, 9 January 1883. On the Liberals' policy in Egypt, see A. Sykes, *Rise and Fall of British Liberalism, 1776-1988*, London and New York, 1997, pp. 102-4.

5   *Pall Mall Gazette*, 10 January 1883 and quoting from the *Morning Advertiser*.

6   Ibid., quoting from the *Spectator*.

7   F.W. Hirst, *Early Life and Letters of John Morley*, II, London, 1927, p. 154.

8   Ibid., p. 155

9   *Newcastle Daily Chronicle*, 15 February 1883.

10 L. Satre, *Thomas Burt. A Miners' MP, 1837-1922*, Leicester, 1999, pp. 78-82.

11 *Newcastle Daily Chronicle*, 13 February 1883.

12 E.F. Biagini, *Liberty, Retrenchment and Reform: Popular Liberalism in the Age of Gladstone, 1860-1880*, Cambridge, 1992, p. 361.

13 Hugh Cunningham, 'Language of Patriotism', *History Workshop Journal*, 12, 1981, p. 8ff. See also Owen R. Ashton, 'W. E. Adams and working class opposition to Empire, 1878-1880: Cyprus and Afghanistan', *Bulletin of North East Labour History Society*, 27, 1993, pp. 49-74.

14 *Newcastle Daily Chronicle*, Meeting of the Labour Representation Committee, 13 February 1883.

15 TWAS, CP/B295, Speech at Durham Miners' Demonstration, 14 July 1883.

16   Ibid., p. 162; *Pall Mall Gazette*, 12 February 1883.

17   *Pall Mall Gazette*, 26 February 1883.

18   SUSC, MP, Morley to Mundella, 20 November 1884.

19   Corder, *Life of Robert Spence Watson*, p. 170.

20   *Newcastle Daily Chronicle*, 25 March 1881.

21   TWAS, CP/B198, Speech in the Commons, 2 April 1879 on 'Local Government Qualifications'.

22   TWAS, CP/B300, Speech by Joseph Cowen to the North of England Commercial Travellers Association, 11 January 1884. See also TWAS, CP/B392, Newspaper cutting (u/k), 1891, with a report of a speech on co-operation by Joseph Cowen.

23   TWAS, CP/F47, Cowen to Dr Lees, 16 March 1883.

24   *The Handbook of the Twenty Sixth Annual Co-operative Congress*, Sunderland, 1894, p. 77 gives a brief history of the Blaydon District Co-operative Society and states that the 'breakaway' society collapsed in 1882…a large proportion of the members 'returned to the old society very probably in a repentant frame of mind'. See also *Newcastle Daily Chronicle*, 19 February 1900.

25   'Gossip's Bowl' by Robin Goodfellow, *Newcastle Weekly Chronicle*, 14 January 1871; TWAS, CP/B120, *Published Returns of Cooperative Societies*, 1872.

26   TWAS, CP/B300, 11 January 1884.

27   TWAS, CP/B392, *Figaro*, November 1891.

28   *Newcastle Daily Chronicle*, 6 May 1870, 5 April 1872, 30 April 1872. His support for women's rights was unwavering. See TWAS, CP/B116, Emilie A. Venturi to Cowen, 13 January 1872.

29   Woodall's amendment was defeated on 13 June by 273:137. See Ian Machin, *The Rise of Democracy in Britain, 1830-1918*, Basingstoke, 2000, p. 95.

30   *Newcastle Weekly Chronicle*, 14 June 1884. See also Martin Pugh, 'The Limits of liberalism: Liberals and women's suffrage 1867-1914', in E.F. Biagini, (ed.) *Citizenship and Community. Liberals, radicals and collective identities in the British Isles, 1865-1931*, Cambridge, 1996, pp. 48, 55-6; Hirst, *Life and Letters of John Morley*, II, p. 225.

31   TWAS, CP/B319, Speech in the Commons, 12 June 1884. The clause was defeated 135:271, with Gladstone, Pease and Morley all voting against.

32   Hirst, *Life and Letters of John Morley*, II, p. 256.

33   Todd, *Militant Democracy*, p. 161.

34   TWAS, CP/B335, Speech, 14 November 1885.

35   Michael Bentley, *Politics Without Democracy, 1815-1914*, London, 1984, p. 256 notes the emergence of a group of Liberal imperialists in the late 1880s. See also, H. C. G. Matthew, *The Liberal Imperialists: The ideas and policies of a post-Gladstonian elite*, Oxford, 1973; T. A. Jenkins, *The Liberal Ascendancy, 1830-1886*, Basingstoke, 1994, pp. 169-72; Richard Price, *An Imperial War and the British Working Class*, London, 1972, p. 5.

36   Judd, *Radical Joe*, pp. 87-8.

37   R. Jay, *Joseph Chamberlain. A Political Study*, Oxford, 1981, p. 37.

38 Ibid., p. 36.
39 Price, *An Imperial War and the British Working Class*, pp. 41-3, 234. It is notable, too, that when H. J. Wilson tried to rally the Sheffield Liberals behind opposition to the Boer War, for example, he encountered formidable opposition.
40 *Tyneside Echo*, 19 January 1885.
41 TWAS, CP/B308, Handbill of the Scottish Liberal Association, 15 March 1884. Cowen, Henry Labouchere and Henry Richard voted with the Conservatives and the Parnellites.
42 John Saville, 'Imperialism and the Victorians', in E. M. Sigsworth (ed.), *In Search of Victorian Values: Aspects of Nineteenth Century Thought and Society*, Manchester, 1988, p. 174.
43 Ashton, 'W. E. Adams and working class opposition to Empire 1878-1880: Cyprus and Afghanistan', *Bulletin of North East Labour History Society*, 27, 1993, p. 17
44 TWAS, CP/B340, 27 November 1885.
45 Richard Shannon, *The Crisis of Imperialism, 1865-1915*, London, 1976, p. 126. See also Richard Shannon, *Gladstone and the Bulgarian Agitation, 1876*, 2nd edn. London, 1975, p. 215.
46 Cowen, *Speeches on the Near Eastern Question*, 11 February 1878, p. 26.
47 TWAS, CP/B141, Speech on the Plimsoll Shipping Bill, 17 April 1873.
48 *Newcastle Daily Chronicle*, Obituary by G. J. Holyoake, 14 March 1900.
49 NCLLS, Local Tracts, L042, 'Mr Cowen MP. Apostle or Apostate? An Exposure', 1880, p. 4. The author is thought to be either James Annand (editor of the *Daily Chronicle* until his enforced resignation in 1877) or W. T. Stead. Both men were at odds with Cowen over the Eastern Question. See Todd, *Militant Democracy*, p. 133.
50 *Newcastle Daily Chronicle*, Obituary by G. J. Holyoake, 14 March 1900.
51 Jenkins, *Liberal Ascendancy*, p. 177; G. R. Searle, *The Liberal Party*, Basingstoke, 2001, pp. 18-19.
52 Jenkins, *Liberal Ascendancy*, p. 178, and summarising the views of D. A. Hamer's study, *Liberal Politics in the Age of Gladstone and Roseberry*, Oxford, 1972.
53 Jenkins, *Liberal Ascendancy*, p. 179.
54 T.A. Jenkins, *Gladstone, Whiggery and the Liberal Party*, Oxford, 1988, ch. 7.
55 Ibid., p. 248.
56 D. G. Boyce, *The Irish Question and British Politics 1886-1998*, Basingstoke and London, 1996, pp. 28-32.
57 TWAS, CP/various correspondence including F51(9), Cowen to Frank Carr, 8 February 1884 stating that the Government had made a grave error in annexing more territory.
58 TWAS, CP/F46(12), Cowen to Josephine Butler, 1 August 1882.
59 TWAS, CP/B330, Speech in Newcastle, 14 February 1885.
60 Cowen, *Speeches on Public Questions and Political Policy*, 3 January 1874, p. 80.
61 Jones, *Life and Speeches of Joseph Cowen*, Speech at Newcastle, 22 December 1883, p. 250.

62   TWAS, CP/B378, Speech on Irish Home Rule, 7 June 1886.

63   TWAS, CP/B398, Speech at The Circus, Newcastle, 22 December 1873.

64   NCLLL, Newcastle upon Tyne Liberal Association, Report of the Sub- Committee, 18 October 1882, pp. 5, 22-3; Todd, *Militant Democracy*, p. 155.

65   TWAS, CP/B340, 27 November 1885 (quoting Montrose).

66   Purdue, 'The ILP in the North East of England', p. 18.

67   Cowen, *Speeches on the Near Eastern Question*, British Empire, Federation and Foreign Affairs, 18 November 1885, p. 261.

68   Ibid., p. 263. See also Bernard Porter, *The Lion's Share. A Short History of British Imperialism, 1850-1983*, 3rd edn. London, 1996; Sheelagh Strawbridge, 'Darwin and Victorian social values', in Sigsworth (ed.), *In Search of Victorian Values*, p. 107ff.

69   TWAS, CP/A966, 'Government Policy in the Soudan', 15 March 1884.

70   TWAS, CP/B340, Election speech 27 November 1885; CP/B335, Election speech, 14 November 1885.

71   Saville, 'Imperialism and the Victorians', p. 165. See also J. F. C. Harrison, *Late Victorian Britain, 1870-1901*, London, 1990, p. 210.

72   Corder, *Life of Robert Spence Watson*, p. 203.

73   TWAS, RSWP/213/79, undated letter to his daughter Mabel.

74   Ashton, *W. E. Adams*, pp. 113, 170-1.

75   Biagini, *Liberty, Retrenchment and Reform*, p. 367.

76   Hirst, *Early Life and Letters of John Morley*, II, p. 248.

77   TWAS, RSWP, Elizabeth Spence Watson to Mabel, 26 November 1885.

78   *Irish Tribune*, various dates including 17 January 1885, 11 April 1885 and 13 June 1885; Todd, *Militant Democracy*, p. 156. On Parnell's strategy, see Shannon, *Gladstone, Heroic Minister*, pp. 388-9.

79   Hirst, *Early Life and Letters of John Morley*, II, p. 268. See also M. Roberts, "Villa Toryism' and Popular Conservatism in Leeds 1885-1902', *Historical Journal*, 49: 1, 2006, p. 227 who notes that Irish and Catholic votes determined the outcome of the 1885 election in Leeds.

80   TWAS, RSWP, Elizabeth Spence Watson to Mabel, 30 November 1885. Morley did contest the Newcastle seat again; he was pushed into second place in 1892 and finally lost Newcastle in 1895. See Shannon, *Gladstone. Heroic Minister*, pp. 517, 575.

81   *Newcastle Daily Chronicle*, Open Letter to the Electorate from Cowen, 30 December 1885.

82   TWAS, CP/F54(15), Joseph Cowen to Thomas Walton, 1 May 1885 referring to the impending libel action brought by the Durham Miners' Association against the *Newcastle Chronicle*. See also Todd, *Militant Democracy*, p. 155; Biagini, *Liberty, Retrenchment and Reform*, p. 323 appraises Cowen's relations with the miners' unions.

83   TWAS, CP/B336, Speech, 16 January 1885.

84   TWAS, CP/F85, William Smith to Cowen, 27 March 1886.

85 TWAS, CP/B373, Slater's Private Detective & Enquiry Association to Cowen, 14 April 1886.

86 On the 1885 election outcome, see Shannon, *Gladstone Heroic Minister*, pp. 389-90; Sykes, *Rise and Fall of British Liberalism*, p. 119. F. S. L. Lyons, *Charles Stewart Parnell*, London, 1977, pp. 340-3.

87 P. Marsh, *Joseph Chamberlain: Entrepreneur in Politics*, New Haven, 1994, p. 214.

88 SUSC, MP, Earl Spencer to Mundella, 31 December 1885; Boyce, *Irish Question and British Politics*, p. 31; Hugh Cunningham, *The Challenge of Democracy. Britain 1832-1918*, Harlow, 2001, p. 130.

89 SUSC, MP, Gladstone to Mundella, 29 December 1885.

90 D. G. Boyce, 'Gladstone and Ireland', in P. Jagger (ed.), *Gladstone*, London and Rio Grande, Ohio, 1998, pp. 117-18; Michael Bentley, *Politics Without Democracy, 1815-1914*, London, 1984, pp. 231-76.

91 TWAS, CP/B373, Secretary, Newcastle Liberal Association to Cowen stating that 516 members of a meeting of 520, had voted in favour of Home Rule, 13 April 1886.

92 TWAS, CP/B365, unidentified newspaper cutting, 12 February 1886.

93 Purdue, 'ILP in the North East of England', pp. 17-42, and his study 'The Liberal and Labour parties in North East Politics 1892-1914', *International Review of Social History*, XXVI: 1, 1981. See also Tony Barrow, 'The Labour Representation Committee at Newcastle upon Tyne 1903', in M. Callcott and R. Challinor (eds.), *Working Class Politics in North East England*, Newcastle upon Tyne, 1983.

94 Jim Coffey, 'Charles Diamond: A legend in his time', *Scottish Catholic Observer*, 19 April 1985; Tom Gallagher, 'Diamond, Charles, Labour politician and newspaper proprietor', in J. M. Bellamy and John Saville (eds.), *Dictionary of Labour Biography*, 11 vols, Basingstoke, 1987, VIII, p. 55; Joan Allen, "Keeping the Faith': The Catholic press and the preservation of Celtic identity in Britain in the late nineteenth century', in Pamela O'Neill (ed.), *Exile and Homecoming*, Sydney, 2004, pp. 78-91.

95 *Tyneside Catholic News*, 'Obituary', 10 March 1934.

96 Edwards and Storey, 'Irish Press in Victorian Britain' p. 173.

97 See *The Irish Tribune. An Irish Journal for England and Scotland*, Saturday, 13 December 1884.

98 TWAS, CP/ F43, Diamond to Cowen, 23 August 1881.

99 A. O'Day, *Irish Home Rule, 1867-1921*, p. 81.

100 TWAS, CP/F57(11), 2 February 1886.

101 *Irish Tribune*, 13 December 1884. It sold for 1d. per issue.

102 Ibid.

103 Ibid., 20 December 1884.

104 Ibid., 14 March 1885, 2 January 1886.

105 Mary J Hickman, 'Incorporating and denationalizing the Irish in England: the role of the Catholic Church', in Patrick O'Sullivan (ed.), *The Irish World Wide. History, Heritage, Identity* (6 vols. Leicester, London and Washington: Leicester University

Press, 1992-2000), V: *Religion and Identity* (1996), p. 209. See also Gabriel Docherty, 'National identity and the Study of Irish History', *English Historical Review*, III. 441, April 1996, pp. 324-49, and especially pp. 327-8.

106 'Catholics and their Press', *Glasgow Observer*, 27 February 1892. See also Edwards and Storey, 'Irish Press in Victorian Britain', p. 175; Owen Dudley Edwards, 'The Catholic Press in Scotland since the restoration of the hierarchy', in David McRoberts (ed.), *Modern Scottish Catholicism 1878-1978*, Glasgow, 1979, p. 169-70.

107 *Glasgow Observer*, 25 April 1885.

108 *Irish Tribune*, 1 January 1887. Diamond founded the *Weekly Herald* in 1888

109 Ashton, *W. E. Adams*, pp. 136-8.

110 *Irish Tribune*, 2 January 1886. On the press and younger readers, see Dina Dixon, 'Children and the press, 1866-1914', in Mark Harris and Alan Lee (eds.), *The Press and English Society from the Seventeenth to the Nineteenth Centuries*, London 1986, pp. 133-48, especially p. 142 which discusses the Catholic press.

111 *Irish Tribune*, 2 January 1886.

112 Ibid.

113 Ibid., Cowen to the Joseph Cowen branch of the INL, Washington, 9 January 1886.

114 On fin de siècle anxieties generally, see Mike Jay and Michael Neve (eds.), *1900. A Fin de Siècle Reader*, London, 1999; Holbrook Jackson, *The Eighteen Nineties*, London, 1939.

115 H. A. Mess, *Industrial Tyneside*, London, 1928, p. 42 notes that 'prosperity narrowed' in the 1880s.

116 *Citizen*, 1:1, 16 October 1886.

117 *Monthly Chronicle of North Country Lore and Legend*, vol.I, Preface, 1887; Ashton, *W. E. Adams*, p. 126.

118 *Monthly Chronicle of North Country Lore and Legend*, vol. V, Epilogue, 1891.

119 Robert Eadie, *A Sketch of Stella Hall with the Career of Joseph Cowen* MP, Newcastle, 1865, pp. 2-3.

120 TWAS, CP/F43-F47, correspondence 1878-1886; AIISH, AP/222/1/208, Cowen to Oliver Heslop, 28 December 1898. Longstaffe was an editor at the *Chronicle*.

121 Jane Cowen, *Tales of Revolution and Patriotism*, London, 1884.

122 AIISH, AP/111/1/217, Cowen to Adams, 24 January 1900. Cowen said he was recovering from a 'breakdown' in his health. He died just a few weeks later.

123 Cowen, *Speeches on the Near Eastern Question*, 'British Empire', 26 June 1897, p. 331.

124 Graham Davis, *The Irish in Britain, 1815-1914*, Dublin, 1991, pp. 215-16.

125 TWAS, CP/F106, 'Wanted-A Leader', *Arrow*, October 1898, vol. 2 complained that the Liberal Association 'practically does nothing'; that it was incapable of providing leadership and Gateshead citizens might just as well take their political guidance 'from *Punch*'.

126 *Newcastle Daily Chronicle,* 19 February 1900. See also the large collection of Obituaries from newspapers in Britain and America, including the *New York Times* in TWAS, CP.

127 Jones, *Life and Speeches of Joseph Cowen,* p. 104.

Appendix I: Activities of Tyneside Radicals (1832-1860)

CHARTIST	NPU	NFAC	URQ	PHRC	NRU
Charles Attwood	✓	✓	✓		
John Blakey	✓		✓		
John Cockburn	✓	✓			
William Cook	✓	✓			✓
George Crawshay		✓	✓	✓	
John K. Crothers		✓			
Ralph Currie	✓				✓
James Charlton		✓			
Thomas Doubleday	✓		✓		✓
James T. Gilmour	✓	✓	✓	✓	✓
Thomas Gregson		✓	✓		✓
Alexander Gunn				✓	
George J. Harney		✓		✓	✓
Thomas Horn	✓	✓			
William Hunter		✓			✓
William Jordan		✓	✓		
Martin Jude		✓	✓		✓
John Kane		✓	✓	✓	✓
Thomas Lishman		✓			✓
Angus McLeod		✓			
Peter Murray			✓		
Robert Peddie		✓			
Jonathan Rayne		✓			
John Richardson		✓			
Josiah Thomas		✓	✓	✓	✓
James Watson		✓	✓	✓	✓

Key:

NPU	Northern Political Union
NFAC	Newcastle Foreign Affairs Committee
URQ	Supporter of David Urquhart
PHRC	Polish and Hungarian Refugee Committee
NRU	Northern Reform Union

Appendix II: Membership of Newcastle upon Tyne Foreign Affairs Committee

John Allison
Peter Anderson
Charles Attwood
Joseph Barlow
James Brown
Robert Catcheside
T. N. Catherall
James Charlton
Robert Charlton
John Cockburn
William Cook
George Crawshay
John K. Crothers
John Fife
John Forster
John Galloway
James T. Gilmour
Thomas Gregson
James Grieves
George J. Harney
Thomas Herdman
William Hunter
William Jordan

Martin Jude
John Kane
Angus Mcleod
Joseph Mills
Peter Murray
Richard Nelson
J. Paley
Robert Peddie
Jonathan Rayne
John Richardson
Richard Bagnall Reed
John Ritchie
John Reid
John Rea
Dr Skelton
John A. Southeron
Joseph Southeron
Josiah Thomas
Arthur Trevelyan
John Wake
Ralph Walters
James Watson
William Watson

Source: TWAS, CP/246

Appendix III: Membership Lists of the Northern Reform Union

South Shields branch (8 March 1858)

Tailor
Trimmer
Shipwright
Moulder
Blacksmith (3)
Builder
Hosier
Publican
Billsticker
Plumber
Joiner
Draper

NB: *names not recorded, occupation list only.*

Hartlepool Branch Executive committee (30 October 1858)

Name	Occupation
Jabez Bridges	Joiner
J. Caldwell	Brass Finisher
J. Callender	Fitter
J. Claugh	Coal Trimmer
C. Hill	Draper
John Hindmarsh	Foreman Tailor
W. Hull	Spirit Merchant
C. Moore	Surgeon
B. Ord	Proprietor of the Free Press
R. Pearson	Stationer
J. Smith	Shopkeeper
-	Foreman Ropemaker

Stockton Branch (12 February 1859)

Name	Occupation
Alderson	Clerk
J. Allison	Corn Dealer
Bell	Publican
J.A. Benson	Merchant
Braithwaite	Wholesale Grocer
Browen	Millwright
J. Byers	Lead Worker
G. Dodds	Solicitor
Falcus	Merchant
Fletcher	Plasterer
W. J. Fenney	Hairdresser
Hinde	Skinner
S. Ingledon	Wharfinger
W. Longstaff	Boot Maker
W. Pybus	Corn Dealer
R. Sewell	Blacking Manufacturer
W. Skinner	Banker
Taylorson	Wholesale Cabinet Maker
Tweedy	Fruit Merchant
Weatherhead	Shopkeeper
Wilson	Bookseller

Source: TWAS, CP/

Appendix IV: Northern Reform Union Petition (28 February 1859)

Houghton le Spring	72
Ebchester	80
Backworth	95
Hartley	124
Westmoor	125
Burradon	133
Dudley	153
Hetton le Hole	163
Prudhoe & Mickley	186
Wylam	232
Easington Lane	239
Windy Nook	250
Jarrow	251
Alnwick	252
East & West Holywell	253
Greenside & Barlow Spen	254
Seghill	269
Birtley & Chester le Street	340
Sheriff Hill & Felling	384
Swalwell	400
Stockton	403
Winlaton	462
Seaton Delaval	475
East & West Cramlington	558
Shotley Bridge & Blackhall	568
Blaydon	570
Hartlepool	682
Hexham	691
Bedlington	705
Hawick	781
Crook	852
Darlington	1054
Blyth	1091
Berwick upon Tweed	1494
South Shields	1665
Middlesbrough	1871
North Shields	2331
Gateshead	2393
Sunderland	2551
Newcastle upon Tyne	8984
Total number of signatures	**34,456**

Source: TWAS, CP/C549

Appendix V: Council Members of the Northern Reform Union

Balks, T. [Seaton Delaval]
Bell, John [South Shields]
Bell, Joseph [Cramlington]
Binns, Stephen [Newcastle]
Blagburn, John [Gateshead]
Blakiston, William [Middlesborough]
Bolton, William [Hartlepool]
Bridges, Jabez [Hartlepool]
Brown, John [Newcastle]
Brown, John [York]
Brownless, John [Darlington]
Carse, Henry [Shotley Bridge]
Charlton, Edward [Newcastle]
Charlton, George [Newcastle]
Cook, William [Gateshead]
Cowen, Joseph [Blaydon]
Crighton, William [Hawick]
Cummins, John [Newcastle]
Curry, Ralph [Newcastle]
Dixon, Thomas [Blyth]
Dodds, George [Newcastle]
Doubleday, Thomas [Newcastle]
Douglass, J. [Sunderland]
Dunn, John [Sherriff Hill]
Elgey, William [Bowden Close]
Emerson, John [Stella]
Ernest, Charles [York]
Falconar, William [Darlington]
Fines, Richard [Seghill]
Fleck, Joseph [Hawick]
Gardner, Robert [Swalwell]
Gibson, John [Gateshead]
Gilmour, J. T. [Newcastle]
Gregson, Thomas [Newcastle]
Grey, Marshall [Newcastle]
Harle, Peter [Wylam]
Hindmarsh, John [Hartlepool]
Holt, William
Horncy, William [Easington Lane]

Hunter, William [Newcastle]
Jude, Martin [Newcastle]
Kane, John [Gateshead]
Larkin, Charles [Newcastle]
Lishman, Thomas [Newcastle]
Mathison, Robert [Berwick]
Messer, Thomas [Burradon]
Mildred, Charles [Darlington]
Moore, John [Windy Nook]
Oxberry, John [Windy Nook]
Ramsay, Robert [Blaydon]
Reed, Richard Bagnall [Winlaton]
Ridley, Ralph E. [Hexham]
Robinson, Martin
Ross, William [Newcastle]
Rule, David
Soppett, Thomas [Darlington]
Summerside, Edward [Winlaton]
Sutherland, Robert [North Shields]
Tennant, John [Seghill]
Thompson, John
Thompson, Joseph [Jarrow]
Thompson, Leonard
Thompson, Thomas [North Shields]
Turnbull, Richard
Walker, James [Carlisle]
Warden, Robert [Gateshead]
Watson, James [Newcastle]
Watt, John [Newcastle]
White, David
Wilde, Anthony [Hetton-Le-Hole]
Wilkie, Thomas [Newcastle]
Wilks, Washington [Carlisle]
Williamson, James [Sunderland]
Wilson, Isaac [Crook]
Wood, Robert [Newcastle]
Young George [East Holywell]

Source: TWAS, CP/C

Appendix VI: Members of the Northern Reform League and Associational life

Name	NRL	TEMP	FS	MI	COOP
John Bennett	✓		✓		
James Birkett	✓				
Thomas Burt	✓	✓			✓
John Charlton	✓	✓		✓	✓
William Cook	✓	✓			
Elijah Copland	✓		✓		✓
Ralph Curry	✓				✓
John Dalglish	✓		✓		✓
George Douglass	✓		✓		
Thomas Gregson	✓		✓	✓	✓
Thomas Herdman	✓	✓			
William Howe	✓	✓	✓	✓	
William Hunter	✓			✓	✓
John Lucas	✓	✓		✓	✓
James McKendrick	✓			✓	✓
Jonathan Rayne	✓		✓		
Richard Bagnall Reed	✓		✓	✓	
Dr. J. H. Rutherford	✓	✓			✓
Robert Sutherland	✓			✓	
Josiah Thomas	✓		✓	✓	✓
Joseph Thompson	✓		✓		✓
James Watson	✓				✓

Key:
NRL: Northern Reform League
TEMP: Temperance Society Member
FS: Friendly Society
MI: Mechanic's Institute
COOP: Executive Member

Appendix VII: Radical activists and their Freemasonry Affiliations

Robert ARMSTRONG	Pride of the Tyne Lodge
Edward ALLSOPP	United Free Gardeners
George ANDERSON	United Order of Oddfellows
BAILEY	Pride of the Tyne Lodge
Richard BLAKEY	United Free Gardeners
John BENNETT	Grand United Order of Oddfellows
George BIRKETT	United Free Gardeners
William CHARLTON	United Free Gardeners
John COATS	United Free Gardeners
John A. COWEN	Lodge of Industry [No 48]
Joseph COWEN, Snr.	United Order of Nottingham Oddfellows, G. M. 1865
Joseph COWEN, Jnr.	Loyal Order of Ancient Shepherds, (Hon. Mbr.)
Matthew CHALDER	Druids Friendly Society
Elijah COPLAND	Ancient Order of Foresters
John DAGLISH	Ancient Order of Foresters
Peter DICKENSON	Ancient Order of Foresters
George DOUGLASS	Ancient Order of Oddfellows
William FORBES	United Free Gardeners
Thomas GREGSON	Ancient Order of Druids
William GUTHRIE	Ancient Order of Foresters
George HAWKS	Ancient Order of Oddfellows
George HEDLEY	United Free Gardeners
William J. HOWE	Ancient Order of Oddfellows 1867/NRL
Robert PROCTOR	Ancient Order of Oddfellows
Jonathan RAYNE	United Free Gardeners
Richard Bagnall REED	Lodge of Industry, (Dep. G. M. of Durham)
William ROBINSON	Ancient Order of Free Foresters
Thomas ROBSON	Ancient order of Oddfellows
Robert STUDDY	United Free Gardeners
Isaac TEMPLE	Ancient Order of Foresters
Joseph THOMPSON	United Free Gardeners
Stephen THOMPSON	United Free Gardeners
Francis WILLIAMSON	United Free Gardeners
Thomas WILSON	Ancient Order of Foresters
Robert WOOD	United Free Gardeners

Select Bibliography

Archival Sources
Bishopsgate Institute, London
G. J. Holyoake Papers

British Library, London
Charles Dilke Papers

Central Reference Library, Newcastle upon Tyne
William Lockley Harle, Correspondence 1826-78
Minute Book of the Northern Union of Mechanics' Institutes

Greater London Record Office
British Anti-State Church Association Records (later the Liberation Society)

Co-operative Archive, Holyoake House, Manchester
Co-operative Congress Records and Society Histories.

International Institute of Social History Amsterdam
Ernest Jones Papers
Jung-Nachlass Papers
W. E. Adams Papers

Tyne and Wear Archives, Newcastle upon Tyne
Chartist Handbills and Posters (11)
Joseph Cowen (1829-1900) Papers
Election Papers including newspapers
Election Papers and Poll Books 1841-1860
Gateshead Board of Guardian Minute Books
Gateshead Council Minutes
Newcastle Corporation Minutes
Newcastle upon Tyne Junior Liberal Club, Annual Reports
Robert Spence Watson Papers
Thomas Wilson Collection, Vol. IV: 1832-35

Special Collections, Robinson Library, Newcastle University
R. W. Martin, North Country Elections from 1826
Cowen Tracts
R. S. Watson Correspondence

University of Northumbria Library
George Howell Collection, Letter Books 1865-79, 1883-4
Holyoake Papers, General Correspondence 1840-79

University of Sheffield, Special Collections
Leader Correspondence
Mundella Papers [MS 6 - 9, MS 22]
Henry Joseph Wilson Collection [MS41]

Printed Primary Sources
Place of publication is London unless otherwise stated.
Adams, W. E., *Memoirs of a Social Atom*, 1903; rept. New York, 1969; Introduction by J. Saville
Adams, W. E., *Our American Cousins*, 1883; rept. New York, 1992; Introduction by O. R. Ashton and A. Munslow
Anon., *Radical Monday. A letter from Bob in Gotham town to his cousin Bob in the country, containing an account. . .*, Newcastle upon Tyne, 1821
Anon., *Handbook of the Twenty Sixth Annual Co-operative Congress*, Sunderland, 1894
Baernreither, J. M., *English Associations of Working Men*, 1889
Black, F. G. and Black, R. M. (eds.), *The Harney Papers*, Amsterdam, 1969
Bonner, H. B., *Charles Bradlaugh. A record of his life and work by his daughter*, 2 vols., 1894
Burnett, J., *A History of the Engineers Strike*, Newcastle, 1872
Burt, T., *Lecture on the Life and Work of the late Joseph Cowen*, Newcastle, 1911
Newcastle upon Tyne Liberal Association, *Newcastle Liberal Association Annual Reports 1878-1893*, Newcastle upon Tyne
Chater, J. W., *Chater's "Canny Newcassel" Diary and Local Remembrancer, For Bissextile or Leap-Year, 1872*, Newcastle, 1872
Cotton, J. S. and Payne, E. J., *Colonies and Dependencies*, 1883
Corder, P., *The Life of Robert Spence Watson*, 1914
Cowen , J., Speeches *on Public Questions and Political Policy*, Newcastle, 1874
Duncan, W., The *Life of Joseph Cowen*, 1904
Cowen, J., (ed.), *Joseph Cowen's Speeches on the Near Eastern Question: Foreign and Imperial Affairs: And on the British Empire*, Newcastle,1909

Devyr, T. A., *The Odd Book of the Nineteenth Century or Chivalry in Modern Days*, New York, 1882

Eadie, R., *A Sketch of Stella Hall with the Career of Joseph Cowen Esq., MP*, Newcastle, 1865

Fordyce, T., *Historical Register of Remarkable Events*, Newcastle, 1876

Friendly Societies of Matrons, *Rulebook of the Friendly Societies of Matrons*, Newburn, 1821

Friendly Society of Women, *Rulebook of the Friendly Society of Women*, North Shields, 1819

Fynes, R., *The Miners of Northumberland and Durham*, Sunderland, 1873; rept. Sunderland, 1923

Gammage, R. G., *The History of the Chartist Movement 1837-1854*, 1st edn. 1854; Facsimile of the 2nd edition, 1894 with an introduction by J. Saville, London and New York, 1969

Gladstone, W. E., *The Approaching General Election: Speeches delivered in Midlothian during the last week of November 1879*, 1879

Gledson, D., *Jubilee Souvenir. A Short History of the New Delaval Equitable Industrial Co-operative Society Limited, 1862-1912*, Pelaw-on-Tyne, 1913

Healey, T. M., *Letters and Leaders of My Day, Vol. 1: 1880-1891*, 1920

Hirst, F. W., *Early Life and Letters of John Morley*, 2 vols, 1927

Holyoake, G. J., *Sixty Years of an Agitators Life*, 2 vols, 1906

Holyoake, G. J., *Self Help by the People: History of Co-operation in Rochdale*, 1858

Hosbach, W., *A History of the English Agricultural Labourer*, 1908

Hyndman, H. M., *The Record of an Adventurous Life*, 1911

Jones, E. R., *The Life and Speeches of Joseph Cowen, MP*, 1885

Jones, W., *Quaker Campaigns in Peace and War*, 1899

Jones, B., *Cooperative Production*, Oxford, 1894

Kropotkin, P., *Memoirs of a Revolutionist*, 2 vols, 1899

Lawrence, E. P., *Henry George in the British Isles*, Michigan, 1957

Lavery, F. (ed.), *Irish Heroes in the War*, 1917

Linton, W. J., *Memories*, New York, 1895

Lloyd, H. D., *Labor Co-partnership*, 1899

Loyal Order of Ancient Shepherds, *Loyal Order of Ancient Shepherds (Ashton Unity) Guide and Directory*, Ashton under Lyne, 1887-8

Madams, J. P., *The Story Retold. An intermediate text-book on Cooperation* Manchester, 1911

McCabe, J., *Life and Letters of G. J. Holyoake*, 2 vols, 1908

McCarthy, J., *A Short History of Our Own Times, from the accession of Queen Victoria to the General Election of 1880*, 1898

Morton, E., *An Adventure in Co-operation among the Working Classes in North Shields*, Pelaw-on-Tyne, 1925

Noble, M., *Short Sketches of Eminent Men in the North of England*, Newcastle upon Tyne, 1885

North of England Temperance League, *North of England Temperance League Centenary Handbook 1858-1958*, Newcastle, 1858

Quin, M., *Memoirs of a Positivist*, 1924

Rae, W. R., *Handbook of the 26th Annual Cooperative Congress*, Sunderland, 1894

Rutherford, J., *The Secret History of the Fenian Conspiracy : Its origin, objects, & Ramifications*, 2 vols, 1877

Scorer, A., 'The Ouseburn Engine Works', *North of England Co-operative Almanack*, Newcastle, 1873

Simpson, W., *Jubilee Souvenir. A Short History of the Cramlington District Co-operative Society Ltd., 1861-1911*, Manchester, 1912

Steel, J. W., *A Historical Sketch of the Society of Friends, 1653-1898*, Newcastle, 1899

Sykes, J., *Local Records; or Historical Register of Remarkable Events*, 2 vols, Newcastle, 1866

Taylder, T. W. P., *The History of the Rise and Progress of Teetotalism in Newcastle*, Newcastle, 1885

Wallsend Industrial Cooperative Society, *Wallsend Industrial Cooperative Society Jubilee Book 1862-1911*, Newcastle, 1911

Watson, R. S., *The National Liberal Federation from its commencement to the General Election of 1906*, 1907

Welford, R., *Men of Mark 'Twixt Tyne and Tweed*, 3 vols, Newcastle, 1892

Whitfield, R., *History of the Lodge of Industry, No 48*, Newcastle, 1934

Wilson, J. A., A *History of the Durham Miners' Association, 1870-1906*, Durham, 1907

Woodcock, G. and Avakumovie, I., *The Anarchist Prince. A biographical study of Peter Kropotkin*, London and New York, 1950

Newspapers and Periodicals

Birmingham Journal
Catholic Herald
Daily Chronicle and Northern Counties Advertiser
Democratic Review of British and Foreign Politics, History and Literature, rept. 1968)
English Republic
Gateshead and Tyneside Echo

Gateshead Observer
Glasgow Observer
Irish Tribune
Miners Advocate
Monthly Chronicle of North Country Lore and Legend
Newcastle Courant
Newcastle Daily Chronicle
Newcastle Guardian
Newcastle Journal
Newcastle Magazine
Newcastle Standard
Newcastle Weekly Chronicle
North of England Farmer
Northern Daily Express
Northern Leader
Northern Liberator
Northern Reform Record
Northern Star
Northern Tribune
Pall Mall Gazette
Poor Man's Guardian, rept. London, 1969
Punch Magazine
Reasoner and London Tribune
Red Republican, continued as *The Friend of the People*, rept. London, 1966 ed. J. Saville
Sheffield and Rotherham Independent
Tyne Mercury
Tyneside Catholic News
Tyneside Daily Echo

Works of Reference

Ashton, O. R., Fyson, R. and Roberts, S., (eds.), *The Chartist Movement. An Annotated Bibliography*, London, 1995

Baylen, J. O. and Gossman, N. J. (eds.), *Biographical Dictionary of Modern British Radicals*, 5 vols, Brighton, 1984-8

Bellamy, J. M. and Saville, J. (eds.), *Dictionary of Labour Biography*, 11 vols, Basingstoke, 1987

Harrison, J. F. C. and Thompson, D., *Bibliography of the Chartist Movement, 1837-1976*, Brighton, 1978

Harrison, B. (ed.), *Dictionary of British Temperance Biography*, Sheffield, 1973

Kunitz, S. J. and Haycraft, H. (eds.), *American Authors, 1600-1900: A biographical dictionary of American literature*, New York, 1938

McCalmont, F. H., *Parliamentary Poll Book*, London, 1879; rept. Vincent, J. and Stenton M., (eds.), Brighton, 1971

Secondary Works

Adelman, P., *Victorian Radicalism: The middle-class experience, 1830-1914*, London, 1984

Allen, E., Clarke, J. F., McCord, N. and Rowe, D. J., *The North-East Engineers' Strikes of 1871: The Nine Hours' League*, Newcastle, 1971

Allen, J., "Keeping the Faith': The Catholic press and the preservation of Celtic identity in Britain in the late nineteenth century', in P. O'Neill (ed.), *Exile and Homecoming*, Sydney, 2005

Allen J. and Buswell, R., *Rutherford's Ladder: The making of the University of Northumbria 1871-1996*, Newcastle, 2005

Allen, J. and Ashton, O. R. (eds.), *Papers for the People. A Study of the Chartist Press*, London, 2005

Allen, J. and Allen, R. C., "Competing identities': Irish and Welsh migration and the North East of England', in Adrian Green and A. J. Pollard (eds.), *Regional Identities in North-East England, 1300-2000*, London, 2007

Anderson, M., *Henry Joseph Wilson: Fighter for Freedom, 1833-1914*, London, 1953

Archer, John E., *Social Unrest and Popular Protest in England 1780-1840*, Cambridge, 2000

Armytage, W. H. G., *A. J. Mundella 1825-1897: The Liberal background to the labour movement*, London, 1951

Ashraf, P. M., *The Life and Times of Thomas Spence*, Gateshead, 1983

Aspinwall, B. and McCaffrey, J. F., 'A Comparative View of the Irish in Edinburgh in the 19th Century', in R. Swift and S. Gilley (eds.), *The Irish in the Victorian City*, London, 1985

Ashton, O. R., *W. E Adams: Chartist, Radical and Journalist, 1832-1906*, Whitley Bay, 1991

Ashton, O. R., Fyson, R. and Roberts, S. (eds.), *The Chartist Legacy*, Woodbridge, 1999

Ashton, O. R., 'W. E. Adams, Chartist and republican in Victorian England', in D. W. Howell and K. O. Morgan (eds.), *Crime, Protest and Police in Modern British Society: Essays in memory of David J. V. Jones*, Cardiff, 1999

Ashton, O. R. and Pickering P. A., *Friends of the People. Uneasy radicals in the age of the Chartists*, London, 2002

Ashton, T. S., *The Industrial Revolution, 1760-1830*, Oxford, 1996

Bailey, P., *Leisure and Class in Victorian England: Rational recreation and the contest for control, 1830-1885*, London, 1978

Ball, A. R., *British Political Parties: The emergence of a modern party system*, London, 1981

Barker, H., *Newspapers, Politics and English Society, 1695-1855*, Harlow, 2000

Barker, M., *Gladstone and Radicalism: The Reconstruction of the Liberal Party in England*, Hassocks, 1975

Barrow, L. and Bullock, I., *Democratic Ideas and the British Labour Movement*, Cambridge, 1996

Barrow, T., 'The Labour Representation Committee at Newcastle upon Tyne 1903', in M. Callcott and R. Challinor (eds.), *Working Class Politics in North East England*, Newcastle upon Tyne, 1983

Beales, D. E. D., 'Gladstone and Garibaldi', in P. J. Jagger (ed.), *Gladstone*, London and Rio Grande, Ohio, 1998

Bean, J. M. W. (ed.), *The Political Culture of Modern Britain: Studies in memory of Stephen Koss*, London, 1987

Beer, S., *Modern British Politics*, London, 1965

Beetham, D., *Max Weber and the Theory of Modern Politics*, Cambridge, 1985

Belchem, J., *Popular Radicalism in Nineteenth Century Britain*, Basingstoke, 1996

Belchem, J., '1848: Feargus O' Connor and the collapse of the Mass Platform', in J. Epstein and D. Thompson (eds.), *The Chartist Experience. Studies in Working-Class Radicalism and Culture, 1830-1860*, London, 1982

Benewick, R., Berki, R. N. and Parekh, B. (eds.), *Knowledge and Belief in Politics: The problem of ideology*, London, 1973

Bentley, M., *Politics Without Democracy, 1815-1914*, London, 1984

Bentley, M., *The Climax of Liberal Politics: British Liberalism in theory and practice, 1868-1918*, London, 1987

Bernstein, G., *Liberalism and Liberal Politics in Edwardian England*, London, 1986

Biagini, E. F., *Liberty, Retrenchment, and Reform: Popular Liberalism in the Age of Gladstone, 1860-1880*, Cambridge, 1992

Biagini, E. F. (ed.), *Citizenship and Community. Liberals, radicals and collective identities in the British Isles, 1865-1931*, Cambridge, 1996

Biagini, E. F. and Reid, A. J. (eds.), *Currents of Radicalism. Popular radicalism, organised labour and party politics in Britain, 1850-1914*, Cambridge, 1991

Boston, Ray, *British Chartists in America, 1839-1900*, Manchester, 1971

Bowler, P. J., *The Invention of Progress: The Victorians and the past*, Oxford, 1989

Boyce, D. G., *The Irish Question and British Politics 1886-1998*, Basingstoke and London, 1996

Boyce, D. G., 'Gladstone and Ireland', in P. J. Jagger (ed.), *Gladstone*, London and Rio Grande, Ohio, 1998

Brady, L. W., *T. P. O'Connor and the Liverpool Irish*, London, 1983

Brake, L. and Codell, J. F. (eds.), *Encounters in the Victorian Press*, Basingstoke, 2005

Briggs, A., *Victorian People: Some reassessments of people, institutions, ideas, and events, 1851-1867*, London, 1954

Briggs, A., *Victorian Cities*, London, 1963

Briggs, A. and Saville, J. (eds.), *Essays in Labour History, in memory of G. D. H Cole*, London, 1969

Brotherstone, T., Clark, A. and Whelan, K., (eds.), *These Fissured Isles: Ireland, Scotland and British History, 1798-1848*, Edinburgh, 2005

Buckland, P. and Belchem, J. (eds.), *The Irish in British Labour History* (Conference Proceedings in Irish Studies, 1), Liverpool, 1993

Busteed, M. A., *Geography and Voting Behaviour*, London, 1975

Cadogan, P., *Early Radical Newcastle*, Consett, 1975

Callcott, M. and Challinor, R. (eds.), *Working Class Politics in North East England*, Newcastle upon Tyne, 1983

Challinor, R., *A Radical Lawyer in Victorian England: W. P. Roberts and the struggle for workers' rights*, London, 1990

Challinor, R. and Ripley, B., *The Miners' Association. A Trade Union in the Age of the Chartists*, London, 1968, new edn. Whitley Bay, 1990

Chase, M., *'The People's Farm': English Radical Agrarianism, 1775-1840*, Oxford, 1988

Chase, M., 'The Teesside Irish in the nineteenth century', in P. Buckland, and J. Belchem (eds.), *The Irish in British Labour History* (Conference Proceedings in Irish Studies, 1), Liverpool, 1993

Chase, M. and Dyck, I., (ed.), *Living and Learning: Essays in honour of J. F. C.Harrison*, Aldershot, 1996,

Church, R. A., *The History of the British Coal Industry, 3: 1830-1913, Victorian Pre-eminence*, Oxford 1986

Clair, C., *A History of Printing in Britain*, 1965

Clarke, J. F., *The North East Engineers' Strike, 1871*, Newcastle, 1971

Cleary, E. J., *The Building Society Movement*, London, 1965

Cole, G. D. H., *A Century of Co-operation*, Manchester, 1944

Cole, G. D. H. and Postgate, R., *The Common People, 1746-1946*, London, 1938

Colls, R., *The Pitmen of the Northern Coalfield: Work, culture, and protest, 1790-1850*, Manchester, 1987

Colls, R., *The Collier's Rant: Song and culture in the industrial village*, London, 1977

Colls, R. and Lancaster, B. (eds.), *Newcastle upon Tyne. A Modern History*, West Sussex, 2001

Colls, R. and Rodger, R. (eds.), *Cities of Ideas. Civil society and urban governance in Britain, 1800-2000*, Aldershot, 2004

Cooke, A. B. and Vincent, J., *The Governing Passion: Cabinet government and party politics in Britain, 1885-6*, Brighton, 1974

Cooper, T., *The Life of Thomas Cooper*, London, 1872, new edn. Leicester, 1971

Cooter, R., *When Paddy Met Geordie. The Irish in County Durham and Newcastle 1840-1880*, Sunderland, 2005

Corder, P., *The Life of Robert Spence Watson*, London, 1914

Cordery, S., *British Friendly Societies 1750-1914*, Basingstoke, 2003

Cowling, M., *1867 Disraeli, Gladstone and Revolution: The Passing of the Second Reform Bill*, Cambridge, 1967

Cragoe, M. and Taylor, A. (eds.), *London Politics, 1760-1914*, Basingstoke 2005

Cunningham, H., *The Volunteer Force. A social and political history, 1859-1908*, London, 1975

Cunningham, H., *Leisure in the Industrial Revolution c.1780-c.1880*, London, 1980

Davis, G., *The Irish in Britain 1815-1914*, Dublin, 1991

Davis, G., 'Little Irelands', in R. Swift and S. Gilley (eds.), *The Irish in Britain 1815-1939*, London, 1989

Davis, J. A. (ed.), *Italy in the Nineteenth Century: 1796-1900*, Oxford, 2000

Dickinson, H. T., *Liberty and Property. Political Ideology in Eighteenth Century Britain*, London, 1977

Dickinson, H. T., *Radical Politics in the North-East of England in the Later Eighteenth Century*, Durham, 1979

Digby, A. and Feinstein, C. (eds.), *New Directions in Economic and Social History*, London, 1989

Dougan, D., *The History of North East Shipbuilding*, London, 1968

Donald, J. and Hall, S. (eds.), *Politics and Ideology, A Reader*, Milton Keynes, 1986

Dunbabin, J. P., *Rural Discontent in the Nineteenth Century*, London, 1974

Dunbabin, J. P., *The Revolt of the Field: the agricultural labourers' movement in the 1870s* , Oxford, 1974

Dunbabin, J. P., 'Electoral reforms and their outcomes in the UK, 1865-1900', in T. R. Gourvish and A. O'Day (eds.), *Later Victorian Britain, 1867-1900*, Basingstoke, 1988

Eastwood, D., *Government and Community in the English Provinces, 1700-1870*, Basingstoke, 1997

Edwards, O. D. and Storey, P. J., 'The Irish Press in Victorian Britain', in R. Swift and S. Gilley (eds.), *The Irish in the Victorian City*, London, 1985

Edwards, O. D., 'The Catholic Press in Scotland since the restoration of the hierarchy', in David McRoberts (ed.), *Modern Scottish Catholicism 1878-1978*, Glasgow, 1979

Eldridge, C. C., *England's Mission: The imperial Idea in the age of Gladstone and Disraeli, 1868-1880*, London, 1973

Ellis, Joyce, 'The 'Black Indies'. The economic development of Newcastle, *c*. 1700-1840', in Robert Colls and Bill Lancaster (eds.), *Newcastle upon Tyne. A Modern History*, West Sussex, 2001

Elliott, M., *Victorian Leicester*, Chichester, 1979

Epstein, J. and Thompson, D. (eds.), *The Chartist Experience. Studies in Working-Class Radicalism and Culture, 1830-1860*, London, 1982

Evans, E. J., *Parliamentary Reform, c. 1770-1918*, Harlow, 2000

Feuchtwanger, E. J., *Democracy and Empire, Britain 1865-1914*, London, 1985

Feuchtwanger, E. J., *Disraeli, Democracy and the Tory Party, Conservative leadership and organization after the Second Reform Bill*, Oxford, 1968

Fielding, S., *Class and Ethnicity. Irish Catholics in England, 1880-1939*, Manchester, 1993

Finn, M., *After Chartism. Class and Nation in English Radical Politics, 1848-1874*, Cambridge, 1993

Flick, C., *The Birmingham Political Union and the Movements for Reform in Britain, 1830-39*, Hampden, CT, 1978

Flinn, M. W., *Men of Iron: The Crowleys in the early iron industry*, Edinburgh, 1962

Forster, M., *Significant Sisters: Active Feminism, 1839-1939*, Harmondsworth, 1984

Foster, J., *Class Struggle and the Industrial Revolution: early capitalism in three English towns [Oldham, Northampton, and South Shields]*, London, 1974

Fowler, W. S. *A Study in Radicalism and Dissent. The Life and Times of H. J. Wilson, 1833-1914*, London, 1961

Fraser, D., *Urban Politics in Victorian England, the structure of politics in Victorian cities*, Leicester, 1976

Freitag, S. (ed.), *Exiles from European Revolutions. Refugees in Mid-Victorian England*, New York and Oxford, 2003

Fyfe, J. (ed.), *Autobiography of John McAdam, 1806-1883*, Edinburgh, 1983

Gallagher, T., *Glasgow. The Uneasy Peace, Religious Tension in Modern Scotland*, Manchester, 1987

Gallagher, T., 'Diamond, Charles. Labour politician and newspaper proprietor', in J. M. Bellamy, and J. Saville (eds.), *Dictionary of Labour Biography*, 11 vols, Basingstoke, 1987

Gallagher, T., 'A Tale of Two Cities: Communal Strife in Glasgow and Liverpool Before 1914', in R. Swift and S. Gilley (eds.), *The Irish in the Victorian City*, London, 1985

Geertz, C., *Local Knowledge: Further essays in interpretive anthropology*, London, 1993

Gerth, H. H. and Mills, C. W. (eds.), *From Max Weber. Essays in Sociology*, London, 1948

Gleason, J. H., *The Genesis of Russophobia in Britain*, Harvard, 1950

Gosden, P. H. J., *The Friendly Societies in England, 1815-75*, Manchester 1961

Gourvish, T. R. and O'Day, A. (eds.), *Later Victorian Britain, 1867-1900*, Basingstoke, 1988

Gray, R., 'The platform and the pulpit: cultural networks and civic identities in industrial towns, c. 1850-70', in Alan Kidd and David Nicholls (eds.), *The Making of the British Middle Class. Studies of regional and cultural diversity since the eighteenth century*, Stroud, 1998

Gray, T., *The Orange Order*, London and Toronto, 1972

Gurney, P., *Co-operative Culture and the Politics of Consumption in England, c.1870-1930*, Manchester, 1996

Hall, S., 'Variants of Liberalism', in J. Donald and S. Hall (eds.), *Politics and Ideology*, London, 1986

Hamer, D. A., *Liberal Politics in the Age of Gladstone and Roseberry*, Oxford, 1972

Harmon, M. (ed.), *Fenians and Fenianism*, Dublin, 1968

Harris, M. and Lee, A. (eds.), *The Press and English Society from the Seventeenth to the Nineteenth Centuries*, London, 1986

Harrison, B., *Drink and the Victorians: The Temperance Question in England, 1815-72*, Keele, 1971

Harrison, B. and Hollis, P. (eds.), *Robert Lowery: Radical and Chartist*, London, 1979

Harrison, J. F. C., *Learning and Living, 1790-1960: A study in the history of the English adult education movement*, London, 1969

Harrison, J. F. C., *Late Victorian Britain, 1870-1901*, London, 1990

Harrison, R., *Before the Socialists. Studies in Labour and Politics 1861-1881*, London, 1965

Harrison, R., *The Independent Collier. The coal miner as archetypal proletarian reconsidered*, Hassocks 1978

Heyck, T. W., *The Dimensions of British Radicalism: The case of Ireland, 1874-95*, Urbana, IL and London, 1974

Hickman, M. J., 'Incorporating and denationalizing the Irish in England: the role of the Catholic Church', in Patrick O'Sullivan (ed.), *The Irish World Wide. History, Heritage, Identity* (6 vols, Leicester, London and Washington, 1992-2000), V: *Religion and Identity*, 1996

Hinton, J., *Labour and Socialism: A history of the British labour movement 1867-1974*, Brighton, 1983

Hobsbawm, E. J., *The Age of Revolution, Europe 1789-1848*, London, 1962

Hobsbawm, E. J., *Labouring Men. Studies in the history of labour*, London, 1968

Hollis, P. (ed), *Pressure from Without in Early Victorian England*, London, 1974

Hollis, P. (ed), *Women in Public, 1850-1900: Documents of the Victorian Women's Movement*, London, 1979,

Hopkins, E., *Working Class Self- Help in Nineteenth-Century England*, London, 1995

Howell, D. W and Morgan, K. O. (eds.), *Crime, Protest and Police in Modern British Society: Essays in memory of David J. V. Jones*, Cardiff, 1999

Howkins, A., *Reshaping Rural England: A Social History 1850-1925*, London, 1991

Hugman, J., 'Joseph Cowen and the Blaydon Cooperative Store: a north East model', in Bill Lancaster and Paddy Maguire (eds.), *Towards a Cooperative Commonwealth*, Loughborough, 1996

Hugman, J., 'Print and Preach: The entrepreneurial spirit of Tyneside politics', in R. Colls and B. Lancaster (eds.), *Newcastle upon Tyne. A Modern History*, West Sussex, 2001

Hunt, C. J., *The Book Trade in Northumberland and Durham to 1860*, Newcastle upon Tyne, 1975

Isaac, P. (ed.), *Six Centuries of the Book Trade in Britain*, Winchester, 1991

Jackson, A., *Home Rule. An Irish History 1800-2000*, London, 2003

Jackson, H., *The Eighteen Nineties*, London, 1939

Jagger, P. J. (ed.), *Gladstone*, London and Rio Grande (Ohio), 1998

James, D., Jowitt T. and Laybourn, K. (eds.), *The Centennial History of the Independent Labour Party*, Halifax, 1992

Jay, M. and Neve, M. (eds.), *1900. A Fin de Siècle Reader*, London, 1999

Jay, R., *Joseph Chamberlain. A Political Study*, Oxford, 1981

Jenkins, T. A., *Gladstone, Whiggery and the Liberal Party*, Oxford, 1988

Jenkins, T. A., *The Liberal Ascendancy, 1830-1886*, Basingstoke, 1994

Johnson, P., *Saving and Spending. The Working Class Economy in Britain, 1870-1939*, Oxford, 1985

Jones, A. G., *Powers of the Press. Newspapers, Power and the Public in Nineteenth Century England*, Aldershot, 1996,

Joyce, P., *Work, Society and Politics: The culture of the factory in later Victorian England*, Brighton, 1980

Joyce, P., *Visions of the People. Industrial England and the Question of Class*, Cambridge, 1991

Judd, D., *Radical Joe. A Life of Joseph Chamberlain*, Cardiff, 1993

Kee, R., *The Green Flag. A History of Irish Nationalism*, London 1972

Kidd, A. and Nicholls, D. (eds.), *The Making of the British Middle Class. Studies of regional and cultural diversity since the eighteenth century*, Stroud, 1998

Kirk, N., *The Growth of Working Class Reformism in England*, London, 1985

Lancaster, B., *Radicalism, Cooperation and Socialism: Leicester Working Class Politics, 1860-1906*, Leicester, 1987

Lancaster, B. and Maguire, P. (eds.), *Towards a Cooperative Commonwealth*, Loughborough, 1996

Lawrence, E. P., *Henry George in the British Isles*, East Lansing, Mich., 1957

Laybourn, K., *A History of British Trade Unionism c.1770-1990*, Stroud, 1992

Lee, Alan J., *The Origins of the Popular Press, 1855-1914*, London, 1976

Leventhal, F. M., *Respectable Radical: George Howell and Victorian working class politics*, London, 1971

Lloyd, T., *The General Election of 1880*, Oxford, 1968

Lopatin, N. D., *Political Unions, Popular Politics and the Great Reform Act of 1832*, Basingstoke, 1999

Lyons, F. S. L., *Charles Stewart Parnell*, London, 1977

Lyons, F. S. L. and Hawkins, R. A. J. (eds.), *Ireland under the Union: Varieties of Tensions. Essays in honour of T. W. Moody*, Oxford, 1980

MacDermott, T. P., 'The Irish Workers on Tyneside in the 19th century', in Norman McCord (ed.), *Essays in Tyneside Labour History*, Newcastle, 1977

Machin, I., *The Rise of Democracy in Britain, 1830-1918*, Basingstoke, 2000

Macfie, A. L., *The Eastern Question 1774-1923*, Harlow, 1989

MacRaild, D. M., *Irish Migrants in Modern Britain, 1750-1922*, London, 1999

MacRaild, D. M., *Culture, Conflict and Migration. The Irish in Victorian Cumbria*, Liverpool, 1998

MacRaild, D. M., *Faith, Fraternity and Fighting. The Orange Order and Irish Migrants in Northern England, 1850-1920*, Liverpool, 2005

Magnanie, L., 'National Cooperative Festivals', in S. Yeo (ed.), *New Views of Cooperation*, London, 1988

Marsh, P., *Joseph Chamberlain, Entrepreneur in Politics*, New Haven, 1994

Matthew, H. C. G., *The Liberal Imperialists: The ideas and policies of a post Gladstonian elite*, Oxford, 1973

Matthew, H.C. G., 'Gladstone, Rhetoric and Politics', in Peter Jagger (ed.), *Gladstone*, London, 1998

McCord, N., *Northeast England. The region's development 1760-1960*, Bristol, 1979

McCord, N. (ed.), *Essays in Tyneside Labour History*, Newcastle, 1977

McCord, N., 'The Fenians and public opinion in Great Britain', in Maurice Harmon (ed.), *Fenians and Fenianism*, Dublin, 1968

McRoberts, D. (ed.), *Modern Scottish Catholicism 1878-1978*, Glasgow, 1979

McWilliam, R. A., 'Radicalism and popular culture: the Tichborne case and the politics of 'fair play', 1867-1886', in E. F. Biagini and A. J. Reid (eds.), *Currents of Radicalism. Popular radicalism, organised labour and party politics in Britain, 1850-1914*, Cambridge, 1991

Middlebrook, S., *Newcastle upon Tyne. Its growth and achievement*, Newcastle, 1950

Milne, M., *The Newspapers of Northumberland and Durham: A study of their progress during the 'Golden Age' of the Provincial Press*, Newcastle, 1971

Moody, T. W., *Davitt and Irish Revolution, 1846-82*, Oxford, 1981

Morris, M. and Gooch, L., *Down Your Aisles. The Diocese of Hexham and Newcastle*, Hartlepool, 2000

Morris, R. J., *Class, Sect and Party. The Making of the British Middle Class, Leeds 1820-1850*, Manchester, and New York, 1990

Morris, R. J., 'A year in the public life of the British bourgeoisie', in R. Colls and R. Rodger (eds.), *Cities of Ideas. Civil society and urban governance in Britain, 1800-2000*, Aldershot, 2004

Morton, E., *An Adventure in Co-operation among the Working Classes in North Shields*, Pelaw-on-Tyne, 1925

Nash D. and Taylor A. (eds.), *Republicanism in Victorian Society*, Stroud, 2000

Neal, F., *Sectarian Violence. The Liverpool Experience 1819-1914*, Manchester, 1988

Neal, F., 'English-Irish conflict in the north-east of England', in Patrick Buckland and John Belchem (eds.), *The Irish in British Labour History* (Conference Proceedings in Irish Studies, 1), Liverpool, 1993

Newsinger, J., *Fenianism in Mid-Victorian Britain*, London, 1994

Nossiter, T. J., *Influence, Opinion and Political idioms in Reformed England. Case studies from the North East 1832-1874*, Brighton, 1975

Oakeshott, R., *The Case for Workers' Co-ops*, London, 1978

O'Brien, P. and Quinault, R. E., *The Industrial Revolution and British Society*, Cambridge 1993

Ó Broin, L., *Revolutionary Underground: The story of the Irish Republican Brotherhood, 1858-192*, Dublin, 1976

O'Day, A., *The English Face of Irish Nationalism: Parnellite involvement in British politics, 1880-86*, Dublin, 1977

O'Day, A., 'The political organization of the Irish in Britain, 1867-1890', in R. Swift and S. Gilley (eds.), *The Irish in Britain 1815-1939*, London, 1989

O'Day, A., *Irish Home Rule 1867-1921*, Manchester, 1999

O'Day, A. (ed.), *Reactions to Irish Nationalism, 1865-1914*, London, 1987

Offer, A., *Property and politics, 1870-1914: Landownership, law, ideology and urban development in England*, Cambridge, 1981

O'Leary, P. (ed.), *Irish Migrants in Modern Wales*, Liverpool, 2004

O' Neill, P. (ed.), *Exile and Homecoming*, Sydney, 2004

O'Sullivan, P., (ed.), *The Irish World Wide, History Heritage, Identity*, 6 vols, London, Leicester and Washington, 1992-2000

Ó Tuathaigh, M. A. G., 'The Irish in Nineteenth Century Britain: Problems of Integration', in Roger Swift and Sheridan Gilley (eds.), *The Irish in the Victorian City*, London, 1985

Palliser, D. M., Clark, P. and Daunton, M. (eds.), *The Cambridge Urban History of Britain*, 3 vols, Cambridge, 2000-1

Peaple, S. and Vincent, J., 'Gladstone and the Working Man', in P. J. Jagger (ed.), *Gladstone*, London and Rio Grande, Ohio, 1998

Pelling, H., *The Origins of the Labour Party, 1880-1900*, Oxford, 1965

Pelling, H., *Popular Politics and Society in Late Victorian Britain*, London, 1979

Perkin, H., *The Origins of Modern English Society, 1780-1880*, London, 2002

Philp, M. (ed), *The French Revolution and British Popular Politics*, Cambridge, 1991

Pickering, P. and Tyrrell, A., *The People's Bread. A History of the Anti-Corn Law League*, Leicester, 2000

Pollard, S., 'Cooperation: from Community Building to Shopkeeping', in Asa Briggs and John Saville (eds.), *Essays in Labour History, in memory of G. D. H. Cole*, vol. I, London, 1969

Porter, B., *The Lion's Share. A Short History of British Imperialism, 1850-1983*, 3rd edn. London, 1996

Porter, B., *The Refugee Question in Mid-Victorian Britain*, Cambridge, 1979

Potts, A. (ed.), *Shipbuilders and Engineers, Essays on the Labour and the Shipbuilding Industries of the North East*, Newcastle 1987

Price, R., *An Imperial War and the British Working Class*, London, 1972

Price, R., *Labour and British Society : an interpretative history*, London, 1986

Prochaska, F. K., 'Philanthropy', in F. M. L. Thompson (ed.), *Cambridge Social History of Britain, 1750-1950*, 3 vols, Cambridge, 1990

Prochaska, F., *The Republic of Britain, 1760-2000*, London, 2000

Pugh, M., *The Making of Modern British Politics, 1867-1931*, London, 1982

Purdue, A. W., 'The ILP in the North East of England', in David James, Tony Jowitt and Keith Laybourn (eds.), *The Centennial History of the Independent Labour Party*, Halifax, 1992

Quinault, R. E., 'Joseph Chamberlain: A reassessment', in T. R.Gourvish and A. O'Day (eds.), *Later Victorian Britain, 1867-1900*, Basingstoke, 1988

Quinliven, P. and Rose, P., *The Fenians In England: A Sense of Insecurity*, London, 1982

Ramsden, J., *An Appetite for Power. A History of the Conservative Party since 1830*, London, 1999

Read, D., *Peterloo: the 'Massacre' and its Background*, Manchester, 1973.

Rich, P. B., *Race and Empire in British Politics*, Cambridge, 1986

Robbins, K., *The Eclipse of a Great Power, 1870-1975*, London, 1983

Rowe, D. J., 'The North East', in F. M. L. Thompson (ed.), *The Cambridge Social History of Britain 1750-1950*, 3 vols, pbk edn. Cambridge, 1990, vol. I: *Regions and Communities*.

Royle, E., *Victorian Infidels, the origins of the British Secularist Movement, 1791-1866, Manchester*, 1974

Royle, E., *Radicals, Secularists and Republicans: Popular free thought in Britain, 1866-1915*, Manchester, 1979

Royle, E., *Revolutionary Britannia? Reflections on the threat of revolution in Britain, 1789-1848*, Manchester, 2000

Rush, M., *The Role of the Member of Parliament since 1868. From gentlemen to players*, Oxford, 2001

Saab, A. P., *Reluctant Icon, Gladstone, Bulgaria, and the Working Classes, 1856-1878*, Cambridge, Mass., 1991

St John, I., *Disraeli and the Art of Victorian Politics*, London, 2005

Samuels, R. (ed.), *Patriotism: The Making and Unmaking of British National identity*, vol. II, London and New York, 1988

Sarti, R., 'Giuseppe Mazzini and his opponents', in John A. Davis (ed.), *Italy in the Nineteenth Century: 1796-1900*, Oxford, 2000

Sassoon, A. S., *Approaches to Gramsci*, London, 1982

Satre, L., *Thomas Burt, Miners' MP, 1837-1922*, Leicester, 1999

Saville, J., *1848. The British State and the Chartist Movement*, Cambridge, 1987

Saville, J., 'Imperialism and the Victorians', in E. M. Sigsworth (ed.), *In Search of Victorian Values: Aspects of Nineteenth Century Thought and Society*, Manchester, 1988

Schoyen, A. R., *The Chartist Challenge. A portrait of George Julian Harney*, London, 1958

Schwarzkopf, J., *Women in the Chartist Movement*, New York, 1991

Searle, G. R., *Entrepreneurial Politics in Mid-Victorian Britain*, Oxford, 1993

Searle, G. R., *The Liberal Party, Triumph and Disintegration, 1886-1929*, Basingstoke, 2001

Shannon, R. T., *Gladstone and the Bulgarian Agitation, 1876*, 2nd edn. London, 1975

Shannon, R. T., *The Crisis of Imperialism, 1865-1915*, London, 1976

Shannon, R. T., *Gladstone, Heroic Minister, 1865-1898*, London, 1999

Shaw, A. G. L. (ed.), *Great Britain and the Colonies, 1815-65*, London, 1970

Sigsworth, E. M. (ed.), *In Search of Victorian Values: Aspects of Nineteenth Century Thought and Society*, Manchester, 1988

Smith, F. B., *The Making of the Second Reform Bill*, Cambridge, 1966

Smith, F. B., *Radical Artisan: W. J. Linton, 1812-97*, Manchester, 1973

Smith, Jeff, 'The making of a diocese 1851-1882', in Robert Colls and Bill Lancaster (eds.), *Newcastle, upon Tyne. A Modern History*, West Sussex, 2001

Stedman Jones, G., *Languages of Class: Studies in English Working Class History 1832-1982*, Cambridge 1983

Stephens, W. B., *Education in Britain, 1750-1914*, Basingstoke, 1998

Stevenson, J., *Popular Disturbances in England 1700-1832*, 2nd edn. Harlow, 1992

Strawbridge, S., 'Darwin and Victorian social values', in E.M. Sigsworth (ed.), *In Search of Victorian Values: Aspects of Nineteenth Century Thought and Society*, Manchester, 1988

Sturgess, R. W. (ed.), *Pitmen, Viewers and Coalmasters*, Newcastle, 1986

Swartz, M., *The Politics of British Foreign Policy in the era of Disraeli and Gladstone*, London, 1985

Swift, R., 'The Irish in nineteenth-century Britain: towards a definitive history', in P. Buckland and J. Belchem (eds.), *The Irish in British Labour History* (Conference Proceedings in Irish Studies, 1), Liverpool, 1993

Swift, R. and Gilley, S. (eds.), *The Irish in the Victorian City*, London, 1985

Swift, R. and Gilley, S. (eds.), *The Irish in Britain 1815-1939*, London, 1989

Swift, R., and Gilley, S (eds.), *The Irish in Victorian Britain. The Local Dimension*, Dublin, 1999

Swift, R., 'Crime and the Irish', in R. Swift and S. Gilley (eds.), *The Irish in Britain 1815-1939*, London, 1989

Sykes, A., *The Rise and Fall of British Liberalism, 1776-1988*, London and New York, 1997

Taylor, A., *Down with the Crown. British Anti-Monarchism and Debates about Royalty since 1790*, London, 1999

Taylor, M., *The Decline of Modern British Radicalism, 1847-1860*, Oxford, 1995

Taylor, M., 'Republics versus empires: Charles Dilke's republicanism reconsidered', in D. Nash and A. Taylor (eds.), *Republicanism in Victorian Society*, Stroud, 2000

Tholfsen, T. R., *Working Class Radicalism in Mid-Victorian England*, London, 1976

Thomis, M. and Grimmet, J., *Women in Protest 1800-1850*, New York, 1982

Thompson, D., *The Early Chartists*, Columbia, 1971

Thompson, D., *The Chartists: Popular Politics in the Industrial Revolution*, London and New York, 1984, Hounslow, 1983

Thompson, D., 'Ireland and the Irish in English Radicalism before 1850', in J. Epstein and D. Thompson (eds.), *The Chartist Experience. Studies in Working-Class Radicalism and Culture, 1830-1860*, London, 1982

Thompson, E. P., *The Making of the English Working Class*, new edn, London, 1980

Thompson, E. P., *William Morris. Romantic to Revolutionary*, New York, 1976

Thompson, F. M. L., *The Rise of Respectable Society. A social history of Victorian Britain, 1830-1900*, Cambridge, Mass., 1988

Thompson, F. M. L. (ed.), *The Cambridge Social History of Britain 1750-1950*, 3 vols, pbk edn. Cambridge, 1990

Todd, N., *The Militant Democracy. Joseph Cowen and Victorian Radicalism*, Whitley Bay, 1991

Todd, N., 'The Red Herring War of 1872: Women's rights, butchers and co-ops in the Northern Coalfield', in B. Lancaster and P. Maguire (eds.), *Towards a Cooperative Commonwealth*, Loughborough, 1996

Tyrrell, Alex, *Joseph Sturge and the Moral Radical Party in Early Victorian Britain*, London, 1987

Tzuzuki, C., *H. M. Hyndman and British Socialism*, London, 1961

Vincent, D. (ed.), *Testaments of Radicalism: Memoirs of Working Class Politicians 1790-1885*, London, 1977

Vincent, J., *The Formation of the British Liberal Party, 1857-1868*, Harmondsworth, 1976

Vincent, J., *Pollbooks: How Victorians Voted*, Cambridge, 1967

Walton, J. K., *Lancashire. A Social History, 1558-1939*, Manchester, 1987

Walton, J. K., *The Second Reform Act*, London, 1993

Walton, John K., 'North', in D. M. Palliser, Peter Clark and Martin Daunton (eds.), *The Cambridge Urban History of Britain*, 3 vols, Cambridge, 2000-1, vol. II

Watson, R. S., *Reminiscences of the late Rt. Hon. Robert Spence Watson, 1837-1911*, York, 1969

Webb, R. K., 'Flying Missionaries: Unitarian Journalists in Victorian England', in J. M. W. Bean (ed.), *The Political Culture of Modern Britain: Studies in memory of Stephen Koss*, London, 1987

Wilson, A., *The Chartist Movement in Scotland*, Manchester, 1970

Winlaton Local History Society, *History of Blaydon*, Gateshead, 1975

Wohl, A. S., *Endangered Lives. Public Health in Victorian Britain*, 1983

Worrall, D., *Radical Culture, Discourse, Resistance and Surveillance*, Detroit, 1992

Wrightson, K. and Levine, D., *The Making of an Industrial Society, Whickham 1560-1765*, Oxford, 1991

Wrigley, C., *A History of British Industrial Relations, 1875-1914*, Brighton, 1982

Yeo, S. (ed.), *New Views of Cooperation*, London, 1988

Young, J. D., *Socialism and the English Working Class, a history of English labour, 1883-1939*, New York and London, 1989

Articles

Ashton, O. R., 'W. E. Adams and working class opposition to Empire, 1878-1880: Cyprus and Afghanistan', *Bulletin of North East Labour History Society*, 27, 1993

Ashton, O. R. and Hugman, J., 'Letters from America: George Julian Harney, Boston, USA and Newcastle upon Tyne, England, 1863-1888', *Proceedings*, Massachusetts Historical Society, 107, 1995

Belchem, J., 'Britishness, Asylum Seekers and the Northern Working Class: 1851', *Northern History*, XXXIX:1, March 2002

Bentley, Michael, 'Gladstonian Liberals and Provincial Notables: Whitby Politics 1868-1870', *Historical Research*, 65:154, 1991

Brock, P., 'Polish democrats and English radicals, 1832-62: A chapter in the history of Anglo-Polish relations', *Journal of Modern History*, 25, 1953

Brock, P., 'Joseph Cowen and the Polish exiles', *Slavonic and East European Review*, 32, 1953.

Burt, R., 'The British Non-Ferrous Mining Industry', *Labour History Review*, 71:1, 2006,

Chase, Malcolm, 'Paine, Spence and the Rights of Man', *Bulletin of the Society for the Study of Labour History*, 52:3, 1987

Chase, Malcolm, 'Wholesome Object Lessons: The Chartist Land Plan in Retrospect', *English Historical Review*, CXVIII:475, 2003

Chase, Malcolm, 'Out of Radicalism: the Mid-Victorian Freehold Land Movement', *English Historical Review*, 106, 1991

Church, R., 'Chartism and the miners: A Reinterpretation', *Labour History Review,* 56:3, 1991

Coffey, J., 'Charles Diamond: A legend in his time', *Scottish Catholic Observer,* 19 April 1985

Cunningham, H., 'Jingoism and the working classes, 1877-78', *Bulletin of the Society for the Study of Labour History,* 19, 1969

Cunningham, H., 'Language of Patriotism', *History Workshop Journal,* 12, 1981

Daunton, M. J., 'Down the Pit: Work in the Great Northern and South Wales Coalfields, 1870-1914', *Economic History Review,* 34, 1981

Davis, J. A., 'Garibaldi and England', *History Today,* 32, 1982

Derry, J., 'Political Biography: A Defence (2)', *Contemporary British History,* 10: 4, 1996

Docherty, G., 'National identity and the Study of Irish History', *English Historical Review,* II:441, April 1996

Dunbabin, J. P., 'The 'Revolt of the Field': The agricultural labourers' movement in the 1870s', *Past & Present,* 26, 1963

Edgar, L., 'Catholic Life in Newcastle 70 years ago', *Northern Catholic History,* 6, 1977

Epstein, J. A., 'The constitutional idiom, radical reasoning, rhetoric and action in early nineteenth-century England', *Journal of Social History,* 23, Spring 1990

Evans, C., 'The Hawks Family of Gateshead and the Tyneside mode of metal production', *Bulletin of the North East Labour History Society,* 30, 1996

Finn, M., "A vent which has conveyed our principles': English radical patriotism in the aftermath of 1848', *Journal of Modern History,* 64:4, 1992

Gilley, S., 'The Garibaldi riots of 1862', *Historical Journal,* 16:4, 1973

Gillingham, J., 'The beginnings of English Imperialism', *Journal of Historical Sociology,* 5, 1992

Halstead J., and Prescott, A., 'Breaking the Barriers: masonry, fraternity and labour', *Labour History Review* (Special Issue), 71:1, 2006

Hammersley, R., 'Jean-Paul Marat's *The Chains of Slavery* in Britain and France, 1774-1833', *Historical Journal,* 48:3, 2005

Hampton, M., 'Liberalism, the press and the construction of the public sphere: theories of the press in Britain, 1830-1914', *Victorian Periodicals Review* 37:1, 2004

Harris, K., 'Joseph Cowen: The Northern Tribune', *Bulletin of the North East Labour History Society,* 5, 1971

Harrison B. and Hollis, P., 'Chartism, Liberalism and the Life of Robert Lowery', *English Historical Review,* 82, 1967

Howell, R., 'Cromwell and the Imagery of 19th Century Radicalism: the example of Joseph Cowen', *Archaeologia Aeliana,* series IV, 10, 1982

Jackson, D. J., '"Garibaldi or the Pope!". Newcastle's Irish Riot of 1866', *North East History*, 34, 2001

Kirk, N., 'In Defence of Class', *International Review of Social History*, 32, 1987

Knox, Elaine, 'The body politic, bodysnatching, the Anatomy Act and the poor on Tyneside' *Bulletin of the North East Labour History Society*, 24, 1990

Lynch, J. G., 'The Irish Population in Darlington 1841-1851', *Durham Local History Society Bulletin*, 43, December 1989

McBride, T., 'Irishness in Glasgow', *Immigrants and Minorities*, 24.1, 2006

MacDermott, T. P., 'Charles Larkin, Radical Reformer 1800-1879', *Northern Catholic History*, 28, August 1988

Maehl, W. H., 'The dynamics of violence in Chartism: A case study in North-east England, 1839', *Albion*, 7, 1975

McClelland, K., 'A politics of the labour aristocracy? Skilled workers and radical politics on Tyneside', *Bulletin of the Society for the Study of Labour History*, 40, 1980

McWilliams, R., 'Liberalism Lite?', *Victorian Studies*, 48:1, 2005

Mowat, R. C., 'From Liberalism to Imperialism: the case of Egypt 1875-87', *Historical Journal*, 16, 1973

Nicholson, W. J., 'Irish Priests in the North East in the 19th Century', *Northern Catholic History*, 21, 1985

O'Brien, P., 'Is political biography a good thing?', *Contemporary British History*, 10:4, 1996

Pentland, G., 'Scotland and the creation of a national reform movement, 1830-1832', *Historical Journal*, 48:4, 2005

Porter, J. H., 'Wage Bargaining under Conciliation Agreements, 1860-1914', *Economic History Review*, 33, 1970

Pickering, P., 'Class without Words: Symbolic communication in the Chartist Movement', *Past and Present*, 112, 1986

Pickering, P., 'Chartism and the trade of agitation in early Victorian Britain', *History*, 76, 1991

Poole, R., 'The march to Peterloo: politics and festivity in late Georgian England', *Past and Present*, 192, August 2006

Porter, J. H., 'The 'revolt of the field': The Devon response', *Southern History*, 7, 1985

Prothero, I., 'London Chartism and the trades', *Economic History Review*, 24, 1971

Purdue, A. W., 'The Liberal and Labour parties in North East Politics 1892-1914', *International Review of Social History*, XXVI:1, 1981

Reidy, D. V., 'Panizzi, Gladstone, Garibaldi and the Neapolitan Prisoners', *Electronic British Library Journal*, 2005

Ridley, D., 'The Spital Fields Demonstration and the Parliamentary Reform Crisis in Newcastle upon Tyne, May 1832', *Bulletin of the North East Labour History Society*, 26, 1992

Ridley, D., 'Shoot the Damn Dogs: The 1734 Dispute at Newbottle Colliery, County Durham', *North East History*, 37, 2006

Roberts, M., "Villa Toryism' and Popular Conservatism in Leeds, 1885-1902', *Historical Journal*, 49:1, 2006

Rowe, D. J., 'Some aspects of Chartism on Tyneside', *International Review of Social History*, 16, 1971

Rowe, D. J., 'Tyneside Chartists', *Bulletin of the North East Labour History Society*, 8, 1974

Smith, J., 'Labour tradition in Glasgow and Liverpool', *History Workshop Journal*, 17, Spring 1984

Steele, E. D., 'The Irish presence in the North of England 1850-1914', *Northern History*, XII, 1976

Thompson, D., 'The Languages of Class', *Bulletin of the Society for the Study of Labour History*, (1) 1987

Wells, R., 'Southern Chartism', *Rural History. Economy, Society, Culture*, 2:1, 1991

Unpublished Theses

Ashton, O. R., 'Radicalism and Chartism in Gloucestershire 1832-1847', University of Birmingham PhD thesis, 1980

Blake, A., 'The Education Question and Liberal Politics in North East England, 1868-1910', University of Newcastle MLitt thesis, 1984

Chase, M. S., 'The Land and the Working Classes: English Agrarianism, c.1775-1851', University of Sussex PhD thesis, 1984

Cooter, R. J., 'The Irish in County Durham and Newcastle', University of Durham MA thesis, 1972

Goodland, G. D., 'Liberals and the Home Rule issue, November 1885 - July 1886: The leaders and the rank and file, with special reference to certain localities', University of Cambridge PhD thesis, 1988

Gurowich, P. M., 'Party and Independence in the early and mid-Victorian House of Commons: Aspects of political theory and practice 1832-68, considered with special reference to the period 1852-68, University of Cambridge PhD thesis, 1986

Jones, C. L., 'Industrial Relations of the Northumberland and Durham Coal Industry 1825-1845', Sunderland Polytechnic PhD thesis, 1985

Jones, P., 'Office holding, Politics and Society in Leicester and Peterborough, 1860-1930', University of Leicester MPhil thesis, 1982

McWilliam, R. A., 'The Tichborne Claimant and the People: Investigations into Popular Culture 1867-1886', University of Sussex PhD thesis, 1989

Muris, C., 'The Northern Reform Union, 1858-1862', University of Durham MA thesis, 1953

Pickard, A. J., 'Liberal Anglicanism 1847-1902: A Study of Class and Cultural Relationships in nineteenth century England', University of Birmingham PhD thesis, 1986

Salmon, I. J., 'Welsh Liberalism, 1865-1896: A study in political structure and ideology', University of Oxford DPhil thesis, 1983

Scott, C. L., 'A comparative re-examination of Anglo-Irish relations in Nineteenth Century Manchester, Liverpool and Newcastle upon Tyne', University of Durham PhD thesis, 1998

Spraggon, K., 'The Radicalism of Joseph Cowen', Newcastle Polytechnic MA Dissertation, 1985

Taylor, A. D., 'Ernest Jones: His later career and the structure of Manchester politics 1861-1869', University of Birmingham MA thesis, 1984

Waitt, E. I., 'John Morley, Joseph Cowen and Robert Spence Watson: Liberal divisions in Newcastle politics, 1873-1895', University of Manchester PhD thesis, 1972

Wilson, K., 'Political Radicalism in North East England 1830-60: Issues in Historical Sociology', University of Durham PhD thesis, 1987

Index

22
105
104
106
107
112
118-9
125
131